THOMAS PELHAM-HOLLES

THOMAS DUKE OF NEWCASTLE
From a painting by Hoare in the National Portrait Gallery

THOMAS PELHAM-HOLLES

Duke of Newcastle

HIS EARLY POLITICAL CAREER

1693-1724

By

STEBELTON H. NULLE

New York University

Philadelphia

UNIVERSITY OF PENNSYLVANIA PRESS

London: Humphrey Milford: Oxford University Press

1931

S.H.N.
Optimis parentibus
HENRICO et MARIAE NULLE
pia cum caritate
D.D.D.

Foreword

It is an astonishing fact that, although more than a century and a half has elapsed since his death, no biography exists of one of the greatest and most interesting political figures of the eighteenth century—Thomas, Duke of Newcastle. The following study of his early life is offered as partial amends for this prolonged neglect.

If, in the succeeding pages, particulars as to the personality of Newcastle during this early period are rather less ample than one could wish, it is because the sources allow no alternative. "In the sixteenth century it was the fashion," wrote Horace Walpole, "to preserve original papers: during the eighteenth it is the fashion to destroy them. Hence we know more of the reign of Queen Elizabeth than we do of the reign of George I." In his own private correspondence it is seldom that the duke becomes discursive or introspective. Furthermore, the memoir writers and diarists for the most part begin their labors with the period which follows the close of this work and deal not with the slender young Minister of the first Hanoverian but with an older and altered man. Similarly, the stout, red-backed volumes of the Newcastle and Hardwicke collections in the British Museum, that seem well-nigh endless in the period of the second George, dwindle almost to insignificance in the 'twenties.

No account of Newcastle's early career could be written without reference to the times in which he lived; but familiar and unnecessary details have been avoided here as far as possible, so as to set the principal figure in bold relief. In sketching the background of the reign of George I, the author has profited by a fresh examination of a mass of manuscript and printed sources, and in some respects has ventured to differ from received opinion. The hitherto unpublished material from the state archives of Hanover and Vienna contained in Professor Wolfgang Michael's splendid *Englische Geschichte im*

18ten Jahrhundert was of the greatest value. Unfortunately, the field of local parliamentary history has found no historian since the days of Oldfield. Much spade-work remains to be done in this quarter, and in his *Parliamentary History of the Borough of Horsham* Mr. William Albery has shown what may be done.

The dates given in this work are all according to the Old Style or Julian calendar. The spelling of the original documents has been followed throughout in all quotations with a view to preserving something of the flavor of that far-off, almost legendary world. With a very few exceptions, the Bibliography contains a list of only those books to which reference has been made in the footnotes. Attention is called to the appended Genealogy, an examination of which reveals how much a family matter the government of Augustan England was.

The author takes pleasure in acknowledging his indebtedness to that goodly company of friendly helpers and advisers, both in this country and in England, who shared his efforts, and in particular to Professor Edward P. Cheyney, of the University of Pennsylvania, and to Professor Witt Bowden, of Atlantic University, for their kindly interest in the progress of the work from its inception, and their generous criticisms and suggestions.

S. H. N.

New York
June, 1930

Contents

Contents

I

Introductory: The Family Background

When on a day in May, 1686, the Lady Grace Holles, daughter of the third Earl of Clare, became the wife of Sir Thomas Pelham, Baronet, two families not unknown in England's annals were joined; but the pair could not have foreseen that, united, the fortunes of their houses would rise still higher, in the person of their eldest son, Thomas, the future Duke of Newcastle, and the subject of this monograph.

The Pelhams were the elder of the two houses; and traced their line, rather dubiously withal, from an ancestor who came to England with the Conqueror, and had been rewarded with estates in Hertfordshire. One Sir John Pelham is supposed to have accompanied the Black Prince to France, and to have been among the "mo than X knyghtes and squyers" that challenged the taking of King John by Sir Denis Morbeck on the field of Poitiers;[1] and ever after the Pelhams bore a buckle in their arms, as a memento of having shared the *spolia opima* of that glorious day. At all events, the family had won wealth and some distinction when the Lancastrians mounted the throne, and gathered additional lands and honors under that dynasty.

The family had now for some time been identified by their broad acres with the county of Sussex. "Johannes Pelham, Chivaler," represented it in the Parliament of 1399,[2] and thereafter there was almost always a member of the family at St. Stephen's, either for the county or one of its boroughs. The Pelhams struck their roots deeply in the soil of Sussex: defending its shores, as Sir Nicholas did Seaford against the French in 1545; winning wealth from its iron mines and forges; proudly carving their heraldic buckle on the towers of its churches; and for generations judging and administering the countryside.

---

[1] Froissart is silent with regard to this paladin. Berners ed., I, *cap.* CLXIV.

[2] *Official Return,* pt. I, 259.

[1]

The rise of the Pelhams to political power in the seventeenth century is typical of that of many other families that composed the oligarchy of the eighteenth. By dint of long activity in Parliament, and by the wealth and prestige gained through fortunate marriage alliances, they ended by taking their places with the peers. Thomas Pelham (*c.* 1540-1624), after holding the shrievalty of his country, sitting in Parliament under Queen Elizabeth, and marrying the niece of Walsingham, her great Minister, was made a baronet by James I, upon the institution of that dignity.

The second baronet (1597-1654) had a considerable Parliamentary career and sat in the Long Parliament until Pride's Purge. He married to advantage several times, one wife being the daughter of King James's Master of Requests, and another that of the elder Sir Harry Vane, the famous Parliamentarian.

With Sir John, the third baronet (1624-1703), the family prestige was increased by his marriage with a daughter of the Earl of Leicester, Lady Lucy Sidney, a sister of the Whig martyr, Algernon Sidney, and of the radiant Sacharissa, whom Waller loved in vain. He lived under all five Stuart sovereigns, weathered two revolutions that convulsed the State, and sat in almost every Parliament before his coach upset and ended his career.

Sir Thomas, the fourth baronet (*c.*1650-1712), the father of the Duke of Newcastle,[3] distinguished himself in Parliament in his younger days as a strenuous opponent of King Charles II, in concert with Sir William Jones, the Attorney-General,[4] his first wife's father. Along with his cousin, the unprincipled Sunderland, and his uncle Henry Sidney, later Earl of Romney and close friend of William III, he supported the Revolution, and was a member of the Convention Parliament.[5] His services

---

[3] For an account of Sir Thomas Pelham, see obituary notice in Boyer, *Reign of Queen Anne,* 10th year, 387-388.

[4] He sat in Parliament 1678-1702, *Official List,* I; Sidney's *Diary,* I, 250, 261-262, 302, and II, 134-135, 199. *Cal. S. P. Dom.,* 1680-1681, 473.

[5] *Somers' Tracts,* X, 12.

and his connections brought immediate reward in the form of a place in the Customs Commission,[6] and subsequently he was thrice a Lord Commissioner of the Treasury.[7] While always a staunch Whig, he was never an extremist, and joined the Tories in the case of Sir John Fenwick in 1696.[8] Nevertheless, in 1706, when the Whigs demanded of Godolphin a greater share of government, he was elevated to the peerage as Baron Pelham of Laughton.[9]

His first wife was the only child and heir of the rich Sir William, and the connection undoubtedly augmented the Pelham estate substantially.[10] When their daughter married the Viscount Townshend in 1698, he was able to give her the large portion of £30,000.[11] But his second marriage with the youngest daughter of the Earl of Clare must have been regarded as a particularly fine match, for the rise of the Holles family to wealth and distinction in the seventeenth century had been even greater than that of his own, although its lineage was not so ancient.

The story of William Holles (c.1471-1542), the founder of the family fortunes and the first to emerge from obscurity, is reminiscent of Dick Whittington. He began life in the Warwickshire village of Stoke, near Coventry; but left the ancestral home for London, where he became successively Warden of the Mercer's Company, Sheriff of Middlesex, Alderman, and then Mayor of London. He died seised of a large estate, scattered in seven counties.[12]

---

[6] *Cal. S. P. Dom.*, 1689-1690, 53.

[7] Luttrell, *Hist. Rel., passim.* In 1694, it was rumored he would be made a baron. H.M.C. *Portland MSS*, II, 167.

[8] *Parl. Hist.*, V, 1034, 1077, 1130. *Somers' Tracts,* XIII, 569.

[9] *Lords' Journals*, XVI.

[10] Temple, *Works* (ed. 1757), II, 532.

[11] Luttrell, IV, 398.

[12] Collins, *Historical Collections,* 55. This and following accounts of members of the Holles family were taken by Arthur Collins, the eighteenth-century antiquary, from Gervas Holles (1606-1675), who wrote a history of his kinsmen.

William, the second son, displayed his father's successful qualities, and was knighted by Edward VI. He married his daughter to a cadet of the Derby family; and his eldest son, Denzil Holles, married Eleanor, the daughter of Lord Sheffield, and granddaughter of the fifteenth Earl of Oxford. Upon the rising of the Northern Earls in 1569 the family won favor at Court by helping to put it down.[13]

John Holles (*c.* 1564-1637), after a career as a soldier, in which he served against the Armada, campaigned in Holland, Ireland, and Hungary, and won a knighthood, anticipated an equally active career at Court. But a promising beginning as Controller of the Household to Prince Henry was extinguished by the death of the heir, and thereafter, for various reasons, he lost favor at Court. The needy James I, however, was willing, in 1616, to sell him the title of Baron Laughton for the round sum of £10,000 and eight years later that of Earl of Clare for another £5,000.[14] His daughter Arabella became the wife of the unfortunate Strafford, and "hot" Denzil Holles, the parliamentary leader, was his second son.

Lacking the ambition of his father and his younger brother, the second earl (1595-1666) devoted himself to the practical but prosaic task of preserving and improving his estate while the Civil War raged about him; and consequently it was said of him that he "was very often of both parties, and never advantaged either."[15]

The third earl (1633-1689) was of a similar turn, and lived and died almost equally without renown. He was, however, the first to throw the family fortunes with the Whigs. He supported the Country Party under Charles II, and welcomed

---

[13] *Ibid.* See also H.M.C. *Buccleuch MSS,* I, 540.

[14] The Earldom of Clare was particularly sought after, being regarded as equivalent to the royal title of Clarence, and Holles carried off the prize that Lord Rich had vainly sought, so that he took instead that of Warwick. Besides Collins, see *G. E. C.,* III and VI, and Goodman, *Court of James I,* 361.

[15] Clarendon, *Rebellion,* V, 342, 346; VII, 174, 187, 242. *Memoirs of Colonel Hutchinson,* I, 164-165.

William of Orange to England; but died before the Revolution was completed.

John (1662-1711), the last and also the most distinguished of the four Holles Earls of Clare, is of particular interest for his influence on the history of his nephew, the future Duke of Newcastle. Strangely combining in his nature both the leading family characteristics, he exceeded all the rest in ambition and in love of gain. From his father, too, descended his staunch Protestantism, and his moderate Whig principles.

For his part in promoting the accession of William and Mary, he was at once rewarded by being made Gentleman of the Bedchamber and Lord Lieutenant and Custos Rotulorum of Middlesex. These were only the first of a long series of rewards and offices that were bestowed upon him during two reigns;[16] although for several years he seems to have taken little part in politics, and devoted himself to his vast estates.[17] Nevertheless, his pride and ambition remained unappeased until he obtained the ducal title. King William refused to make him Duke of Clarence,[18] but finally yielded to his importunities and in 1694 made him Marquess of Clare and Duke of Newcastle.[19] Four years later he received the Garter.

The ultimate source of Duke John's prestige must be sought in his wealth and parliamentary influence. Five generations of thrifty Holleses had not lived in vain, and, true to form, their heir was able to augment considerably his enormous patri-

---

[16] His *cursus honorum* is impressive: High Steward of E. Retford and Lord Lieutenant of Notts (1694); Commissioner for Greenwich Hospital (1695); Lord Lieutenant of the E. Riding of Yorkshire (1698); Steward of Sherwood Forest and Governor of Hull (1699); Lord Lieutenant of the N. Riding of Yorks (1705); Warden and Chief Justice in Eyre of the royal forests north of the Trent, High Steward of Dorchester and Lord Lieutenant of Middlesex (1711). See Luttrell and *Cal. S. P. Dom., passim,* and H.M.C. *Portland MSS, passim.*

[17] H.M.C. *Seventh Rept.,* 205.

[18] *Ibid.,* and Luttrell, III, 300 (Apr. 28, 1694).

[19] *Cal. S. P. Dom.,* 1694-1695, 121. Bramston, *Autobiography* (Camden Soc., 1845), 378. Hereafter he will be referred to on occasion as Duke John, to distinguish him from his nephew, Thomas.

mony. He married Margaret, the favorite daughter of Henry Cavendish, the second Duke of Newcastle of that creation; and upon the latter's death in 1691, inherited the bulk of his estate, thereby adding about £10,000 a year to his income.[20]   A few years later, his second cousin, Baron Holles of Isfield, the grandson of the great Parliamentarian, died childless, and made him his devisee.   As a result, Newcastle was generally reputed to have the greatest estate in the kingdom.[21]   He hunted in almost royal style;[22] and on one occasion entertained the King for five days at his great seat at Welbeck Abbey, with the lavishness of a fellow monarch.[23]   On the other hand, like his great contemporary, the Duke of Marlborough, Newcastle was notoriously covetous, even to the extent of demanding of his duchess on one occasion an explanation for an outlay of six shillings for oranges and lemons![24]

With estates scattered all over England, his influence on parliamentary elections was enormous.[25]   His support was sought by rival Whig leaders, but by none so assiduously as Robert Harley.   Their correspondence, preserved in the *Portland MSS*, commenced in April, 1704, and with it began a political and personal alliance that ended only with the duke's death.   It was Harley's plan, apparently, that the grandee play Crassus to his Cæsar, and form part of his personal following in a coalition of moderates of both parties.   Perhaps his scheming brain

---

[20] H.M.C. *Denbigh MSS*, 565a. Luttrell, II, 270 (Aug. 4, 1691). G.E.C., III, 249-250.

[21] Macky, *Journey*, 35, and Burnet, *Own Times*, VI, 69.

[22] H.M.C. *Portland MSS*, V, 65.

[23] From the numerous references, this event seems to have made a great impression on contemporaries, *e.g. Lexington Papers*, 140; *Cal. S. P. Dom.*, 1695, 91; H.M.C. *Portland MSS*, II, 189; Luttrell, III, 537.

[24] Macky, *ibid.*, H.M.C. *Portland MSS*, VIII, 280, Goulding, *Countess of Oxford*, 2.

[25] *e.g.* at Westminster in 1695 (H.M.C. *Portland MSS*, II, 173); at Westminster, Lincoln, and counties Yorks, Derby and Notts in 1701 (*Ibid.*, 180-182); and H.M.C. *Coke MSS*, 417); Co. Yorks, Leeds, Halifax and Craven in 1706 (*Portland MSS*, II, 197); at Pontefract in 1708 (H.M.C. *Bagot MSS*, 341); at Boroughbridge, Westminster and Sussex in 1710 (*Portland MSS*, II, 217-218, and 222); etc.

had already hatched the plan for the marriage of his eldest son
with the duke's daughter and presumptive heir.[26] On the other
hand, the ambitious Newcastle, eager for office and convinced
that a "Whig game was intended at bottom," became Lord
Privy Seal in 1705, and remained so until his death. Thus he
served in two of the most critical as well as the most brilliant
administrations that England ever had: that of Marlborough
and Godolphin; and its successor, led by Harley and St. John.
It is noteworthy that he won the praise of Bishop Burnet for
his cautious and exact fulfillment of the office. The year after
his appointment, he was chosen by Harley as one of the thirty-
one commissioners that negotiated the union with Scotland.
A loyal Whig to the core, Newcastle was at this time in correspondence with the Court of Hanover;[27] and there is no evidence that he ever intrigued with that of St. Germain, as did
many of his associates. Powis House, in Lincoln's Inn Fields,
was purchased for £7,000 and became the centre of Whig
social life in London.[28] The alliance with Harley enabled him
to get his brother-in-law, Sir Thomas Pelham, promoted to the
peerage,[29] and to stifle a "snivelling project" to give the Electoral Prince of Hanover the title of Duke of Clarence.[30] Newcastle was resolved that if he could not have it himself, nobody
else should, and the future sovereign had to be contented with
the Dukedom of Cambridge!

Newcastle had but one child, the Lady Henrietta Holles,
born in 1694, a handsome, sensible girl, whose only fault in the
eyes of Dean Swift lay in her ruddy hair.[31] Whatever her

---

[26] H.M.C. *Portland MSS,* II, 184, *et seq.*

[27] *Stowe MSS* (Hanover Papers), No. 222, f. 394b and 404 (Elector to
Newcastle); and H.M.C. *10th Rept.,* pt. 4, 140-141 (Electress Sophia and
Elector to Newcastle); and H.M.C. *Portland MSS,* II, 180 and 182.

[28] Luttrell, V, 547 (May 8, 1705); Feiling, *Tory Party,* 376; Leadam,
Hist. of Eng., 67.

[29] H.M.C. *Portland MSS,* II, 189 (Harley to Newcastle).

[30] *Ibid.,* 196-197 (Harley to Newcastle), and 189 (Newcastle to Harley).

[31] Swift, *Journal to Stella,* 277. She became the mother of Prior's "noble,
lovely, little Peggy."

complexion, however, she was the finest "fortune" in England, and her hand was sought with eagerness by the most noble suitors. Rumor went so far as to include the Elector or his son among them, while even the arrogant Duke of Somerset sought her hand for his heir.[32]

Such, in brief, was the propitious family background which helped to shape the career of the future Duke of Newcastle. Thus, to begin with, he belonged by birth to a small and powerful aristocracy, and his tastes, education, and career were largely decided by this fact. The tradition of political activity was strong in both families, as has been seen, and not every man could reckon a Strafford and a Denzil Holles among his connections. Both families, too, had adopted Whig principles in the days of the Green Ribbon Club, and one had provided the cause with its noblest martyr. Later they helped to bring about the Revolution, and in the uncertain times of William III and Anne were among the most loyal champions of the Revolution Settlement and of the Protestant religion. So the future duke took to political life almost as a matter of course, and his party affiliations were likewise predetermined.

If it is true that "England is governed in times of excitement by its people, and in quiet times by its property"; or, as Harrington taught, that the distribution of power must correspond with that of property, it was natural and inevitable that Thomas Pelham should become one of the governors of his country. For if the Holleses had been uniformly good husbandmen, neither were there wastrels among the Pelhams of the seventeenth century, and their crabbed account books may still be seen in the British Museum.[33] Pelham was thus the heir of two great, unencumbered estates, and the wealth he inherited made possible a public career of an influence undreamed of by his ancestors.

---

[32] H.M.C. *Buccleuch-Queensberry MSS*, II, 766. H.M.C. *Portland MSS*, II, 184, 192-193, 199, and 224-225. *Wentworth Papers*, 58.

[33] *Add. MSS*, 33,137, 33,146, and 33,151-153.

II

Minority

Thomas Pelham, the future Duke of Newcastle, Secretary of State and Prime Minister of Great Britain, was born in London,[1] July 21, 1693.[2] His father had been presented with only two daughters by his first wife; and following his second marriage four more daughters had preceded the appearance of the boy, who was given the favorite Pelham baptismal name of Thomas.

He first saw the light at a time of fear and uncertainty for his native land, with foreign invasion and domestic conspiracy in the very air. While great lords like Marlborough and Godolphin meditated treason, hosts of lesser men disliked the foreign King, and felt the Revolution Settlement to be unstable. Abroad, the Grand Alliance was struggling with the unconquered Sun-King, and the campaign of 1693 had ended as ingloriously for the Allies as its predecessors. The roar of the guns at Neerwinden had barely died away. It was his destiny to be among those who preserved the Revolution and helped to bring the House of Hanover through the perils that encompassed it.

Of his childhood nothing whatever is known, for he left no formal memoirs or anecdotes, and none were set down by another hand. His mother died when he was but seven years of age,[3] having given birth in the meanwhile to another son,

[1] Clare College (Cantab.) *Admission Book*.

[2] The date of his birth is variously given by later writers. In Collins' *Historical Collections*, 175, the date is given incorrectly as July 1, 1693. In his *Baronage*, on the other hand (ed. 1727, 375), it is given as July 21, 1694, and in Lower's *Notices of the Pelham Family*, as Aug. 1, 1693. The correct date is to be found in Coxe, *Pelham Administration*, I, 3, and in the *D.N.B.* Boyer's *Reign of Queen Anne* (10th Year, 388), gives simply July, 1693. The date given above is substantiated in H.M.C. *Portland MSS*, V, 476, and also in a letter from his cousin Lucy Pelham to her brother, referring to a dance in celebration of the occasion in 1718. (*Add. MSS*, 33,085, f. 2.)

[3] She died in Soho Square, Sept. 13 or 17, 1700, at the age of 32. Boyer, Luttrell, IV, 687.

Henry, who was also to be a Prime Minister, and to a fifth daughter. Her early death brought young Thomas more under the care of his father, whose political activities and connections must have stirred the boy's imagination. Thus, from the outset, Pelham learned to view politics, not as a science, but as a practical problem and an endless toil and conflict.

At an early age, he was sent to Westminster School, which, in Queen Anne's day was as much in vogue among the aristocracy as Eton.[4] Carteret, his future rival, and John Hervey, whose mordant *Memoirs* were to traduce him, were his companions on the playing-field. But the famous Busby, who had fostered the youthful talent of Locke and Atterbury and the muse of Dryden and Prior, was no longer there, his place as Headmaster having been taken by Thomas Knipe. It would be interesting to know what progress the future statesman made in his classical authors and what friendships he established;[5] but it would be of still greater interest to know if he availed himself of his privilege as a Westminster boy, and listened to the stormy debates of those exciting times ensconced under the gallery in old St. Stephen's Chapel.[6]

At the age of sixteen, the academic scene was shifted, and he was "admitted nobleman and pupil to Mr. Laughton" at Clare Hall, Cambridge, where he probably went into residence with the seventeen fellows and thirty-nine other scholars either at Easter or October, 1710.[7] Clare Hall, as it was then called,

---

[4] Coxe, *Pelham Administration*, I, 2. H.M.C. *Portland MSS*, V, 76. Previous to this the two sons of Lord Pelham seem to have been under the private instruction of a resident tutor, Richard Newton (1676-1753), afterward famous as the Principal of Hart Hall (Oxon.) and as an educational reformer. *Gent. Mag.*, LIV (1784, pt. I), 84.

[5] Pelham seems to have formed an attachment for Robert Freind, the Undermaster, who succeeded Knipe in 1711. In 1737, Freind addressed a Latin ode to him, beginning with the words of Horace to Maecenas: *"Dux bone, et rerum columen mearum,"* and referring to his many favors. *Gent. Mag.*, VII, 631. See also *ibid.*, III, 152.

[6] For this interesting privilege see Claude Greening, in *London Morning Post*, Apr. 25, 1899 (quoted in Porritt, *Unreformed H. of C.*, I, 579).

[7] *Clare College Admission Book.* Dates also given in Venn, *Alumni Cantabrigiensis*, 336.

was the second oldest foundation at Cambridge, and was described by a German visitor of that year as "a somewhat low, but yet fine building," with a library that was small but stocked with "many good books, especially Italian and Spanish."[8]

Richard Laughton, the tutor under whom Pelham was placed, had made such a reputation as an advocate of the Newtonian philosophy and as a disciplinarian that many young men of family were sent to Clare, although it was one of the lesser colleges of the University, so as to be under his tuition.[9] Among Pelham's fellow students were John Hervey, who had followed him from Westminster, John Hobart, later first Earl of Buckinghamshire, Martin Folkes, afterward President of the Royal Society, and several future churchmen, among them Anthony Ellys, who became Bishop of St. David's and Charles Naylor, on his way to the Deanery of Winchester.

Life in the decadent university of the eighteenth century reproduced the idleness and frivolity of the *beau monde* of the capital;[10] and, inasmuch as Pelham was not obliged to look to academic attainment for a livelihood, it is extremely doubtful whether he read as hard as he pursued the joyful courses of his fellows. The eccentric William Whiston, who succeeded to the chair of Newton and was himself a fellow at Clare, severely criticized the "irregularities" which he found there; and recommended a greater devotion to divine services, strict temperance and sobriety, and diligent improvement in learning.[11] The University cannot be said to have aroused in Pelham any considerable cultural interests, as he seems never to have been much of a patron of literature or art or of their devotees. On the other hand, it was there, no doubt, that he acquired the fondness and capacity for the pleasures of the table and the bottle

---

[8] Zacharias K. von Uffenbach, quoted in Mayor, *Cambridge under Queen Anne*, 146.

[9] *D.N.B.*, XXXII, 204, and H.M.C. *5th Report* (*Field MSS*), 400a.

[10] For student life at Clare in 1714-16, see H.M.C. *Clare College MSS*, 112-113.

[11] Whiston, *Memoirs*, 88. (From a sermon preached at Clare, Dec. 17, 1698.)

that he soon afterward displayed. Steele, in 1715, referred to him as "fortified by letters"; but this probably reflects the client's fervor rather than the unembellished fact. It is uncertain how long he remained in residence at Cambridge; and, after the events about to be narrated, the responsibilities of two great estates and family boroughs which were thrust upon him were enough to banish all thoughts of further academic life.

Equestrian accidents have altered the course of English politics more than once, and the sudden death of Duke John, in the prime of life, was of the highest importance in the career of his nephew. The duke was thrown and injured while riding to hounds in Sherwood Forest, but continued the chase for some time before he was let blood. That night, which was Friday, he was given over; but he lingered until the following Sunday, the 20th of July, 1711, when he died.[12] His lordly monument at the left of the entrance to the north transept of Westminster Abbey, where he lies buried, is the creation of his own proud precaution; and, as he would have wished, it was regarded as the finest in England.[13]

When his will was opened, it was found that he had left the bulk of his vast estate, estimated at from £25,000 to more than £40,000 a year,[14] to Thomas Pelham, the eldest son of his sister Grace. His widow was left, over and above her jointure, only Orton House and newly acquired property in county Huntington, and the use of the family plate and jewels for life. To his daughter he left lands in the counties of Stafford, York and Northumberland, worth about £5,000 a year, and a portion of £20,000.[15]

---

[12] H.M.C. *Portland MSS*, V, 65 (Lady Pye to Mrs. Harley), and the *Whole Life and Noble Character of John, Duke of Newcastle*, 5.

[13] *London Daily Journal*, no. 597 (Fri. Feb. 14, 1724), and *London Daily Post*, no. 1373 (Th. Feb. 20, 1724), also Boyer, *Pol. State*, XXIV, 98.

[14] H.M.C. *Denbigh MSS*, 568a—a newsletter of 1691, which puts it at about £20,000. Burnet, VI, 69, says "above £40,000." Boyer, *Pol. State*, II, 78, says £25,000.

[15] Copy of the will preserved at Somerset House. An epitome is printed in Collins, *Historical Collections*, 182-183.

The terms of the will seem to have been a surprise to contemporaries, and it is not altogether clear why the duke made Pelham his residuary devisee. The fact that he required him to adopt the name of Holles makes it probable, however, that Newcastle, as the last male of his line, wished, with characteristic pride, to perpetuate his name, and to endow its bearer with the riches which would uphold its dignity. Thereafter, the heir always subscribed himself Pelham-Holles; and after he attained the dukedom himself, as Holles-Newcastle.[16] It was also provided in the will that in the case of the death of Pelham without issue, the estate was to fall to his brother Henry; and in a similar contingency to the two sons of the testator's sister Elizabeth, Lady Barnard. As young Thomas was not the oldest nephew of the duke, this order of inheritance and remainder would seem to indicate a partiality for him that cannot be explained, save on the theory that he had made a very favorable impression on his uncle.

The will proved to be an Apple of Discord, and gave rise to a prolonged legal war between the heir and the disappointed relatives, which was not settled for years.[17] The dowager duchess, who was a woman of irascible temperament, was outraged at losing the Cavendish lands which she had from her father; and at once set about contesting the will on the ground that his testament precluded disposing them out of her hands. The Pelhams were conciliatory, and for a year and more continued to hope and to work for an accommodation. The case was heard in Chancery in February, 1713, and the duchess was ordered to produce the deed settling the Cavendish estate, "at which she was so much exasperated that she was resolved to

---

[16] Confirmed by a private Act in 1719. The same year Newcastle was evidently in some doubt in the matter, and got an opinion from Sir Edward Northey, who thought that the title of honor could be used without the name Holles; but advised its continued use. *Add. MSS*, 33,137, f. 292-293.

[17] For the case as a whole, see: Auditor Harley's *Account* in H.M.C. *Portland MSS*, V, 657-659, also *ibid.*, 92 and III, 230-233; *Add. MSS*, 33,084, f. 189; 33,441, f. 3; and 33,064, ff. 1-5. *Lord's Journals*, XIX, 521. H.M.C. *Clements MSS*, 262.

appeal from the order to the House of Lords." The peers' decision was rendered in May; the appeal was dismissed, and the orders and proceedings in Chancery upheld. A sequestration was issued against the dowager, to which she put in an answer; and an examination concerning the deed, which somehow got lost about this time, was ordered by Chancery.

In the meantime, the Harleys, whose designs on the hand and fortune of the Lady Harriet (as she was usually known) have already been noticed, were not idle. Robert Harley, who had been given the Treasurer's staff and the Earldom of Oxford in May proceding the death of Duke John, was a vainglorious and ambitious man, entirely devoted to his family. Making due allowances for the bitter personal enmity which Boling-broke had for Oxford, his comment on the last-named character-istic is worth noting: "Whether this man ever had any de-termined view besides that of raising his family, is I believe, a problematical question in the world. My opinion is that he never had any other."[18]

Indirect evidence attests that plans for the marriage had long been maturing in the Treasurer's mind, and so far success had attended his efforts to keep off all other suitors. The death of the duke, who was well disposed toward the project,[19] obliged the Harleys to make haste, as the dowager seemed inclined to accept the Duke of Somerset's offer; while Pelham repeatedly expressed to the duchess his own willingness to be the lucky man, and settle all difficulties at once. This being the posture of affairs, Harley wrote the duchess letters filled with fulsome compliments and friendly concern, and stimulated her natural inclination to go to law with the Pelhams rather than to accept an accommodation.[20] The poor woman was no match for one of the subtlest minds of the age; and was soon brought round

---

[18] *Letter to Sir Wm. Windham,* 19. Cf. Feiling, *Tory Party,* 313 and 384, and H.M.C. *Portland MSS,* VII, 32-33, 40 and 41. In Nov., 1714, Harley's debts were declared on good authority to be over twice his assets. H.M.C. *Portland MSS,* VII, 208.

[19] According to Auditor Harley, the Treasurer's brother, the duke pro-posed the match himself. *Ibid.,* V, 657.

[20] *Ibid.,* II 230, ff., and V. 53-54 (Monckton to Harley).

to support the match, and to believe Oxford "superior to any person in England." The marriage took place at Wimpole on August 31, 1713; and it would be interesting to know which caused the Treasurer the keener pleasure, the brilliant match his son had made or the conclusion of the great Peace of Utrecht, signed a few months before.[21]

The Harleys were now in a position to take up the Lady Harriet's quarrel with her cousin over the Cavendish estates which had been willed to him, but which she claimed *in toto*.[22] However, the willingness of the Pelhams to treat concerning part of the estate, rather than risk the uncertainties of more litigation, led by mutual agreement to the appointment of Lord Cowper as arbitrator. A settlement was reached in July, 1714, just before the fall of Oxford. By the composition, Lord Harley got the whole Cavendish estate, valued at £10,000 a year and containing £40,000 worth of timber. In return, Lady Harriet's portion of £20,000, charged on the Holles estate, was remitted to Pelham, together with lands worth another £20,000.[23]

Just before the wedding, the dowager had become estranged from her daughter and the Harleys; and their subsequent agreement with Pelham, by which, as she said, "Harley takes from Pelham my estate as a gift from Pelham," aroused her beyond measure, so that her hatred for the former was as great as her quondam admiration.[24] Her Grace's cause was finally heard and lost in a Court of Delegates, which rendered its decision on May 21, 1715; and the following year she died unmourned, leaving what remained of her estate to the Lady Frances Spencer, her sister's daughter.

[21] "As soon as the last hand was given to the fortune of his family," wrote Bolingbroke, "he abandoned his mistress (*i.e.* Queen Anne), his friends, and his party, who had borne him so many years on their shoulders." (*Letter to Sir William Windham, 23.*)

[22] For this dispute see *Add. MSS,* 33,064, ff., 9-11, 15-16, 19, 21, 23, 27, 29, 31, 36.

[23] Swift, *Corres.,* II, 183-184. H.M.C. *Portland MSS,* V, 472 (newsletter of July 15, 1714). The agreement was confirmed by private Act in 1719. *Lord's Journals,* XX, 44.

[24] H.M.C. *Bath MSS,* I, 248.

For some time the Baron Pelham, now an old man past sixty, had been in ill-health and confined to his seat at Halland, in Sussex. Suddenly, on February 2, 1712, he "fell ill of a pain in his stomach, and dyed three hours after."[25] After providing generous portions and trust funds for his four daughters, and another £5,000 and annuities for his second son, Henry, the residue of the estate, aside from minor bequests,[26] he devised to his eldest son.

So it was, that at an age when other young gentlemen of family were still to be found at the universities completing their education, or roaming the Continent in charge of a tutor, young Pelham became the master of two great estates, and a figure to be reckoned with in politics. Moreover, by the death of his father, he now became the second Baron of Laughton, and a peer of the realm.

Duke John, William Monson of Bloxborn, Herts, and George Naylor of Hurstmonceux, who had married Pelham's eldest sister, were named executors, and also guardians of the heir during his minority. But by a codicil, there was added to this group a fourth (or actually a third, in view of the death of the duke), whose office did not end when his charge became of age, but lasted as long as life itself. This was faithful Thomas Bowers.[27] Born at Shrewsbury about the time of the Restoration, he had been a fellow of St. John's, Cambridge; and upon settling at Hellingly, in Sussex, a living of which the Pelhams enjoyed the patronage, he became the friend and adviser of the family. After preaching the funeral of the old lord, he seems to have endeavored to supply his place in the counsels of the new.[28] In 1713, he became Archdeacon of Canterbury.

---

[25] Boyer, *Reign of Queen Anne,* 10th Year, 387.

[26] An interesting feature of the will is the leaving of £100 to the poor of Laughton, East Hoathly and Bishopstone, a similar sum to put out twenty poor boys of Sussex, and £50 to the charity schools there. Even in death the Pelham attachment for the county is revealed.

[27] Lower, *Sussex Worthies,* 120.

[28] In July, 1715, Bowers wrote the younger man a fatherly letter of remonstrance on account of his extravagance, ending by referring to the "tender affection I have had for you almost from your infancy, and now

Throughout life, Pelham seems to have found it necessary to have a close confidant and adviser; and he was fortunate indeed in this, his first one, although as will be seen, he did not always follow his advice!

The exact value of Pelham's estates at this period cannot be determined. Contemporaries estimated it at £25,000 a year and more.[29] But from an examination of the detailed accounts of his land stewards for the year ending Lady Day, 1726—the earliest data available—the rent-roll of all his estates save those in Sussex, which were not included with the rest, was charged at £36,240.[30] In a report submitted in July, 1723, the value of the rents from that county was computed at about £2,500 a year in addition,[31] making a grand total of £38,740.[32] In 1712, the sum would probably be somewhat more, rather than less than this, owing to Pelham's prodigality.

The estates extended over no less than eleven counties, including the broad patrimony of the Pelhams between Lewes and Hastings, in Sussex, and the still greater Holles lands, which embraced a large part of the shires of Nottingham and Lincoln, and smaller estates in Dorset, Yorkshire, Wiltshire, Hertfordshire, Derby, Kent, Suffolk, and Middlesex as well.

So far, the background and the conditions surrounding the period of Pelham's minority have received attention to the exclusion of purely personal aspects. Unfortunately, history has drawn a veil over this side of his early life, and it is not until he is twenty and more that he begins to figure as an indi-

yt. sincere friendship I have had for you after you are grown up." *Add. MSS,* 33,064, f. 82.

[29] Boyer, *Pol. State,* II, 78, says £25,000. Erasmus Lewis (*Swift Corres.,* II, 183-184) says twice as much as Lord Harley, who put it at £16,000. Horace Walpole, *Memoirs of George II,* 141, says about £30,000.

[30] *Add. MSS,* 33,320, ff. 1 to 22a.

[31] *Add. MSS,* 33,064, f. 249-250. See also *ibid.,* ff. 258-259 (Newcastle to Lady Lincoln).

[32] This is substantially Basil Williams' estimate (*E.H.R.,* XII, 450). The *Cambridge Chronicle* of Nov. 26, 1768, says that the estate was worth £50,000 when he came into it. *Add. MSS,* 5,832, f. 114b. There is no evidence of his having any personal interests in banking, the trading companies, or colonization.

vidual in the sources.   It is significant that when he makes his first appearance, he is already absorbed in politics.

During his minority, his political activities and expenditures would be curtailed somewhat; but it is certain that he had some share in influencing the general election of the fall of 1713,[33] which the Whigs hoped to gain on the strength of the outcry against the commercial clauses of the Treaty of Utrecht.

There is a very interesting letter from Richard Steele, already famous for the *Tatler* and the *Spectator,* which sheds some faint light upon Pelham the politician of this period, but lamentably too little.   The author, who had first attracted Pelham's interest by his political activities,[34] seems to have become dissatisfied with him as a patron, and announced his intention of going into active politics, concluding in his impulsive way: "I am going out of your dependence, and will tell you with the freedom of an indifferent man that it is impossible for anyone who thinks, or has any public spirit, not to tremble at seeing his country in its present circumstances in the hands of so daring a genius as yours."[35]   The full significance of this is not altogether clear; but it was something to be called a genius by Richard Steele!

The almost universal desire for peace had won the election for the party that had made it, but the defeated Whigs renewed the campaign with fresh and more successful tactics.   They began a furious propaganda which was to cut across all older party lines and separate men for generations into two opposing camps —into Hanoverians and Jacobites.   They sought to discredit their opponents by associating them indiscriminately in the popular opinion with the hatred of Popery and Wooden Shoes; and Whig pamphlets, Whig ballads, and Whig demonstrations all struck the same violent note of horror and of warning.

Into this agitation Pelham plunged with all his character- istic warmth and party zeal.   Joining with thirty other gentle-

---

[33] H.M.C. *Portland MSS,* V, 377 (Monckton to Oxford).   Bateson, *Changes in the Ministry,* 167, quoting *Add. MSS,* 33,003, f. 386.

[34] Steele, *Correspondence,* II, 379 (Steele to Clare).

[35] H.M.C. *Blenheim MSS,* 23b (Steele to Pelham, June 4, 1713).   See also H.M.C. *Seventh Report,* pt. I, 239a.

men as ardent in their attachment to the principles of the Revolution and the Hanoverian Succession as himself, he helped to found, in the latter part of 1713, the Hanover Club,[36] one of those little coteries of scholars, gentlemen, and wits that at once moulded and illuminated the public opinion of the day. There were five other peers besides himself, and the membership included Lords Castlecomer and Lincoln (his brothers-in-law), the younger Craggs, Paul Methuen, William Pulteney, Steele and Addison, and "old" Horace Walpole. The society had its officers and rules, and met once a week at Charing Cross, where the members planned their remarkable manifestations in the Whig interest.

The first of these demonstrations seems to have occurred on November 17th, chosen because it was the anniversary of the proclamation of the Protestant champion, Queen Elizabeth. The day was ushered in by the ringing of bells in and about the city; and after nightfall houses were illuminated for the occasion, and a bonfire was kept blazing before the headquarters of the Club. The climax came when three sinister-looking effigies, tricked out to represent the Pope, the Devil, and the Pretender, were put in the middle of a "machine" blazing with hundreds of flambeaux and links, and paraded through the principal streets to Cornhill and back, while thousands of loyal subjects followed in the wake vociferating: "God preserve the Queen, the Church and the Protestant Succession in the illustrious House of Hanover!" and "No Popery and no Pretender!"[37]

The occasion of Queen Anne's birthday, February 6, 1714, was seized for a similar outburst of party spirit,[38] and there undoubtedly were others that went unrecorded. If Horace Walpole, the letter writer, may be trusted on this point, it was Pelham's purse that partly inspired and largely paid for all this fervor,[39] and if so, to him must go a generous share of the credit for "keeping up," as Oldmixon put it, "the Whig spirits in

---

[36] Oldmixon, *Hist. of Eng.*, III, 509, and Macky, *Journey*, 188.

[37] Boyer, *Pol. State*, VI, 381-383.

[38] Oldmixon, *op. cit.*, III, 536.

[39] Walpole, *Memoirs of George II*, I, 141.

London and Westminster, and consequently throughout the whole kingdom."

Pelham was also active in patronizing the literary champions of Whiggism, like Steele, who, having made his peace, shortly after addressed him as a youthful but patriotic Mæcenas. "All the world is witness," he wrote, "that it hath been your Lordship's early inclination to find out and encourage the lovers of your Country, to comfort them under the neglect of their friends and support them against the resentment of their enemies. . . . . Whoever has exerted himself for the publick has, at your house, a friend and benefactor."[40]

A most critical period was now at hand in the domestic affairs of England. Events were taking place which threatened the Succession and filled the future with danger and uncertainty. They can only be dealt with here, however, insofar as they concern Pelham himself. The Queen had recovered from her illness of the spring of 1713; but on Christmas eve she was seized again, and the Tories were once more thrown into despair. The exultation of the Whigs on this occasion caused the resentful woman upon her recovery to turn to the counsels of Bolingbroke, thereby adding fuel to the feud already raging in the Cabinet. Her confidence in Oxford had been wavering for some time, as a consequence of his remissness and disrespect; and in the course of a few months this was to lead to his downfall. He had received a warning the previous September, when the Queen had refused his pressing request for the revival of the Dukedom of Newcastle in favor of his family,[41] and the resentment he had shown on that occasion only helped to preserve that dignity for Pelham.

His administration became gradually weaker; and while the two arch-gamblers continued their dramatic struggle for supremacy, government was almost at a standstill. The physical decline of Harley, brought on by prolonged excesses, undoubt-

---

[40] Steele, *Corres.*, II, 380.

[41] It is uncertain whether Harley made the demand for himself or for the son who married the duke's daughter just a month before. See H.M.C.

edly contributed to his distraction; but it is interesting to speculate on the influence of his private conflict with Pelham as a
conducive factor. The younger Craggs felt certain that the
harassed Treasurer had come to terms over the settlement of
the Holles estate in order to relieve himself from some of his
distress.[42]

Finally, on Tuesday, July 27, the long-expected blow descended, and Oxford was dismissed. It seems that when his
disgrace was finally determined, the Queen designed to soften
it by granting him the dukedom he desired, and, upon his coun-
sel, to make Lord Pelham Earl of Clare. Why this last step
should have been contemplated, and whether it formed a tacit
part of the agreement by which the estates were settled, is not
known; and in all events, nothing was heard of the project
afterward.[43]

While these scenes were enacted at Kensington and Whitehall, an event of another nature was taking place at Lord Pelham's country seat at Halland. The young master had arrived
at that interesting age at which he was

> "Loosen'd from the minor's tether
> Free to mortgage or to sell,"

and he felt that £2,000 could not be spent more fittingly than by
inviting in the countryside to help him celebrate the occasion.
A Gargantuan entertainment was provided, "where were
dressed seven oxen, fifteen sheep, six calves, eight bucks and so
proportionate of fowls, etc. There were eighty stands of sweet-
meats on the first table and so proportionable on the rest;
forty-nine hogsheads of strong beer, seven hogsheads of claret,
besides champaign, burgundy and four hogsheads of punch,
etc."[44]

Portland MSS, V, 329 (Drummond to Oxford); 334 (Newsletter); and
468 (Oxford's *Account of Public Affairs*). Also Bolingbroke, *Letter to
Sir Wm. Windham,* 20. *Cf.* Feiling, *Tory Party,* 464.

[42] Craggs to Pelham, July 15, 1714. *Add. MSS,* 32,686, f. 16.

[43] Boyer, *Pol. State,* VIII, 73-74. Michael, *Englische Geschichte,* I, 357,
based on Bothmer to Robethon, Aug. 7, 1714, Hanoverian Archives.

[44] H.M.C. *Portland MSS,* V, 476.

These festivities were symbolic of the whole career of the hero of the occasion. Fondness for popularity and display, love of convivial pleasures such as these, and utter heedlessness of the expenses they engendered were among Pelham's greatest weaknesses. But they were amiable weaknesses, and it is precisely this impression that we get from the very first contemporary estimate of him that has survived. "He is very silly, but very good natured," wrote Lady Mary Wortley Montagu to her husband about this time.[45] Long afterward, Lord Waldegrave commented on the same trait of good nature and willingness to forgive injuries; and it is noteworthy that when the news of his death reached his old kinsman, the Earl of Chesterfield, the latter in his musings should have singled out this selfsame characteristic.[46]

The full political importance of this feature will be realized when it is remembered that it made possible the duke's alliance with the masterful Walpole, and later that triumphant partnership with Pitt, a union which must have often been made wellnigh intolerable by the violent and domineering temper of the younger man.

In justice, it may be urged that the brevity of his residence at Cambridge, his failure to make the *grand tour* with its broadening effect, and the early death of those near relatives whose restraining influence would have counted, were responsible for his less engaging characteristics.[47] Furthermore, in spite of the ample opportunities which his upbringing provided, Pelham was never, like Bolingbroke at first, or like the third Earl of March—better known as "old Q"—(to mention an extreme case), a gross or vicious man of pleasure. In spite of his life as a *bon vivant,* he actually outlived his generation.

---

[45] Lady Mary Wortley Montagu, *Letters,* I, 211.

[46] Waldegrave, *Memoirs,* 13. Maty, *Misc. Works of Chesterfield,* III, 418-419. Also, Bradshaw, *Chesterfield's Letters and Characters,* III, 1424.

[47] In this connection it is interesting to consider the psychological results of his experiences during early childhood as a carefully-nurtured only son and brother.

III

Newcastle's Position in Local Politics in 1715

"I vow 'tis a melancholy consideration that mankind will inhabit such a heap of dirt for a poor livelihood." It was with these words, written to his wife in a fit of disgust, that Lord Cowper reprobated Sussex in a letter from Kingston-on-Thames in the spring of 1690.[1] Once a hive of varied industry, with navies riding in her harbors, Sussex had indeed fallen into evil days since the Middle Ages; and her inhabitants lived humdrum lives in drowsy, stagnant towns, only relieved from their low state now and then by a rousing electoral canvass. From the early years of the Rebellion down to the alarming days of the French Revolution, the county is almost altogether missing from the pages of national history.

A number of factors seem to have contributed to this state of things. One was the decay of her indigenous industries. "The guns that smote King Philip's fleet," and many a beautifully wrought fireback and abbey grille, as well as countless homelier objects, were products of her native ironmasters. And the forests in which King Harold's men had hidden after Hastings had supplied the fuel for the forges. But the Civil War, the competition of the Swedish mines, and the more abundant supplies of ore and charcoal in Shropshire and Staffordshire, had, by 1740, reduced the county to ten furnaces, and an output of but 1,400 tons a year.[2]

Another factor in the general decline was the ruin of the ports, due to the slow encroachment of the sea, and the gradual filling-up of the once teeming estuaries with sand. In 1715, the borough of Arundel petitioned Parliament for relief, with the warning that "the mouth of the river (*i.e.*, the Arun) is so stopped-up that, without some speedy care be taken, the navi-

---

[1] Campbell's *Lives of the Chancellors,* quot. in *Sussex Archaeol. Coll.,* XI, 183.

[2] For this and other industries see *Vict. County Hist.,* II, 199 and 249. *Cf.* Ashton, *Iron and Steel in the Industrial Revolution,* 36-38.

gation-trade will be totally lost, which will be a great loss to
the said borough and the adjoining part of the county."[3]   In
1723, Hastings petitioned in a similar vein,[4] pointing out that
"there is no harbour remaining for the convenience of shipping
on the coast of Sussex and Kent from Portsmouth to Dover,
except that of the town of Rye, which is of late years gone to
decay, and daily swerves up with slub."   In 1698, it was officially reported that for two miles there was not more than from
two to four feet of water in the Rye fairway at low tide.[5]   This
is confirmed by the *Atlas Maritimus,* a report to the Admiralty
by the Commissioners who surveyed the coast in 1728.   Rye,
it declares, "were it not for the badness of their harbour, would
be a town of great trade.   Their harbour, from being once able
to receive the whole navy of England, is now so choked up with
sand . . . . that it is almost useless."[6]

As a result of this depression of trade and industry, Sussex
became almost entirely agricultural, as it is still, indeed, today.
Lumber, cattle and grain had become its most important
products, as Defoe found while on his famous tour.   As a
fishing center, Sussex had been important since the Doomsday
survey; and this industry continued to be fairly prosperous, but
affected like everything else by the ruin of the harbors, so
that many fishermen had to eke out a livelihood by smuggling.
Nevertheless, it could still be said that "a Sussex carp, a Chichester lobster, an Amerley (*sic*) trout, are famous."[7]

The influence of this profound economic blight can be traced
in the political character of the county.   There must have been
many a voter in the impoverished boroughs obliged out of sheer
need to commend himself to his wealthier neighbor or influential
outsider; and exchange his franchise for a job, or for relief
from a pressing debt.[8]   Furthermore, the prosperity of a whole

[3] *Commons' Journals,* XVIII, 192.

[4] *Ibid.,* XX, 128.

[5] *Vict. County Hist.,* II, 159, quot. *Sloane MSS,* 3,233.

[6] *Sussex Archaeol. Coll.,* XI, 180.

[7] Chamberlayne, *Present State,* 20.

[8] *E.g. Add. MSS,* 33,064, ff. 39-40, and f. 49.   Hutchinson, *Collection,* 46.

community might depend upon the favor of a lord, and the election largesse must sometimes have proved a godsend. It was said of New Shoreham that the villagers got rich every seven years by pocketing the gifts for their votes.[9] At Bramber the ale-house keeper boasted that he made £300 on a single pipe of Canary during the bye-election in 1724.[10] Lastly, the very smallness of the boroughs made it easier to buy up the few voters or tenements. The son of the soil, too, is cautious and suspicious of change, and more inclined to pursue the even tenor of his political way than the enterprising townsman.

Sussex has a long coast-line, with many harbors, both large and small, and the shore of France is not far distant. Given these circumstances, and mindful of the general trade depression, the existence of widespread smuggling was to be anticipated. Contraband wares were exported as well as imported, and the business flourished notoriously, in spite of the King's laws and the King's men. As might be expected, the chief illegal export was wool, grown on the high, grassy downs. In 1660, an Act had been passed entirely prohibiting the export of wool, and two years later illicit trade in the article was made a felony. This, as well as the milder legislation of William III (7 & 8 Gul. III., c. 28), had no effect, and there were few convictions. The law of 1698 (9 and 10 Gul. III., c.40), providing that no person living within fifteen miles of the sea in Kent and Sussex should buy any wool without entering bond with sureties that no wool bought should be sold to anyone within fifteen miles of the sea, was openly and flagrantly defied. In 1721, for example, it was reported to the Privy Council that French sloops, with thirty or forty men each, not only trafficked with ships in the Channel, but actually sent their boats ashore, with eight or ten armed men to assist the smugglers, who now came down in gangs to the seaside even in the daytime, in defiance of the laws, and often set a guard on

---

[9] *Sussex Archaeol. Coll.,* VIII.
[10] Defoe, *Tour,* I, 130.

the officers of the Customs.[11]   Two years later, Defoe found the Customs officers riding about like huntsmen, beating up their quarry.   The *owlers*, as their human game was called, sometimes actually assaulted and killed the officers in turn, so that the latter were often obliged "to stand still and see the wool carried off before their faces, not daring to meddle."[12]

Import smuggling had been increased by the wars of Marlborough, and was carried on largely in tea, brandy, silks, and lace.   The extent of the traffic is revealed by the numerous references in the *Calendar of Treasury Papers,* where, in September, 1735, a correspondent of Sir Robert Walpole recalls the fact that about a year previously, on visiting relatives in Kent and Sussex, he had observed that wherever he went "they drank no tea but what was run."[13]

So important and audacious was the trade that it became a factor in local politics.   Public opinion was opposed to the duties, and justices hesitated to commit popular smugglers, while politicians found it necessary to intercede for those who had fallen into the clutches of the law.[14]   Moreover, it is quite reasonable to believe that the existence of a lucrative but unlawful trade helped to bring about an unprincipled attitude toward other corrupt practices, and a general decline of public virtue in the field of politics as well, especially in and about the port towns.

Two hundred years ago the roads of England were universally bad, but those of Sussex, especially in the lower-lying Weald, had long possessed, and justly, a most unenviable notoriety.   "Souseks full of dyrt and myre," wrote Leland quaintly in the days of Henry VIII, while Cowper spoke of the northern part of the county as "a sink of about fourteen

---

[11] *Privy Council Register,* no. 87, George I, no. 3, 194.

[12] Defoe, *Tour,* I, 123.

[13] *Cal. Treas. Papers,* 1735-1738, 47.

[14] For examples see *Add. MSS,* 32,688, ff. 158, 166, and 212. *Cf.* Torrens, *Hist. of Cabinets,* I, 435.

miles broad, which receives all the water that falls from two long ranges of hills on both sides of it."[15] Communication by land with the outside world was almost entirely confined to damp, sunless lanes, bad enough in dry summers but impassible in winter. When Prince George of Denmark visited Petworth in the winter of 1703, a member of his entourage wrote an account of the state of the roads that is worth quoting *in extenso*. He described the journey as being "through the worst ways I ever saw in my life. We were thrown but once indeed in going; but both our coach, which was the leading one, and his Highness's body coach would have suffered very often if the nimble boors of Sussex had not frequently poised it up, or supported it with their shoulders, from Godalming almost to Petworth; and the nearer we approached the Duke's house, the more inaccessible it seemed to be. The last nine miles of the way cost us six hours to conquer them; and indeed we had never done it if our good master had not several times lent us a pair of horses out of his own coach, whereby we were able to trace out the way for him."[16] While on his well-known tour in the early twenties, Defoe saw an ancient lady of quality near Lewes "drawn to church in her coach with six oxen, nor was it done in frolick or humour, but meer necessity, the way being so stiff and deep that no horses could go in it."[17]

The absence of means of easy travel must have brought about a state of no little isolation, which, combined with the factors already mentioned, would tend to make the political control of the county easier. Particularism and local tradition would be fostered, while personal sentiment would go a long way in politics, the lead of the local squire or county magnate being regarded as a requirement of loyalty almost feudal. Moreover, when the county elections came round, many voters who

[15] Campbell, *Lives of the Chancellors,* quot. in *Sussex Archaeol. Coll.,* XI, 183.

[16] *Sussex Archaeol. Coll.,* XIV, 15.

[17] Defoe, *Tour,* I, 129.

were known to be unfriendly could be left at home, helpless in
a sea of mud; while their more loyal or pliant neighbors would
be provided with the means to get to the polls through the
opulence and foresight of the magnate.

As might be expected, the towns of Sussex were with few
exceptions referred to with contempt by travelers of those days
as poor, insignificant places, sunk in torpor and in mire.   It
mattered little that many a fine old Norman church or abbey
lay half in ruins within their confines, proclaiming a consequence long gone by. Defoe found Rye, Winchelsea, and Hastings to "have little in them to deserve more than a bare mention." Winchelsea was only "the skeleton of an ancient city," the
gates standing "near three miles from one another over the
fields, where the ruins are so buried that they have made good
corn fields of the streets, and the plough goes over the foundations over the first floor of the houses."[18]   In 1728, a Sussex
tradesman, describing the coast towns,[19] spoke likewise in his
diary of the "ruins of Winchelsea, which had lost even the appearance of a city, even the rubbish of it."   West of the place,
he goes on, "we have nothing of note but Hastings, a small
town, and though the chief of the Cinque Ports, yet of no other
consideration, having neither trade nor harbour, fort nor castle,
not need of any."

Macky and Defoe alike found Steyning and New Shoreham
to be poor, miserable little market-towns, the primary interest
of the latter being shipbuilding, just as when John Lackland
landed there on his way to a throne, over five hundred years
before. Both travelers single out little Bramber for opprobrium,
describing it as even more wretched than the two other places,
"there being scarce a house in it fit for a stable." The most
pretentious house was said to be the tavern, and altogether the
place boasted "not above fifteen or sixteen families in it, and of

---

[18] Defoe, *Tour,* I, 124 and 130-131.

[19] *Sussex Archaeol. Coll.,* XI, 181. Many years later, Coventry Patmore
described Winchelsea in similar but more poetic language as "a town
in a trance, a sunny dream of centuries ago; but Rye is a bit of the old
world living pleasantly on in ignorance of the new."

them not many above asking you for an alms as you ride by."[20]

Chichester, with its Roman walls and fine Norman cathedral church was at this time interested in the grain trade, its once famous malting and needle-making industries having largely vanished.[21]   Lewes, at the edge of the downs, and crowned with its castellated acropolis, fared best of all, as a small but pleasant and beautifully situated town.

What manner of men dwelt in these drowsy hamlets?   To those who knew them best, the generality of the sons of Sussex in the days of the first two Georges seem to have been distinguished by their uncouth ways and their devotion to the bottle.   Of booklearning, there was little enough among the farmers, and when the good burgesses of Seaford addressed their candidates in 1722, their handwriting was a scrawl, and about half of them signed by mark.[22] The yeomen of the better sort were regarded as squires, and loved to boast of their honorable lineage among their familiars at the pothouse.   Burton, the theologian and classicist, writing in the middle of the century, had little good to say of them, and referred with a scholar's scorn to "the inelegant roughness and dull hilarity of their conversation," and their innocence " both of academical discipline and London courtesies." He attributed their boorishness to "their intercourse with servants so assiduous and with clergymen and gentlemen so rare.   Being illiterate they shun the lettered," he goes on, enjoying the antithesis, "being sots the sober.   Their whole attention is given to their cattle and everything else fat, their own intellect not excepted." But, as if to relieve this unpleasant picture, the gallant doctor had to admit that there was something admirable about the women of Sussex, who, although modest and industrious, had all the feminine blandishments of attire, and were "both by nature and education better bred and more intelligent than the men."[23]

---

[20] Macky, *Journey,* I, 99, 103, 109. Defoe, *Tour,* I, 130. *Sussex Archaeol. Coll.,* VIII, 264.

[21] *Sussex Archaeol. Coll.,* XXX, 149-150. Defoe, *Tour,* I, 135.

[22] *Add. MSS,* 35,584, f. 249.

[23] *Sussex Archaeol. Coll.,* VIII, 257.

This being the case among the squires, it is not to be wondered at that Spershott, describing the Chichester of his boy-
hood in the days of George I, represents the plain town laborers
and the yokels as homely and free in their conversation; and
much given to such barbarous diversions as bull- and badger-
baiting, and cock- and dog-fighting, and rough street-sports like
cudgelling and football.

Drinking to excess, the vice of the century, was universal
here with all classes; and "revelings and night freaks too
common." Wine and strong beer were the favorite potations
at the numerous public houses. "It was not uncommon with
some farmers, when they came to town, to get drunk and stay
two or three days till their wives came to fetch them home."[24]

With an unprosperous and untutored electorate, of such
easy standards of personal morality, it is not remarkable that
political morality in Sussex was no higher. These conditions
among the voters go a long way to explain the existence of the
corrupt practices to be described below.

Dotting the countryside, and dominating the social and political scene no less than the stone keeps of their ancestors, stood
the mansions of the great governing families. Here lived the
Sussex grandees six months out of the year, enjoying a pre-
eminence that was almost feudal, and receiving the homage
of the lesser folk about them. Although paramount in the
southeast, the Pelhams were by no means the only great county
family, for Sussex could boast of possessing the principal
residences of the first three peers of the realm. The premier
duke and Hereditary Marshal of England, Thomas, eighth
Duke of Norfolk (1683-1732), had a seat in the southwest
at the venerable, half-ruined castle of Arundel, where Mont-
gomery and Fitzalan had once kept their state. The second
peer of England, the haughty Charles, sixth Duke of Somerset

---

[24] *Ibid.,* XXIX, 228-230. The Sussex watering-places were to perform
wonders for these men and women, who could not go to Bath or Tun-
bridge; but the vogue of Brighthelmstone, Bognor, and Hastings was still
in the future.

(1662-1748), likewise occupied the ancient seat of the Percys at Petworth, in the northwest. The third peer, Charles, first Duke of Richmond (1672-1723), was established after 1720 at Goodwood; and the Earl of Scarborough at Stanstead, near Shoreham, not to mention peers of lesser rank.

The presence of these great nobles naturally resulted in making Sussex one of the most aristocratically controlled counties in England, all the more so since there was no enterprising industrial or moneyed interest to furnish competition. As long as the magnates were in accord politically, the parliamentary situation rested in the hollows of their hands.

After this short consideration of certain social and economic factors of significance in relation to politics, the parliamentary situation itself may now be examined.

It was one of the anomalies of the old unreformed system that Sussex, with twenty-eight members, stood so near the head of all the English counties in the number of representatives in the House of Commons. This number was made up of the two county members, eighteen from the boroughs of Arundel, Bramber, Chichester, East Grinstead, Horsham, Lewes, Midhurst, New Shoreham, and Steyning, and eight from the four Cinque Ports lying within her boundaries, namely, Hastings, Rye, Seaford, and Winchelsea. Only three other counties exceeded this number—Cornwall having forty-four, Wiltshire thirty-four, and Yorkshire thirty.

With the inconsequence so characteristic of many time-honored English institutions, this disproportionate number was due not to her relative importance in the eighteenth century, but in the Middle Ages. In the days of the first three Edwards, when the representation of Sussex and the Cinque Ports was becoming fixed, and when the inland counties were thinly populated, the share of Sussex in the greater numbers and flourishing trade of the southern and southeastern seaboard entitled her to this preëminence.

The county franchise belonged, as it had for three hundred years, to the resident freeholders possessing estates of the clear annual value of forty shillings. The majority of these voters resided in the eastern part of the county, in the rapes of Lewes, Pevensey, and Hastings.[25] At the beginning of the eighteenth century, the average number of electors that appeared at the hustings varied from about two thousand to over three thousand.[26]

As has been seen, Sussex was one of those counties where large estates, held by great landowners, were numerous; and where, in consequence, aristocratic pressure on the electorate was tremendous. Among the oldest and wealthiest of these ruling families were the Pelhams. It is of the first importance in the political history of the family that their *latifundia* lay largely in southeastern Sussex, the very section where most of the forty shilling freeholders were to be found.[27] It was due to this that the Pelhams had been able practically to dictate their own election and that of their allies at almost every county choice for generations.[28] Furthermore, the different branches of the family had intermarried with the other county families like the Ashburnhams and the Morleys, and so consolidated their position until it was almost impregnable.

Although Chichester was the county town, it was inconveniently situated in the extreme west of Sussex; so that most of the freeholders had to travel from thirty to seventy miles, at great expense and over almost impassable roads, in order to vote. To remedy this, it had been provided in early Tudor times that the county court be held alternately at Lewes and Chichester (19 Hen. VII., c. 24). This arrangement had not been successful altogether, and an Act of William III (7 & 8 Gul. III., c. 25, secs. 3 & 4), had forbidden the adjournment of the poll without the consent of the candidates, in an effort

---

[25] *"Reasons humbly offered, etc."* and *Add. MSS,* 33,058, ff. 203-208.

[26] Whitworth, *Succession of Parliaments,* 223. Cooper, *Parliamentary History,* 2. In 1705, 2,914 voted; in 1708, 1,717; in 1713, 2,780; and in 1714, 3,002. In *Add. MSS,* 33,058, f. 208, the number for 1714 is given as 3,283.

[27] *Add. MSS,* 33,166, ff. 5-13.

[28] Duckett, *Penal Laws,* 440-441.

to prevent irregularities on the part of the sheriff. It is significant that when the freeholders of the east petitioned Parliament against this Act, they were answered by counter-petitions from the westerners, who declared their rivals wished to elect *both* members.[29] It is obvious upon which side the Pelhams would be.

The borough franchise in Sussex was on a fairly broad basis for the old parliamentary régime, but in actual practise both the boroughs and the Cinque Ports had passed almost entirely out of the control of their inhabitants. Of the nine parliamentary boroughs, six (Arundel, Bramber, Chichester, Lewes, New Shoreham, and Steyning) were scot-and-lot boroughs; and the rest (Grinstead, Horsham, and Midhurst) burgage boroughs, while in the Cinque Ports the franchise was nominally exercised by all the freemen.

The burgage boroughs, in Sussex, as elsewhere, were the easiest to control, as, in the first place, the number of electors was small, and as the burgages in all of them were almost wholly in the possession of local landowners.

At East Grinstead, the northernmost borough, Lionel, seventh Earl and first Duke of Dorset (1688-1765), controlled twenty-nine of the thirty-six burgage tenements. At election time, his Grace's agents brought his deeds to the polls and carried them away afterward, without scrutiny. Most of the voters were non-resident and had to be imported at the duke's expense at election time, in the same conveyance with his steward and the latter's clerks. After a collation, likewise at the ducal charge, they were taken home the way they came.[30]

At Horsham, although the Duke of Norfolk was lord paramount, most of the burgesses voted independently until 1705, when the Tory Eversfields first succeeded in getting control and returning their nominees. Owing to the fact that the number of burgage tenures was disputed, the Eversfield interest was challenged in 1713 by the local Whig family of Ingram.

---

[29] *Commons Journals,* XV, 595. Horsfield, *Sussex,* II, App. 23.

[30] Cooper, *Parl. Hist.,* 18-19. Duckett, *Penal Laws,* 441.

In 1715 another contest occurred, and this time the Ingrams were successful in unseating their rivals by a petition. Inasmuch as the two groups were nearly balanced, an amicable *modus vivendi* was arranged, partly through a marriage alliance, by which their combined hold on the borough was established. Whigs and Tories then obtained a seat apiece for the next eight Parliaments.[31]

Midhurst was the seat of the Viscounts Montagu, who owned the 120 tenements and nominated the members in the 17th century. Early in the 18th century, however, the control was alienated to John Meers Fagg, of an influential county family; and when his daughter married Sir John Peachey of West Dean, the third baronet of that name, in 1752, there were no contests for over half a century, the two families supplying the members themselves, the inhabitants being content to have the farce of election performed by the deputy of the proprietors.[32]

The scot-and-lot or inhabitant householder boroughs were only less easy to control, and if the parliamentary borough did not happen to be coextensive with the actual town, so much the better. All the would-be borough master had to do, once he had most of the property in this restricted area, was to fill the houses with tenants who would obey orders. Inasmuch as there were no large scot-and-lot boroughs in Sussex, the number of householders in any of them was suitably small.

Arundel, which today has such a mediaeval aspect, was the first borough of this kind, and is interesting as one of the boroughs which Newcastle was to influence later through a marriage connection. Sir John Shelley, fourth baronet (1692-1771), of an old Sussex family seated a few miles east at Michelgrove, married the duke's youngest sister, Margaret Pelham, in 1727, and sat for the borough from then until 1741.[33]

---

[31] Albery, *Parl. Hist. of Horsham,* chs. III and IV, *passim.* Oldfield, *Rep. Hist.,* V, 35-36. Duckett, *ibid.*

[32] Cooper, *Parl. Hist.,* 28. Oldfield, *Rep. Hist.,* V, 53-54. Duckett, *op. cit.,* 441.

[33] *Eng. Hist. Rev.,* XII, 460, ff.

The hypenated scot-and-lot boroughs of Bramber and Steyning were notable for their scandalous reputation even under the old unreformed system, as well as for their singular proximity. Lying at the foot of glorious downs, and consisting of a single street, the centers of the two boroughs were less than a mile apart. Bramber was divided into two parts, the northern one forming a part of Steyning, and distant about half a mile from the other part.[34] Unlike the notorious boroughs of Weymouth and Melcombe Regis in Dorset, they were not municipally united in spite of their propinquity, and in the last years of the old order the members were even elected on a different franchise in the two boroughs.

At Bramber, the franchise was vested in the inhabitants of ancient houses or those built on ancient foundations, paying scot and lot. In our period, the bulk of this property was divided between two rival families, headed by Sir Richard Gough, and Thomas, first Viscount Windsor, and the contests between the two interests were numerous. Henry Sidney, who had been active in Bramber politics, gives an amusing account of an election there in 1689, in which his relative, Sir John Pelham, seems also to have been interested. On that occasion there was great expenditure in bribery and treating, and one candidate paid £10 a man. A generation later, Defoe found Bramber "scandalously mercenary."[35]

At Steyning also there were frequent contests between rival patrons, the knightly family of Fagg being especially influential after the Restoration, if the number of times its members were returned means anything. In 1712 the Duke of Richmond spent £500 in an unsuccessful effort to elect Lord Bellew. The duke's chaplain came eight days before the election and promised the voters, not an otherworldly recompense, but five or six guineas a man, forthwith. A week later his Grace, who had

---

[34] Oldfield, *op. cit.*, V, 42 and 51-52. Dallaway, *Sussex*, II, pt. 2, 157.

[35] Cooper, *op. cit.*, 11. Oldfield, *op. cit.*, V, 51-52. Sidney, *Diary*, I, 114-120. For contests at Bramber see *Com. Journ.*, XVIII, 155-156 and XX, 20.

all his royal father's easy-going ways, appeared in person and went from house to house, soliciting votes. That night, on the eve of the election, the grandfather of the reforming third duke regaled the voters and their wives at the George Inn, the character of the entertainment being revealed by a witness at Westminster, who testified "the company had nothing to eat, but they drank all night."[36]

Chichester was too close to Goodwood not to come under the Richmond influence, along with its bishop and cathedral clergy. The voters objected to this, and there was an occasional contest by minor interests, especially that of the May family.[37] The second duke, while still Earl of March, was himself chosen for one of the seats in 1722; and when his father drank himself to death the following year there was a bye-election which caused Newcastle some concern. The latter, always on the lookout to extend his power, had used his interest to get his faithful old mentor, Thomas Bowers, elevated to the see of Chichester the year before; and his influence thus introduced into the city was being exerted in behalf of Lord William Beauclerk, the second son of the Duke of St. Albans. One Mr. Woodyer wrote him, announcing his intention to stand, and the duke had to appeal to the new bishop to induce him in a tactful manner to retire. "Ye vacancy being made by ye D. of Richmond, I thought indeed it was reasonable he should recommend his successor. . . . I find all our friends think we should espouse ye D. of Richmond's interest as being ye most solid support of ye Whigg interest in Chichester."[38]

Lewes is interesting as the only borough in Sussex in which the Pelhams, through the ownership of most of the houses, enjoyed complete right of direct patronage. One of their numerous tribe or their relatives or friends had been regularly returned from the borough since the Restoration.[39]

---

[36] Cooper, *op. cit.*, 34-35. *Com. Journ.*, XVII, 117 and 213-214.

[37] Cooper, *op. cit.*, 15-16.

[38] *Add. MSS*, 32,686, ff. 252-253.

[39] Cooper, *op. cit.*, 24. Oldfield, *Rep. Hist.*, V, 13. In 1719, in a letter subscribed by 132 electors, the constables and inhabitants of Lewes wrote

The voters of the port of New Shoreham seem to have been most free with their favors, and to have passed willingly from one allegiance to another. In the picturesque words of his Grace of Richmond,[40] it was "a whore that is anybody's for their money." So shameless did the practice finally become, that in 1771 the borough was thrown into the hundred, following the revelation of the activities of the "Christian Club." In the first quarter of the century two wealthy Londoners who owned lands and houses at New Shoreham were very influential. The first was Sir Gregory Page, baronet, of Greenwich, a director of the East India Company, and therefore in a position to get shipbuilding contracts for the town; while the other was Sir Nathaniel Gould, of Stoke Newington, a Turkey merchant and director of the Bank of England, both of whom sat for the borough at different times.[41] Newcastle does not seem to have been interested there until the election of 1734.[42]

The Cinque Ports, set aside by the Conqueror as the special and privileged guardians of the English shore, had long since outlived their original usefulness. They still, however, proved to be of the highest value in providing convenient means of packing the Administration benches in the House of Commons, and consequently presented a picture of almost unparalleled jobbery and misrule. Only one of the original five, Hastings, lay in Sussex. Two others in that county, Rye and Winchelsea, had been added later, but placed on an equality with the others; while Seaford, the fourth, was really only a "limb" or "mem-

---

Newcastle as follows: "Having heard your Grace's letter publickly read to us, (we) do not only herein return your Grace our hearty thanks for the honour you have done us in recommending soe fit a person as Mr. Yorke to serve as one of our representatives in this parliamt. for this town for the present vacancy, butt alsoe begg leave to assure your Grace that wee do unanimously and entirely approve of him, and shall be ready on all occasions to show the regard we have to the favours your Grace has pleased to lay upon us." *Add. MSS,* 35,584, f. 179.

[40] *Add. MSS,* 32,688, f. 46.

[41] Cooper, *op. cit.,* 30-31. Cheal, *Shoreham,* 231-232. *Com. Journ.* XIII, 357.

[42] *Add. MSS,* 32,688, f. 46.

ber" of Hastings, but remarkable as the only subsidiary port that sent members to Parliament.

Until the Revolution the Warden claimed the right to nominate one or both of the parliamentary representatives from each port, but one of the first Acts of the new reign was to abolish this practice.[43] This was only preliminary to bringing the ports into more complete subjection to the Admiralty, and from that time on nomination was largely an Administration affair. Control was achieved by setting up a large custom-house establishment in each port to supply sinecures for election purposes. Places in the Excise and Post Office provided patronage for still other faithful supporters of Government. "Caleb D'Anvers" once declared in the *Craftsman*[44] that "the number of dockmen and cinque ports officers is as regularly computed at our county election as a gentleman reckons his own tenants; and what is still worse, many of our boroughs are totally governed by this mischievous dependence. They have places in the Cinque Ports, or they work in the docks, and are therefore looked upon as the property of the Admiralty. The candidate comes to them with a letter from thence, and it is well known that they must either pay obedience to it, or forfeit their bread. · · · They have their orders, and dismission is almost the certain consequence of non-compliance."[45]

The right to vote was legally vested in all the freemen, or barons, as they were called, in the ports; that is, all persons legally liable to share the expenses of the town. Freedom was determined by (1) birth in the town of a father free at birth; (2) ownership of a freehold tenement; and (3) by purchase, redemption or gift. But, as a matter of fact, the privilege was actually kept in the hands of a few by dishonest discrimina-

---

[43] 2 Gul. and Mar., sess. 1, c. 7.

[44] The *Craftsman*, no. 381, vol. 11 (Oct. 20, 1733).

[45] The docility of the Cinque Ports is illustrated by George Onslow's election for Rye in 1754. "At the recommendation of the Duke of Newcastle, . . . I was chosen most honourably, for my election cost me not a shilling save my moiety of the entertainment." H.M.C. *Onslow MSS*, 520.

tion on the part of the magistrates. The magistracy itself was
a nest of corruption. It was supposed to consist of a mayor
and twelve jurats in each port; but the practice was to reduce
this number as low as possible, so that the several shares of the
spoils of office would be the greater. And, although the mayors
were prohibited by statute (9 Ann. c. 20) from holding office
two years in succession, the law was evaded by rotating the office
among relatives. The magistrates were generally common, un-
educated fellows, and they chose the freemen from among the
poor in order to control them the better.[46]

The land comprised in the rape of Hastings had been in the
possession of the Pelham family ever since Henry of Bolingbroke awarded it to Sir John Pelham in 1412, for his numerous
services. So extensive was the estate that an applicant for the
post of rent-collector in 1717 declared the employment he
sought involved a ride of twenty-five miles over thirty-seven
parishes, in order to see the 667 tenants.[47] The influence of so
great a landlord was naturally immense, as will later be seen,
and so the members usually supported the Government interest.

There is plenty of evidence of a slightly later date that the
Duke of Newcastle's control was made possible in part by using
his influence to prevent the admission of political opponents to
the freedom of the port of Hastings; and it is entirely probable
that such methods were used at an earlier period, not only there,
but in the other ports as well. On January 29, 1733, Thomas
Pelham, the duke's cousin, wrote to John Collier[48] at Hastings
with regard to a mandamus which had been applied for by
two men, to compel the mayor and jurats to admit them to
freedom: "My Lord Duke desires me to acquaint you that
his Grace hopes you will take the effectual methods for preventing the admission of any freemen by virtue of such man-
damuses as you mention are already serv'd on the mayor and

---

[46] For the political situation in the Cinque Ports, see Cooper, *op. cit.*, 38,
and Oldfield, *Rep. Hist.*, V, 349-367.

[47] *Add. MSS*, 33,064, f. 80.

[48] For this man, see below, p. 140.

jurats, in favour of John Sargent and John Shorter. Mr. Strange was retain'd some time ago for any affairs we might have depending in the Law Courts here, relating to Hastings, and leaves before the next election; but if you can likewise have the Attorney & Sollicitor Gen'l for this particular businesse, my Lord Duke has no sort of objection to it."[49]

Rye was a Treasury borough, all freemen with few exceptions having soft berths in some revenue department. In order to provide places for so many men, the number of Treasury warrants for appointees at this stagnant port in 1723 was exceeded in all England only by those for the flourishing port of Bristol![50]

Seaford resembled Hastings in that the nomination was exercised in the Administration interest by a neighboring family, that of Thomas of West Dean, from whom it descended, upon the death of Sir William in 1706, to the Harrisons of Sutton. The Pelhams also owned large estates at Seaford, and one of their seats was located hard by, at Bishopstone; and accordingly, a Pelham was occasionally returned in the seventeenth century. Newcastle seems to have endeavored from the beginning to increase his influence here, as will be seen, but did not get complete control until 1747.[51]

Winchelsea was another Treasury borough, of special interest for having fallen to a great extent under the control of George Dodington, a director of the East India Company, who had himself returned in 1705 and several times after. His nephew, the notorious Bubb, got his first parliamentary experience when he was sent to St. Stephen's from Winchelsea, in 1715. After returning from his embassy at Madrid, he was re-elected, but chose to sit instead for Bridgewater, Somerset. This seat he held continuously until 1754, and in the meantime his political

---

[49] *Collier Correspondence,* I, 90-91.

[50] Chamberlayne, *Present State,* 516-518. Rye had a Collector with a salary of £60 and a Deputy-Collector and twenty other officers with salaries totaling £2,040. At Bristol, 105 officers got £2,757/11.

[51] Cooper, *op. cit.,* 46. *Sussex Archaeol. Coll.,* VII, 109, and Oldfield, *op. cit.,* 44-48.

connections, all stalwart Administration Whigs, were returned for Winchelsea through his influence.[52]

Something may be said here of the direct influence of Newcastle and other peers in elections, already alluded to several times. Strictly speaking, there seems to have been no legal bar to the intervention of peers in the county choice[53] but the resolution that was passed by the House of Commons at the beginning of each session "that it is a high infringement of the liberties of the Commons of Great Britain for any lord of Parliament, or any lord lieutenant of any county to concern themselves in the election of members to serve for the Commons in Parliament." Nevertheless, the practice was continued because the lower chamber was packed with the nominees of noblemen. The activities of the Duke of Richmond at Steyning were typical of practices that were immemorial, and which, in the eighteenth century, were usually taken as a matter of course. A particularly flagrant case occurred at Lewes in 1705, when the Dukes of Somerset and Richmond, *en grande tenue,* sat boldly on the very bench at the county poll. Everyone present expected them to carry all before them until Turner, the High Sheriff, who failed somehow to let the stars they wore blind him to his duty, ordered them away.[54]

Such then, was the political *milieu* in Sussex in which the future Duke of Newcastle began his operations. It will be observed that his power in county affairs, by virtue of which he was able to influence regularly the return of members, was due to his inheritance of the broad Pelham acres. He was the head of all the Pelham clan, and his exalted rank in the peerage and in the State gave him an authoritative position in their midst. He was their fountain of patronage and preferment. It will also be observed that in our period, so far as the Sussex boroughs are concerned, his undisputed control was limited to one—

[52] Cooper, *op. cit.,* 51. Oldfield, *op. cit.,* V, 413. Sanders, *Dodington,* 9, and 57-58. Sir C. H. Williams, *Works,* I, 21-25. H.M.C. *Egmont MSS,* I, 31.

[53] Pollard, *Evolution of Parliament,* 2d ed., 110.

[54] H.M.C. *Portland MSS,* IV, 185 and 190.

Lewes—which he likewise inherited; though his preponderance was great, but by no means absolute, in Hastings. At Seaford he was seen endeavoring to augment his influence, while at Chichester the young Duke of Richmond was observed at the outset of his career as Newcastle's lieutenant. Elsewhere the boroughs of Sussex were in other hands, albeit mostly Administration-Whig hands. In later life, in the commanding position of minister of state and arbiter of the political destinies of the highest, he was able to influence other borough patrons, such as the Ingrams.

Another source of Newcastle's power in the county lay in his office of Vice-Admiral of the Coast of Sussex. His grandfather, Sir John Pelham, and Duke John had both been Vice-Admirals before him, and after his appointment in January, 1715, he held the post for life. The functions of the office were mainly financial and judicial, but involved the patronage of the subordinate judges and marshals who actually did the work.[55] There was a source of profit as well, which might be of a somewhat dubious character. The Vice-Admiral claimed the sole right to seize all flotsam, jetsam, and lagan found along the coast, as perquisities of the Admiralty, but he probably had a keener eye for the share due to him.[56]

But Newcastle's estates in Sussex were not merely of interest to him as sources of power and wealth. He had all the English nobleman's affection for the countryside, and a special devotion to Sussex. He once explained his feeling in a letter to his favorite sister, Lucy, Countess of Lincoln. After referring to the question of settling some estates on his brother, he wrote: "The parting with one of my houses in Sussex wld., I doubt not, be thought only reasonable but of very little consequence to me, especially by those who have admired and blamed my partiality to that county." But he claimed Sussex as the place

---

[55] For the subject of Vice-Admiral, see Marsden, *Eng. Hist. Rev.*, XXII, 736-757 and XXIII, 468 *sqq.*

[56] Newcastle found it worth while to carry on a prolonged litigation for the possession of three half-anchors of brandy found floating near Hastings in 1722. *Add. MSS*, 33,058, ff. 259, 275, and 293.

where his ancestors had lived before him, and as the place where he wished to retire when out of public business, and concluded: "Love of popularity and publick views have not been the only inducemts. to me to live in Sussex."[57]

There can hardly be any doubt that this love for the ancestral shire, its traditions, its fields, its game, was one of the real sources of his strength, for it really demonstrates the healthy sense of comradeship between the rustics and the great peer. The Duke of Somerset, with his Horatian aversion for *profanum volgus,* might command their awe, but never their affection or the political power that accompanied it. In the case of a man like Newcastle, it was a most kindly and harmonious relationship; for the multitude had not yet learned discontentment, but humbly accepted the lot to which it had pleased a divine tactic to assign them. Like Burke, they liked to think of aristocrats as "the great oaks that shade a country and perpetuate their benefits from generation to generation." Likewise, between the head of the Pelhams and the gentry, there were ties of blood and a loyalty founded upon many affectionate recollections of favors given and received.

Newcastle inherited three country seats in Sussex, where, year in and year out, like Chaucer's Franklin, he played the amiable rôle of St. Julian among his neighbors and dependents. Of these establishments the fortified brick manor house of Laughton Place was the oldest; but after serving as the family seat since 1534, it had been given up in the time of the duke's father for the more livable Halland. Evelyn mentions this Tudor mansion among other "sweet and delectable country seats"; but in spite of its eleven hundred acres of deer-stocked park, the duke found it "so dirty as not to be lived at above a month or six weeks in ye summer." Nevertheless, it became famous as his favorite residence when in the county.[58] Bishop-

---

[57] *Ibid.,* 33,064, f. 257.

[58] So it was that Walpole, in a letter to Newcastle in 1723, spoke of his great new seat of Houghton in Norfolk as "a little Halland, & full of all sorts of suitors, visitors and what not." *Add. MSS,* 32,686, f. 274 (July 10, 1723).

stone, his third establishment, was too small to be of much use to him save as a hunting lodge.

In 1715, with comparatively few seats subject to his nomination or influence, Newcastle (then Earl of Clare), was only at the beginning of his parliamentary and electioneering career. He had not yet begun that long tenure of the greatest offices, which gave him such solid influence in so many boroughs and counties. Neither could he command the support of the innumerable bishops and lower clergy, who were to owe the incidence of the apostolic succession to him. Such being the case, his early activities cannot be expected to display the perfection of a later date.

It is proposed to examine next in some detail the electioneering methods used in Sussex at the outset of his career for the choice of the first Parliament of George I. The manuscripts, which provide such ample material for the study of later elections, are, for this period, unfortunately scanty; but they nevertheless reveal a political machine already in excellent working order. The young peer, whose practical experience in such matters could hardly as yet have been very extensive, is seen in full control of this machine, and showing himself as a talented apprentice in that art of which his consummate mastery was later to make his name a byword for all time.

Whatever he may have lacked in experience was amply provided by his trained agents in the county—men who probably had served old Sir John and the first Baron Pelham in the same capacity. Little of them but their names and their prodigious exertions is to be gathered from the manuscripts. Anthony Trumble, a Hastings attorney, seems to have been his lordship's principle factotum at this time.[59] Another was Captain James Pelham, a distant cousin of the peer.[60] Both men were untiring in his service—writing letters, interviewing voters, paying off bills, and keeping him constantly advised of the progress of the campaign. Their work was begun months before the dissolu-

---

[59] *Add, MSS,* 33,058, f. 201, is his commission of agency.

[60] Namier, *Structure of Politics,* II, 523 note.

tion of Parliament, and when one election was over they began laying the wires for the next. But there were times when the contest waxed hot, and the presence of no mere subordinate, however skillful, would suffice; and on these occasions it was necessary for the commander-in-chief to take the field in person. The very sight of the great man, not to mention the redoubled issues of strong drink, was enough to revive the ardor of his followers, and throw the enemy into confusion.

One form of electioneering, in the best traditions of Old England, was never allowed to lapse, but was carried on all the year round:

> His table dormant in his halle alway
> Stood redy covered al the longe day

Both at Halland and at Bishopstone it became the custom of "giving small beer and doles of wheat to all the people of the country about them, without stint or limitation, and of entertaining all comers and goers, with their servants and horses." This jovial but ruinous practice not only used up annually the combined rent of both goodly estates, amounting to a thousand pounds sterling, but absorbed an equal sum besides![61]

Another practice, the political benefits of which were more or less continuous, was that of making substantial presents to the boroughs. In March, 1715, Trumble was directed to pay the cost of recasting a bell for the church of All Saints at Hastings. Since the bell would cost over twenty pounds, the agent was charged to arrange with the mayor where the news was to be sent, so that it should not spoil for want of telling![62] Ostensibly to encourage navigation at the same port, the Earl of Clare also let it be known that he planned to build a ship of 140 tons burden the summer following the election. This brought on requests for shares.[63] About the same time, at the instance of the Hastings magistrates, he applied unsuccessfully to the

---

[61] *Add. MSS*, 33,137, f. 472.

[62] *Ibid.*, 33,064, f. 50.

[63] *Ibid.*, 33,064, f. 52.

Ordnance Commissioners to furnish the town with powder and ammunition.[64]

If as yet there were no bishops in his train, as lord of many manors the earl had extensive influence over the lower clergy through his patronage to numerous livings.[65]   Such men were as good as so many electioneering agents, and had the additional persuasiveness of ghostly authority.   The fidelity of at least one devoted man of God is well brought out in a letter from John Gallop, "clerk of the church" in Hastings, written immediately after the election.   "My lord, my humble service to your honour, and at the Request of the freemen, your friends, I shall, the next Lord's day, God willing, perform their desires and my owne in singing the 20th Psalm, the first 4 verses, and the last 4 verses of the 118th psalm—this is the joyfull day indeed, and I am sure a joyfuller day to Hasting, to all people's Satisfaction, hath not been for many years.   I wish you with all my heart all Joy and happiness, long to live, and all designs and purposes may prosper to the end of your Issues, and God give his blessing to your honour, which shall be the prayer of your most humble servant."[66]

Especially before the election, many voters were flattered by complimentary or persuasive letters from his lordship or his agents, a cheap and easy way of bringing some of them around. It is extraordinary what an intimate knowledge of the family connections, financial interests, and personal peculiarities of the most plebeian voters was possessed by the peer and his agents.[67]

"The strategem of winning men by places," mentioned by Lord Clarendon, was a familiar weapon in the electioneering armory of the Earl of Clare.   The voters had a keen sense of their importance before elections, and some were not backward about demanding assistance or preferment; while others were more coy, or were attached to some different interest, and so

[64] *Ibid.*, 33,058, f. 231 and 33,064, f. 61.
[65] *Sussex Archaeol. Coll.*, LV, 233-257.
[66] *Add. MSS*, 33,064, f. 43.
[67] *Ibid.*, f. 50.

had to be solicited with divers inducements to win their compliance. An interesting example of the last-named kind is revealed in a vigorous letter from Trumble to one John Gyles, a
clerk in the South Sea offices in London, together with the
conciliatory one he got in response.[68] Gyles's uncle and some
other relatives, apparently freemen at Hastings, were opposing
Lord Clare in the interests of Sir Joseph Martin, who had got
the clerk his place. All arguments with the uncle having failed,
the nephew was urgently pressed to come down and use his
influence with the old gentleman, with the promise of something
more substantial than a paltry clerkship for his pains.

The election once over, the faithful were not forgotten.
Trumble was kept busy looking to the mortgages hanging over
the heads of loyal voters, conferring with Archdeacon Bowers
about the relief of widow Balier, and so on.[69] Petitions continue to come in from voters who felt they too had a claim to
reward,[70] and refused to be overlooked.[71]

In spite of these inducements, there were some voters who
either could or would not listen to reason, and in such cases
intimidation was resorted to. One John Casswell wrote the

---

[68] Add. MSS, 33,064, ff. 38 and 39-40. See Appendix C for both letters.
[69] Ibid., f. 60.
[70] A most interesting example of these is a letter from one Thomas
Curtis, at Hastings, to the earl at Halland, forming Add. MSS, 33,064,
f. 54. "Honrable Lord Pallam, Earle of Clare," it begins, "my oumble
Duty to you and your Brother. this Cum to bag of your Lord Ship one
my banded Kneese to make frinds for me to Mr Comton and Mr Butlar
and Mr Hanrey Pallam, that I may git in to a smole in ploy—ffor I have
bin much out of order since I came from the County Choyce that my
youran that Cum out of my body have bin Nothing but blud and watter,
so I bag that you Dow not for git the words you towld mee the first day
you came to Towne for I hop I was the bast frind in the towne that
sarved your Lord Ship in both Choyses, as Mr Trumble now vary wale.
all at praysant from your Ever and Duty full Sarvant to Command. (P.S.)
If your Lord Ship place to see mee Before you goo to London, order mee
a Line or tow, and I will com oufar in privat. if not the Lord of Heavan
blis you and Sand you Safe to goo and Cum is the prayer of your Duty
full Sarvant. (P.P.S.) I would fane see you if your Lord Ship think fit."
[71] Add. MSS, 33,064, f. 49.

earl that he could not help in the county election because the opposition threatened to put him out of his house, and also got his creditors to press him for payment.[72] Geoffrey Glyd, who kept the "Royal Oak" at Hastings, wrote to the same effect after the election, complaining that the brewer, being incensed at his failure to support Sir Joseph, threatened to distrain his goods and evict him if he did not pay at once the £37 he owed him. These are both cases of the opposition trying to terrorize the supporters of the Pelham interest; but the earl could put the screws to unlucky tenants and debtors himself, in the same way, if the need arose. If the voter were a placeholder, he would think twice before taking any action against the interest of his patron, who thus exercised coercion in another form.

But probably the most successful, as well as the most spectacular device to capture and retain voters was the election entertainment, immortalized by the brush of Hogarth. Appealing to the incurable festive and gregarious instincts of mankind, it could be used to inspire the wildest spirit of enthusiasm and loyalty. It was a source of Clare's success that he never failed to provide the expected festivities, nor hesitated from pride of caste to play the genial host, and pledge the most plebeian audience in many a flowing bowl. But the cost was enormous. " 'Tis not to be imagined," wrote Henry Sidney's agent at Bramber, in 1689, "what those fellows, their wives and children will devour in a day and night, and what extraordinary reckonings the taverns and alehouses make, who, being burgers, are not to be disputed with on that point." He goes on to describe a convivial scene, to the like of which young Clare must already have been more than a mere spectator: "You would have laughed to see how pleased I seemed to be in kissing of old women, and drinking wine with handfulls of sugar, and great glasses of burnt brandy, three things much against the stomach, yet with a very good will, because to serve him I most honored."[73]

---

[72] *Ibid.*, f. 46.
[73] Sidney's *Diary*, I, 117, 119.

So far, nothing has been said of the future Duke of New-castle's early influence outside of Sussex, in which county it has been examined in detail. Although his interest in Notting-hamshire and Yorkshire was considerable, it is with the south-ern county that his name is generally associated, and it was there that he often directed the campaign in person. Sussex always came first in his affections. "I will never abandon Sus-sex," he assured his admirers in Nottingham, when they asked him for his brother as their candidate.[74] Moreover, the two northern counties were too far from the capital and the main scene of action to hold the duke there for long.

Nottinghamshire, with about half the area and a population estimated in those days at eighty percent of that of Sussex,[75] was largely his property as the heir and successor of the Holles earls and Cavendish dukes.[76] His seat was the great chateau overlooking Nottingham, built after the Restoration by Wil-liam Cavendish,[77] Duke of Newcastle, upon the ruins of an ancient stronghold supposed to have been erected originally against King Alfred by the Danes. The county sent eight members to Westminster—two for the shire itself and six for the three boroughs of Nottingham, Newark-on-Trent, and East Retford.

The control of the county proper, as was natural, was largely in the hands of its greatest proprietor; although the friendly Whig Duke of Kingston, seated at Thoresby, a relative of Newcastle's, also had to be considered.[78] Furthermore, the Whigs did not have everything their own way, as in Sussex. Time had not extinguished the spirit of Royalism which was so strong during the Civil War, when the county had been staunchest for King Charles;[79] for it will be remembered that

---

[74] *Stowe MSS*, 247, f. 165.

[75] Chamberlayne, *Present State*, 16 and 20. *Somers' Tracts*, X, 596-597.

[76] For details of his estates in Notts, see *Add. MSS*, 33,320, ff. 3b and 5b.

[77] A picture of the Castle forms the frontispiece of the first volume of the *Victoria County History* of Notts. See also Deering, *Nottinghamia*.

[78] *Stowe MSS, supra.*

[79] *Memoirs of Colonel Hutchinson*, I, 163.

it was at Nottingham that he had raised his royal standard, on a stormy day in August, 1642. The Tory interest, headed by Lord Middleton of Wollaton,[80] was very powerful, and Newcastle and the Whigs crossed swords with it not only in 1715, but in 1722 as well. "It was myself," boasted the old duke in 1767, referring to his early career, " and I may also say myself alone, who rescued the county of Nottingham, and all the boroughs in it, out of the hands of the Tories: the county from Willoughby and Levinz; the town of Retford from Levinz and Digby; the town of Newark from Willoughby; the town of Nottingham from Warren and Sedley."[81]

In addition to his tremendous prestige as lord paramount, Newcastle also filled the exalted offices of Lord Lieutenant and Custos Rotulorum, as Duke John and the Cavendish dukes had done before him. He was also Lord Warden of historic Sherwood Forest, which lies in the western part of the county. As the King's representative, he had the right of appointment to the coveted offices of deputy-lieutenant, and of granting commissions in the county militia, besides nominating all the justices of the peace.[82] Later, when he became a power at Court, he could also influence the choice of sheriff, who was of more than usual political significance here; being returning officer not only for the county, but for the borough of Nottingham as well.[83]

Nottingham was a good-sized, flourishing town, with considerable trade and industry, lying on the navigable river Trent. Its ale and malt had a widespread reputation for excellence, and were consumed as far away as Lancashire and Yorkshire; while

---

[80] Sir Thomas Willoughby, 2d baronet and first Baron Middleton (1670-1729). H.M.C. *Portland MSS,* V, 339.

[81] *Add. MSS,* 33,003, f. 386, quoted in Bateson, *Narrative of Changes,* 167-168.

[82] Webb, *Parish and County,* 286-287, 373-375, and 381. 14 Car., II, c. 3, and 15 Car., II, c. 5.

[83] *Add. MSS,* 32,686, f. 59. *Eng. Hist. Rev.,* XII, 546, quoting *Add. MSS,* 32,688, ff. 536 and 543.

the production of stockings, glass, and earthenware was also of some importance.[84]

Such a borough presented political problems and difficulties unknown in Sussex. In the first place, the town was large and prosperous, and, unlike the degenerate little market-towns of Sussex, sought to emancipate itself from aristocratic servitude.[85] The franchise was very popular, being exercised jointly by the freemen (both by birth and by service), and the forty-shilling freeholders; so that there were about a thousand resident and two hundred nonresident voters.[86] Then too, as Newcastle himself declared, Nottingham was the most Tory town in the county.[87] Under such conditions, it was not possible to obtain the obedience of the borough by the methods so successfully followed in Sussex. Although small money-bribes were widely distributed among the voters at election time, this practice was too expensive to be long persisted in. Hence, if Newcastle was to enjoy the patronage of the borough, he had to win confidence and popularity by means of constant *largesse*. How he did this is revealed in the following *Humorous Account of Revels at Nottingham Castle*, found in the *Hardwicke Papers*.[88]

"The siege of Nottingham Castle in the year 1720, when the present duke of Newcastle held out for about eight weeks against the whole posse of the county; and even the town and county of the town of Nottingham, vizt., the whole corporation, the mayor, aldermen, &c, who were all called in for assistance, and came as a recruit to the county at large. First, with much difficulty, we waded up to the very mouth thierrow (*sic*. through?) the counterscarpe *ore tenus*, brimful of champaigne &c, and then with knife and forke in hand, we stormed the pye crust fortification, which was arm'd and guarded with very fat,

---

[84] Defoe, *Tour*, II, 550, and Deering, *Nottinghamia*, sec. V, "Of the Trade and Manufactures of this Town," pp. 91-101.

[85] Oldfield, *Rep. Hist.*, IV, 323.

[86] *Add. MSS*, 32,686, f. 25.

[87] *Stowe MSS*, 247, f. 165.

[88] *Add. MSS*, 35,838, ff. 424 and 424b. Boney or Bunney Park was the massive residence of Sir Thomas Parkyns, nearby.

rather white, venison: when we found the castle so well stor'd with all sorts of viands and provisions, we wonder'd not he held so long a campaign, since he called to his aid the Duke of Burgundy, French &c, who brought in all their wines to his assistance. Most were shot in their legs, and others terribly cut in their heads, so that they could not retreat without being carried out, some in handbarrows, others in wheelbarrows, and a certain aid de camp at the gate could not reach his head-quarters tho but a little way into the town. And my lady dutchess lending her Berlin to Mr Burnel, the present high sheriff's father, to carry him to Mr Alderman Bearn's, he so very much defiled it, both upwards and downwards, that the coachman with much difficulty cleansed it, but could not sweeten it without setting Rosemary Lane on fire, and burning aromaticks in it. And the females which came as spectators to the siege, many were so very much intoxicated that they stript themselves and showed the naked truth that they were prepared for combate, which occasioned a certain man of the law to say he would bring his action sur le case on behalf of his housekeeper. I glory in that I was the only person that came off sober, without wound or scar, and had got safe home, had not my coachman been made drunk, that he overturn'd me before I got to Bunny fort." (etc.)

The scot-and-lot borough of Newark-on-Trent, the last borough created under the old system, had fallen into corrupt ways almost at once.[89] It was the property of the Duke of New-castle, and its members were his nominees.[90] The small free-man borough of East Retford was also under his control.

The duke's estates in the West Riding of Yorkshire were not so extensive as in some counties, but they fortunately included two of the thirteen boroughs of that county. Aldborough (the Roman Isurium) and Boroughbridge, mere hamlets, lay in the same parish and were but half a mile apart, but the franchise was different in each. Aldborough was a scot-

---

[89] *Savile Corres.*, 43-48.
[90] Oldfield, *Rep. Hist.*, IV, 327-329. *Stowe MSS*, 247, f. 165.

and-lot borough, and Boroughbridge a burgage borough; but the same ducal master owned the houses in the former and the burgages in the latter.[91]

It is interesting to observe that after the death of Duke John in 1711, his friend and associate, Robert Harley, apparently set about managing his county and borough influence in Notts and Yorkshire in his own interests, with the approval of the dowager; but of course all that came to nothing with his fall from power.[92]

Summing up, finally, the degree of Newcastle's influence in the infancy of his career as election manager to the Whig party, it has been seen that his political ascendancy extended to three counties, and involved the disposition, approximately, of twenty seats.[93] With such a train of clients at his back, and an unexhausted purse, with strings unloosed, it is not strange that his friendship was eagerly sought by the Whig factions that fought for the control of the country, and that he was able to make such rapid progress on the road to power.

---

[91] Oldfield, *op. cit.*, V, 329, and 332.

[92] H.M.C. *Portland MSS,* IV, 519; V, 245, 328, 338, 344.

[93] *Viz:* County Sussex; Lewes; Hastings; Seaford; County Notts; Nottingham; Newark; East Retford; Aldborough, and Boroughbridge. Confirmed in a letter he wrote to Lord Stanhope on Oct. 14, 1719: "I will take ye liberty to say yt I myself will make the difference of sixteen votes." *Add. MSS,* 32,686, f. 152.

IV

Political Apprenticeship 1714-1716

Queen Anne breathed her last on the first of August; and on the same day, after the list of Justices was opened by the Archbishop, the Lords and Justices issued a proclamation, with the name of Baron Pelham of Laughton signed among the rest, proclaiming George the First as King. The new sovereign came to his crown and kingdom, in the rhetoric of Bolingbroke, "with as little contradiction and as little trouble as ever a son succeeded a father in the possession of a private patrimony."

On that day also, Pelham took his seat for the first time[1] with the Lords of Parliament, and was now enrolled among the self-styled hereditary counsellors of the Crown. The first business of that memorable day was the administration of the oaths of allegiance and abjuration, and he was thus among the first emphatically to manifest his loyalty to the new King.

The formation of a Court and a government was the momentous subject which now engrossed aristocratic minds, and Bernstorff, the head of the King's Hanoverian councillors, refers in his *Autobiography* to the incredible multitude of applicants who imagined themselves "fit for anything and everything."[2] Unlike the case in 1689, when neither party had an exclusive claim to William's favor, King George had the best of reasons for launching the Whigs upon their long monopoly of power. But the four lean years since Sacheverell's impeachment had so whetted their appetites for office that Whig fought with Whig for the privileged places under the new establishment.

There were few, if any, differences in the principles or programs of the various competitors, for the key to the domestic politics of England from the Revolution to the Reform Act must be sought not so much in parties and principles but in the

---

[1] *Lords' Journals,* XX, 4.

[2] Quoted in Ward, *Great Britain and Hanover,* 73.

alliances and antagonisms of aristocratic factions or family connections and their hangers-on. The members of each group were bound in loyalty to their leader by blood or self-interest, rather than to the Crown they all wished and claimed to serve.

At the head of one of these groups stood John, Duke of Marlborough. The greatest captain of his age, he had also conducted its most brilliant Administration, and now, after two years of watchful retirement, he returned to England, indifferent alike to parties and principles, but hoping to resume his former preëminent rôle. His old place of Captain-General had been restored to him as the first official act of the new King, and important Household appointments were distributed among his daughters and their noble husbands.

Second in command of this group was the imperious Charles Spencer, third Earl of Sunderland, a thoroughgoing Whig, and, like his father before him, a skilful and intriguing politician. The influence of the duke, his father-in-law, had helped him to become Secretary of State in the Queen's day, and he now coveted the same high office under the new régime.

Pelham seems to have been on close personal terms with the Marlboroughs at this time,[3] and it is significant that not long after he was discreetly courted by the crafty duchess in the interest of her grandchild, Lady Harriet Godolphin, the only daughter of the duke's heir.[4] Furthermore, he was related both by blood and marriage with Sunderland,[5] a fact of considerably more political importance in those oligarchic days than at present.

The second coterie of real political importance was led by Charles, second Viscount Townshend, and his brother-in-law, Robert Walpole. Both were veteran leaders of the Whig cause in Queen Anne's reign, and, what was more, Townshend

---

[3] Craggs' letter of July 15, 1714, would indicate as much. *Add. MSS,* 32,686, f. 16.

[4] *Coxe MSS,* xlvi, quoted in Thomson, *Memoirs,* 538.

[5] They were second cousins, both being great-grandsons of Robert Sidney, second Earl of Leicester. Sunderland's first wife, Arabella Cavendish, was also a sister of the Dowager Duchess of Newcastle, Pelham's aunt.

had won the especial confidence of the King's all-powerful
Hanoverian advisers. Pelham stood unquestionably in the
very closest relations with Townshend, whose first wife had
been his half-sister Elizabeth; and the two were likewise kinsmen through common descent from the famous general, Lord
Vere of Tilbury. Further evidence of his intimacy with this
group is to be seen in his visits to Townshend at Rainham and
London, and in the familiar letters he received from Walpole's
brother Horace, the diplomatist.[6]

There is no period in Pelham's early life concerning which
less is to be known than that which falls in the space of the
stirring year 1714. One thing is certain, however, and that is
the fact that his birth, wealth, and political influence, not to
mention his services to the dynasty, would make him anticipate
some substantial recognition from the King he had helped to
his throne. Owing to his youth and inexperience, he could
by no means expect a place in the Administration at once;
however, there were titles and appointments in the Household
that were highly acceptable. But still, preferment was to be obtained through the King's advisers, and Pelham, between two
luminaries, had to decide into which orbit he would fall.

The reasons which induced him to make his choice will
never be exactly known, but for the next two years he was a
close adherent of the Administration of Lord Townshend,
who, on September 17, 1714, was sworn Secretary of State
in the place of Bolingbroke. The offer of marriage was allowed
to lapse, although Pelham admitted that the notion of having
posterity descended from his Grace of Marlborough had great
weight with him. Sir John Vanbrugh, a confidant of both
parties concerned, who may be said to have acted in his own
character of Coupler in this affair, found that the young peer

---

[6] In a letter of August 17, 1714, to Pelham at Halland, Walpole, after
supplying the news, refers to a secret understanding with Lady Ashburnham, not to be revealed to his "spouse." He concludes: "I must, in behalf
of ye town, tell you that your presence is mightily wanted and desired."
Add.. MSS, 32,686, ff. 20-21, also f. 98 (same to same).

had thoughts about marriage unusual with men of quality and fortune. After his experiences with the behavior and understanding of the ladies of the Court and town, he told the knight, he despaired of finding a consort that measured up to his expectations, and so the matter was put off until another day.

The elevation of Townshend to the place of first Minister was a surprise and disappointment to Marlborough, and dashed the hopes of his ambitious son-in-law. Probably neither appreciated the singular favor in which the viscount stood with the all-powerful Hanoverian Ministers, as a "safe" man and a straightforward supporter of the Succession, or understood what a dangerous and suspicious reputation they themselves enjoyed in the same quarter. Townshend proceeded with the task entrusted to him of forming a Ministry. Instead of his old place, Sunderland, who had sat in the mighty Junta, was offered the indignity (as he deemed it) of the Viceroyalty of Ireland, which he accepted only upon the understanding that he need not leave England. The other secretariat, that of the Southern Department, was bestowed, on Horace Walpole's recommendation, upon General James Stanhope, who had won distinction as a commander and diplomatist in the Peninsula. Robert Walpole, whose financial genius was already recognized, had to be satisfied temporarily with the subordinate but lucrative post of Paymaster of the Forces; but the very next year, upon the death of Halifax, he became First Lord of the Treasury.

At this juncture, just two months after his accession, King George set foot for the first time in his new dominions. He disembarked at Greenwich, and Pelham was undoubtedly among those nobles and gentlemen who accompanied His Majesty on his walk from the landing to the Palace hard by. The next morning, he had the honor of kissing the royal hand, along with those favored few that "received such marks of royal favour . . . as their firm and unshaken adherence to the succession had merited."[7] Among the rest was Oxford, and

---

[7] Boyer, *Pol. State,* VIII, 248-251.

the spectacle of his contemptuous dismissal by the King must have afforded some satisfaction to the young peer.

On the whole, the new Administration was a remarkably strong and able one; but the King found, upon his arrival, that unmistakable signs of disunion had already made their appearance in its ranks, and that the contest of the Whigs *in* place and those *out* of place was beginning to develop. An egregious and fatal blunder had been made in failing to gratify the craving of Marlborough and his lieutenant for power, and neither was the man to swallow his mortification. The duke was stung into resuming his traitorous correspondence with the Pretender. He even sent him money for the Stuart cause, but he was nevertheless too calculating and self-centered to hazard everything he was or hoped to be in an uncertain and desperate enterprise.[8]

In spite of this, the influence of the fascinating Captain-General with his next-door neighbor, the King, was so great that many voices were raised against it.[9] Still other Whigs protested loudly at the choice of this or that Minister, while all parties railed at the inordinate ascendency of the hated foreign advisers that surrounded the King. Lastly, the Hanoverian Tories were bitterly disappointed at their practical exclusion from the Cabinet, despite their fidelity. They were not deceived by the factitious device of giving Nottingham the place of Lord President, and Shrewsbury that of Master of the Horse, in order to lend the Cabinet a nonpartisan aspect.

Pelham, however, had no reason to be numbered among the

---

[8] *Stuart Papers,* I, 335, 338, 340, 394-395, 401, and II, 135. Bolingbroke wrote "James III" that he doubted Marlborough's sincerity, and that though "his inclination lead him right . . . that inclination is warp'd by several unfortunate habits. The love of money and the love of power will, I doubt not, prevail, and make him keep aloof, till your affairs are in such a posture as to make even them operate for you, and in that case you would not want him." *Ibid.,* I, 390 (Aug. 15, 1715).

[9] For the discordant notes see: H.M.C. *Portland MSS,* V, 501 (Oxford to ?Stratford); *Wentworth Papers,* 425-430, and 439 (Bathurst to Strafford); *Stuart Papers,* I, 436 (Berwick to James III); H.M.C. *Portland MSS,* VII, 206.

malcontents, for on the 19th of October, the day before the
Coronation, he was created Viscount Houghton and Earl of
Clare.[10]   With due allowance for the fulsomeness of such
documents, a translation of the patent is worth quoting in part.
"As to himself," it runs, "being the worthy representative of
both houses (*i.e.* Pelham and Holles), while he was yet a
beardless youth, he was happily emulous of entering upon the
practice of his family's virtues as his best inheritance: and he
exhibited such ripened proofs of an extraordinary genius that
his uncle, the Duke of Newcastle, seemed in no measure to
regret not having male issue, since he had a nephew endowed
with such perfections to fill the place of the most endeared
son.   He therefore appointed so promising a youth, who had
already deserved so well of his country, and in time to come
will deserve better, to be the heir of his very great estate."[11]
The most interesting passage is that, however, which seems to
assert that Pelham declined the offer of a higher title, pre-
sumably a dukedom, made him at this time.[12]

Within the next few months, Clare, as he may now be called,
was invested with the family honors of Lord Lieutenant and
Custos Rotulorum of the counties of Middlesex and Nottingham, Lord Warden of Sherwood Forest, and Vice-Admiral
of the Coast of Sussex.

Queen Anne's last Parliament, which had been continued in
accordance with the Act 7 & 8 Gul. III, c. 15, was finally dissolved January 5, 1715, and ten days later a Proclamation
summoning a new one was issued, calling upon the voters to
"have particular regard to such as showed a firmness to the
Protestant Succession when it was in danger."

The election which ensued, coming closely upon the appeals

---

[10] This and other original patents conferring honors upon Pelham in
our period, except the ducal patent, are in *Add. MSS*, 33,063, ff. 1 to 7.

[11] Translation in Guthrie, *Complete History of the English Peerage*, II,
155-6.

[12] The original reads: *"ut ad excelsiorem posthac honoris gradum invitus
licet evehatur quem a nobis ipsi jam oblatum minus ambire quam mereri
voluit."*

and promises of the Pretender, may be regarded as a national
vote of confidence in the new government. It was also Clare's
first chance to demonstrate his ability and value to the Administration as an election manager.

Now that the Whig party was in power, his efforts were
facilitated in Sussex by the presence of the Whig Lord Lieutenant and Whig justices of the peace, while in Notts he held
the Lieutenancy himself. The political influence of the Lord
Lieutenant and of the deputies and justices of the peace he
nominated was notorious, and these offices were constantly
subject to manipulation in the interests of the Administration
in power. The return of Henry Campion, a Tory gentleman
of modest estate, for Sussex in the last election—that of 1713
—would have been impossible, according to the writer in the
Somers Tracts "had there been above five Whig Justices of
the Peace and three Deputy Lieutenants in the county."[13]

Nevertheless, the Tories had high hopes for success. The
elections of 1710 and 1713 had sent up large majorities in their
favor, and now they expected to carry most, if not all, of the
county seats. In the last session of the Parliament just dissolved, they had vied with the Whigs in a display of zeal for
the King's business, and it had been Windham and Bromley
who had proposed the increase of his Civil List. The Tories
began their agitation long before the King arrived in England,
and, being at that time in possession of the offices, and having
the support of the Church, they enjoyed a strong position.
Dr. Sacheverell went up and down the land, warning his
hearers of the menace of Lutheranism, and it was hoped that
he would repeat his triumph of four years before.[14]

Clare lost no time in beginning operations in Sussex, where

---

[13] *Somers Tracts,* XIII, 567-568. On the same subject, see Webb, *Parish
and County,* 375 and 381, and H.M.C. *Onslow MSS,* 502. When George III
attacked the Whig oligarchy, one of his first steps was to take the advice
of Henry Fox to "strip the Duke of Newcastle of his three Lieutenancies."

[14] For the Tories' activities see Lady Cowper's *Dairy,* 19; Boyer, *Pol.
State,* IX, 160; Michael, *Eng. Geschichte,* I, 463-465, and 489, and II, 32-34;
Wentworth Corres., 411, 415, and 430; and H.M.C. *Portland MSS,* V, 501.

he appears to have spent most of his time after the early part of August, while his agents were busy simultaneously in his northern county. From the accounts that have survived, the contest in Sussex, so far as Clare is concerned, centered about the fight with the Tories for the possession of the two seats for the county. The Whig candidates were Spencer Compton (later Earl of Wilmington) and James Butler, while Bertram Ashburnham and one of the Eversfields stood in the Tory interest. The election is interesting as being the last conducted upon strict party lines for years to come, and so hot was the encounter that his Lordship wrote Trumble that he would rather have him "give five guineas a man than let Mr. Ashburnham have any."[15] The poll was held at Chichester, which meant that provision had to be made for the transportation of many freeholders who would otherwise be unwilling or unable to make the trip. An examination of itemized bills, like the one following, that were afterward presented to him, is the most graphic way of bringing out something of the fashion in which Clare handled this problem.

"Account of several Charges on ye Freeholders by my Lord Clare's orders on ye Election for ye County of Sussex, 17 of February, 1714/5 by Tho: Grebell[16]

To Expenses on ye Freeholders ye day before we set out	5	15
To Daniel Sandown for his team..................	15	
To ye carpenter for fitting of seats...............		5
To Thirty five hired horses, at 15s each...........	26	5
To 20 freeholders in & with ye Waggon to bear there Charges	20	
To 35 freeholders for there charges of horse and them selves, each 30s......................	52	10
To 40 poor freeholders for hiring people in there absence, & there own loss of time, 8 days, at 2s per day	32	

---

[15] *Add. MSS,* 33,064, f. 47.
[16] *Add. MSS,* 33,058, f. 225, also ff. 223-224 and 227-228.

To severall other expenses on ye freeholders at Chi-
       chester, Arundel, Shoram, Newhaven, Born,
       and Hastings.............................   17   15

To one Kedwel of Winchelsea....................   1   1   6

To a messenger sent to my Lord Clare about the
       ffellows of Hasting.......................   10

                                                    ————————
                                                    171   1   6

To the fferrys of Rye & Winchelsea..............   1   5

                                                    ————————
                                                    172   6   6

To Mr. Edward Martin of Winchelsea............   1   1   6

                                                    ————————
                                                    173   8   0

To Mr. Butlar, our Town Clerke" (amount wanting)

The election lasted two days, and the final poll showed:
Compton, 2066; Butler, 2143; Ashburnham, 1106; Eversfield,
1224; an overwhelming victory for the Whigs. Altogether,
280 freeholders living out of the county appeared for the occasion, many, very likely at Clare's expense.[17] It was doings
such as these that caused one simple Sussex yeoman to con-
fide to his diary that the Whigs were generally supposed to
have won "by all manner of indirect practices, particularly
of the E— of Cl—e, their grand patron."[18]

The other contest which absorbed the earl's attentions occurred at Hastings, where his first cousin, Henry Pelham of
Lewes, and Archibald Hutchinson, an independent Whig, were
standing in his interest, with Sir Joseph Martin, the sitting
member, as the opposition candidate. The peer came down
in person on the 11th of January and, after a reception from
the magistrates, gave a "splendid and generous" entertainment
in return.[19] This was not the only expenditure in connection

---

[17] *Ibid.*, ff. 203-208.

[18] *Sussex Archaeol. Coll.*, XXV, 171-172, *Diary of Thomas Marchant,
of Little Park, Hurstpierpont.*

[19] *Add. MSS*, 33,064, f. 38, also f. 47.

with the canvass. The thirsty freemen were plied with liquid arguments at the "Oake" and the "Bell" by the energetic Mr. Trumble, and out-of-town voters were sent for. When the votes were counted, it was found that the earl had not spent his money to no purpose, and he had the pleasure of seeing both men he had supported returned.

Meanwhile, the struggle for the Tory stronghold of Nottingham was being waged by his lordship's agents in the interests of John Plumptre and George Gregory, the Whig candidates. The situation is best described in a letter written in November by Plumptre himself.

My Lord: This week Mr. Gregory and I have imploy'd in going round the town from house to house, that we might not fail of speaking to every elector. We, each of us, gave a shilling to drink to such as would acept of it, which cost us about fifty pounds, and there are about 200 voters living out of town, most of whom must be applied to the same way. The town generally is well enough inclin'd towards us, & if ye men would poll according to their promises we have already a majority; but if ye enemy comes with money, all will be turn'd adrift again. It is the general belief here that we shall have no opposition, which makes the market low, so that many proselytes might be gain'd over at a small expence, but we dare not begin with one, for if it should be known that we have given but ten shillings to anyone, all ye poor men who have promised us already would have ye same or turn against us, which would run to a charge too unreasonable at a time when we are in hopes of no contest. However, as it is not fit that your lordship should be ignorant of any circumstances of our condition, it is my duty to acquaint your lordship that if our antagonists begin not to stir of 10 days or a fort-

night longer, that delay will so sink the expectations of those who gape for money that it will, in all
probability, afford an opportunity of fixing, for less
than seven hundred pounds, the burrough in good
hands for severall years to come.[20]

The total outlay, however, was rather more than estimated,
actually coming to nearly £865,[21] but Clare, to whom money
was no object, probably felt that the victory which was bought
by this undisguised bribery was well worth it.

The privilege of sitting for one of Clare's nomination boroughs in Yorkshire was eagerly bespoken by "lame ducks" in
the party. Lady Mary Wortley Montagu urged her impecunious husband to persuade him that he was "obliged in Honour"
to get him chosen at Aldborough.[22] The elder Craggs, too,
after failing at Newport, "gave his poor soul to the devil if
he had not rather owe his seat to Clare than to any man in
England," and hoped he would favor him at Aldborough, in
the event of Stanhope being doubly elected there and at Cockermouth.[23] Both parties appealed to Townshend to use his influence with his youthful ally. The author of the *Crisis* too,
now a knight, was pleased at being set up for Boroughbridge,
where he was chosen as a matter of course.[24]

Throughout the country, the election of 1715 was a sweeping success for the Whigs, who were returned with a majority
of 150 seats in the House of Commons. Their opponents
had bartered the future for the present. Their zeal for Hanover came too late, and the old cry of "No Popery" claimed
them for its victim. "I see plainly that the Tory party is
gone," wrote Bolingbroke mournfully, and gone it was, for

[20] *Add. MSS*, 32,686, ff. 25-26.
[21] *Add. MSS*, 33,060, ff. 13-18. An inadequate *précis* of this and the above
is given in H.M.C. *Chichester MSS*, 223.
[22] Lady Mary Wortley Montagu, *Letters*, I, 211.
[23] *Add. MSS*, 32,686, ff. 29 and 31 (Craggs to Clare and Townshend to
Clare).
[24] *Add. MSS*, 32,685, ff. 13-19.

fifty years to come. In the boroughs, the Whigs generally had a majority of two to one, and of the sixteen members of the Cinque Ports, only one avowed Tory was chosen.[25] No less than eighteen seats, or nearly one-eighth of the total Whig majority, was due to the activities and expenditures of the Earl of Clare, who was victorious everywhere save for the county of Nottingham, where the Tories won a triumph which proved to be their last. Not only so, but the Speaker of the House of Commons, and one of His Majesty's Principal Secretaries of State owed their seats to him.[26]

After taking his seat with the peers, Clare's name appears but twice in the *Lords' Journals* before the 6th of April; but after that date his name is rarely missing from the roll. His parliamentary duties now required constant residence in London, and the work of remodeling and repairing Powis House, renamed Newcastle House after its purchase by Duke John, was begun late in 1714, under the direction of Sir John Vanbrugh.[27] This three-story Restoration mansion, still standing in tarnished splendor at the northwest corner of Lincoln's Inn Fields, was one of the finest town houses of its day, although it would fall far below the standard of the Parisian hotel of a French grandee of the same period. But, though the house still stands, the great square it overlooks has been transformed, for, at the beginning of the eighteenth century, Lincoln's Inn Fields, although flanked by the residences of the nobility, was an ugly, open, expanse, strewn with rubbish and haunted by blackguards.[28] Notwithstanding the fact that Vanbrugh hoped to have the place ready at the beginning of 1715,

---

[25] Boyer, *Pol. State,* IX, 160-161.

[26] Stanhope was actually doubly returned, and elected to sit for Cockermouth. Monson, the earl's brother-in-law, then sat for Aldborough.

[27] For Newcastle House, see Macky, *Journey,* 122, and Marks, *Historical Notes,* 60-61. There is a reproduction of an early 18th century engraving by Sutton Nicholls in Firth's ed. of Macaulay's *History,* III, 1213.

[28] Marks, *ibid.,* 27, and Gay, *Trivia,* Book III, lines 133-144. It was a rendezvous of duellists, and Duke John himself had once settled an affair of honor there. Luttrell, *Hist. Rel.,* II, 451.

it was not occupied until later in the year,[29] and not actually completed for more than another twelvemonth. Newcastle House must be numbered among those historic houses where kings and princes once were welcomed, and whose halls have known alike the candle-lighted revels of the highborn gentlemen and ladies of the Augustan age, and the comings and goings of stately bishops, diplomats and statesmen, who resolved the destinies of England there.

Here and there, beyond these aristocratic confines, lay the foul haunts of the London mob, called by one who knew it "the most cursed brood in existence."[30] Ordinarily indifferent to political change, the rabble was now brought out of its loathsome rookeries by the cry that never failed to rouse its fury: —"The Church is in danger!" The devotion to the Established Church at this time may be laid not only to the fundamental religious conservatism of the vulgar, but to the industrial competition of popish rustics and Irish immigrants, who poured into the Metropolis at a time when the importation of printed calico and linen was causing distress among the London weavers.[31] Late in 1714, also, there was a serious cattle-plague raging in London and its environs, which caused great hardship and distress.[32] Hundreds of cows had to be killed by the justices of the peace, and although at first the owners were indemnified out of the Civil List, later this was discontinued. Furthermore, prejudice against foreigners in general mounted the very steps of the throne, while the Lutheranism of the new sovereign was alleged to be as dangerous as the Catholicism of his rival.

---

[29] *Add. MSS*, 33,064, ff. 44 and 123. Newcastle wrote from thence Sept., 1715 (*Add. MSS*, 33,060, ff. 34-35). In the meantime, on occasion at least, he seems to have stayed with Lord Townshend (33,064, f. 81).

[30] Saussure, *Foreign View*, 111.

[31] George *London Life,* chs. III and IV, *passim.* Boyer, *Pol. State*, XVII, 627-640. *Cf.* H.M.C. *Trevor MSS,* 2 (H. Walpole to R. Trever), in explanation of the riots of 1736.

[32] *Cal. Treas. Papers*, 1714-1719, 31-34, and Michael, *Eng. Geschichte*, I, 488.

As Lord Lieutenant and Custos Rotulorum of Middlesex and the Liberties of Westminister, it was Clare's duty to assume command of the forces of the county in this emergency. On April 8, at the head of his deputy-lieutenants, he had an audience with the King, and presented an address composed by Steele, in which His Majesty was assured that "no endeavour on his part should be wanting to prevent and suppress the least tendency to commotion."[33]

Nevertheless, within a fortnight, there began[34] a series of popular disturbances of more or less violence, on almost every "public" day, and which were attributed by the distracted Ministry to the machinations of the Jacobites. Curiously enough, the Tories were equally certain that they were deliberately fostered by the Whigs to complete their ruin.

There was a great High Church riot on April 23, the anniversary of Queen Anne's coronation, which began at Snow Hill conduit and spread westward to Holborn Bars, and eastward to the middle of the City. A lesser outbreak[35] occurred on the birthday of the popular hero, James, Duke of Ormonde, the Pretender's secret *chargé d'affaires* in England. A month later, on the anniversary of the King's birth, there was further violence, and it was said that the bells tolled but faintly, or not at all, while churchwardens pretended that the ropes were lost. On the day following, the anniversary of the Restoration, there were greater illuminations and bonfires than on the previous one, especially in the City, where windows that were not lit up were smashed, including those of the Lord Mayor. So overpowering was the mob that the Life Guards that patrolled the streets were insulted and forced to join in the cry of "High Church and Ormonde."[36] On the tenth of June, the Pre-

---

[33] Boyer, *Pol. State,* IX, 273-275. *Cf.* Aitkin, *Steele,* II, 57.

[34] There had been Jacobite outbreaks in various parts of the kingdom as early as the preceding October and November. *Stuart Papers,* I, 335, and Michael, *op. cit.,* I, 448.

[35] Boyer, *Pol. State,* IX, 335-336.

[36] Tindal, *Hist. of Eng.,* IV, pt. 2, 245. H.M.C. *7th Rept.,* 247a. Boyer, *Pol. State,* X, 588.

tender's birthday, militia was needed to quell a great riot that resulted in several deaths and numerous arrests.[37]

These tumults were not confined to London, but broke out at various places in the provinces during the summer,[38] exacerbated, no doubt, by the proceedings against the members of the late Administration.[39]   So alarmed was the Ministry by the vigilant Lord Stair's reports of the Jacobite preparations in France, and so apprehensive of even graver disorders at home, that the King went in person to the House of Lords, where his speech was read exhorting Parliament to take measures for the defence of the nation, "under a rebellion actually begun at home, and threatened with an invasion from abroad."   On the same day, July 20th, Clare and some of his deputy-lieutenants were summoned to a Great Council which met at St. James's that evening.[40]   The Riot Act of 1553 was revived, and on the 25th proclamations were issued for suppressing rebellions and rebellious tumults, commanding papists to depart from London and Westminster and their immediate environs, and for putting the laws into execution against them and Non-Jurors.[41]   In accordance with the Commons' Address, the King ordered twenty-one new regiments to be levied, and ordered the trained bands to be ready for an emergency.[42]   Loyal addresses poured in, Lord Clare's among the rest, assuring the King that the orders regarding the papists and Non-Jurors would be enforced.[43]

---

[37] Michael, *op. cit.,* I, 489.

[38] At Birmingham, Shrewsbury, Manchester, and in Worcestershire and Staffordshire. H.M.C. *7th Report, Egmont MSS,* 239b (Berkeley to Perceval), and H.M.C. *Townshend MSS,* 158-159. *Add. MSS,* 38,507, f. 136. H.M.C. *Portland MSS,* V, 513 (T. Salt to his father). In July, travelers in Lancashire ran the risk of being roughly handled by the Jacobites if they refused to cry "Down with the Rump" with them. Michael, I, 485.

[39] Michael says (I, 486): *"Wollte man ein einziges Ereignis als die Ursache der folgenden Rebellion hinstellen, so wäre es unstreitig die Minister-anklage."*

[40] *Add. MSS,* 32,686, f. 35, and Michael, *op. cit.,* I, 508-509.

[41] *Add. MSS,* 35,838, ff. 414b-415.

[42] Tindal, *Hist. of Eng.,* IV, pt. 2, 433.

[43] Boyer, *Pol. State,* X, 111-112.

While these vigorous public measures followed one another in rapid succession, an equally effective manoeuvre of a private character was put into effect. A number of officers and gentlemen organized the Whig rabble,[44] in an effort to turn the tables against the "Jacks," as their opponents were called. In view of his past and subsequent experiences as the organizer of a Whig mob, it is altogether possible that this array was concerted and inspired by the Earl of Clare himself. As a result of all this, Stanhope was able to write Stair on July 28th that commotion was largely at an end.[45]

In describing the way in which men earned a peerage, Lord Brougham once spoke of "service without a scar in the political campaign, constant presence in the field of battle at St. Stephen's chapel; but above all, right votes in right places."[46] If House of Lords is substituted for St. Stephen's, Clare could lay claim to all these qualifications. Furthermore, if unsparing munificence in the cause of the Administration has ever merited reward, he could surely aspire to promotion, for, not long after this, Bishop Atterbury asserted that the young earl had spent the enormous sum of £100,000 in the service of the Hanoverian family.[47] These considerations, and the influence of Townshend, led to his being created on August 11th Marquess of Clare and Duke of Newcastle-on-Tyne.[48]

It can be, and has been, asserted that his elevation to the highest dignity in the gift of the Crown was out of all proportion to his age and attainments; but such a step was regarded as natural enough in the days of the "Venetian oligarchy," when family connections and aspirations, rather than prolonged and meritorious labor in the interests of the State, were the surest passports to promotion. The worthless Philip, second Marquess of Wharton, "the scorn and wonder of our

---

[44] H.M.C. *Lennard MSS*, 366 (June 21, 1715).

[45] Michael, *op. cit.*, I, 510.

[46] *Hansard*, 3rd ser., VIII, 244 (Oct. 7, 1831).

[47] *Stuart Papers*, V, 611.

[48] *Lords' Journals*, XX, 166-167.

days," was made a duke two years later while still in his 'teens
and secretly in allegiance to the Pretender, for no other reason
than that the Ministry hoped to attach him and the fourteen
seats he controlled[49] to its interest. Newcastle at least had
pursued public objects with unflagging energy and his promotion was a proof of his rising credit with the Ministry.

While Newcastle was thus establishing himself in the confidence of the Ministry, Fate was playing into his hands by
striking down some of the most conspicuous of the elder Whig
statesmen, men who had played the leading rôles on the political scene since the Revolution. Godolphin had survived his
fall by but two years, and now Burnet, Halifax, Wharton, and
Somers, in rapid succession, sank into the grave, while Oxford
lay in the Tower and his baffled rival tasted disillusionment at St.
Germain. This mortality, coming as it did at the outset of
his career, made smoother sailing for ambitious younger men
like Newcastle, whose progress was facilitated thereby.

Now, on September 6, 1715, after months of anticipation on
both sides of the Channel, "Bobbing John" raised the standard
of the White Rose in his own braes of Mar. By the first
of September the rebellion had gained sufficient headway to
embolden part of the insurgents to make their way across the
Border into England, and other invasions were expected in
Devonshire and the West. However impotent and foolhardy
the Rising of 'Fifteen appears today, the suspense and perturbation of contemporaries was genuine enough.

The danger of invasion was not the only one to be reckoned
with, for as Lord Chancellor Cowper, a careful observer and
honest adviser, told the King, should any disgrace befall his
troops, insurrections would immediately follow in many places
in England,[50] for no less than two-thirds of the country was
said to be hostile to the new régime.[51]

The unpopularity of the redcoat since the days of Oliver

---

[49] *Stuart Papers*, II, 471 (Wharton to Mar).

[50] Lady Cowper's *Diary*, 181.

[51] Michael, *Eng. Geschichte*, I, 488.

still caused Englishmen, in the hour of this double danger, to turn to their raw militia and untrained squires; and therefore it was Newcastle's duty, as Lord Lieutenant of the counties of Middlesex and Nottingham, to muster and equip their trained bands, and if necessary lead them to the fray.[52]

During August, the duke was kept busy sending out offers of deputy-lieutenancies and commissions in the militia.[53] Inasmuch as he could not take personal charge of both his lieutenancies at once, he sent instructions to his subordinates in Nottinghamshire, reminding them that their county was "a passage into Scotland, and therefore capable of doing great service." He undertook to procure such quantities of arms as were necessary, and closed by enjoining them to support the King and his government as "the only means to secure what is dear to us, both as Englishmen and Protestants."[54]

The militia of Middlesex consisted of two regiments of foot and a troop of horse, and that of Westminster one regiment and a troop. Newcastle was now, on September 21, charged by the Privy Council to put these forces in readiness, and to seize the persons and arms of all papists, Non-Jurors, and others suspected of disaffection.[55] The next day he called his deputies together for the first time and delivered a spirited address, reminding them of the impending danger and exhorting them to venture their all in the service of King and country, showing favors to none. "This pathetick, concise, and yet comprehensive speech from so young a nobleman was received with admiration and applause, and made a lively impression on the minds of the assembly."[56]

---

[52] For the military duties of the Lord Lieutenant see: Chamberlayne, *Present State*, 131-132; *Statutes of the Realm*, 14 Car., II, c. 3 and 15 Car., II, c. 5.

[53] *Add. MSS*, 32,686, ff. 37, 40, etc.

[54] *Add. MSS*, 33,060, ff. 34-35 (Sept. 20, 1715).

[55] Boyer, *Pol. State*, X, 322-324. Lord Chancellor Cowper and the Attorney- and Solicitor-General all held these seizures illegal. Lady Cowper's *Diary*, 180.

[56] Boyer, *op. cit.*, 324-326, where the speech is given in full. *Cf.* Steele. *Corres.*, II, 376-378.

Inspired by this patriotic appeal, the lieutenancy did not spare itself in carrying out orders, meeting daily, and sometimes even twice a day, for business throughout September and October at the Covent Garden Coffee House. More than eight hundred suspects were examined, to be either committed, bailed, or discharged. In his capacity of Custos Rotulorum, Newcastle was also the principal civil officer of the county of Middlesex, and the justices of the peace under him were kept busy tendering oaths, not only to suspects but also to all householders, lodgers, apprentices and men-servants over the age of eighteen.[57]

Meantime, the inexperienced patriots of Nottinghamshire, in the absence of their natural leader, were not having the same success in putting the county in a state of defense; although they lost no time in rounding up the luckless papists and placing them in safe custody. Newcastle had failed somehow to provide them with full powers to call out the militia, and not only were they unprovided with arms, but horses were lacking and the officers were altogether innocent of tactics and discipline.[58] Moreover, there were but four bridges over the Trent, and should they be destroyed it would be very difficult to get troops across, as the river was seldom fordable at this season. In view of all this, some of the deputies doubted their power to cope with a possible insurrection in Derbyshire and begged that a regiment be sent to their assistance.[59]

The exasperation and apprehension growing out of these circumstances caused the deputies, justices, and other gentlemen of County Nottingham to form, on October 20th, the first "Voluntary Association for the Defense of his Majesty's Person and Government."[60] This step seems to have been taken in imitation of the Associations of 1585 and 1680, two

---

[57] *Add. MSS*, 33,060, ff. 52-53 (Nov. 8, 1715). Boyer, *op. cit.*, 581-588.

[58] *Add. MSS*, 33,060, f. 38 (Deputy-lieuts. at Mansfield to Newcastle, Oct. 13, 1715).

[59] *Ibid.*, f. 40 (Oct. 19).

[60] Boyer, *Pol. State*, X, 435-437.

earlier occasions when the Protestant religion was in danger.[61]
The members agreed to arm themselves at their own private
charge and to put themselves under leaders of their own choice,
for the purpose of suppressing any tumult or rebellion in or
near the county.

The example of the loyalists of Nottingham was later followed throughout the kingdom, and the government hastened
to give these organizations the stamp of its approval by com-
missioning the leaders under the Lords Lieutenants. Newcastle, with all the prodigality that characterized his public as
well as his private disbursements, now offered to pay the cost
of sending half-pay officers to Nottingham, when the Secretary
at War would have put the burden upon the towns.[62] Finally,
on November 12, the day before the invaders capitulated at
Preston, the duke was able to notify the deputies that the rest
of the arms that they required were on their way and would
soon reach them, "except some bayonets and swords."[63]

In the meantime, Newcastle was among the first to follow
the lead of County Nottingham, and organized early in November "the Voluntary Association of the Nobility, Clergy, Gentry
and others, inhabitants within the County of Middlesex and the
City and Liberty of Westminster." The Association register
lay open at the coffee house for weeks, and thousands of citizens
subscribed their names. It was observed that the clergy were
of all men the most reluctant to come forward. While the
government fostered such demonstrations of fidelity, it was
understood that they were to be undertaken at the expense of
the Lord Lieutenant, and the duke must have paid heavily for
his display of patriotic zeal.[64]

In spite of numerous and well-laid precautions, the storm of
Jacobite disorder, after a brief lull, broke out afresh in London

[61] See Innes, *Eng. under the Tudors,* 331-332, and Lodge, *Pol. Hist. of
Eng.,* VIII, 217.

[62] Tindal, *Hist. of Eng.,* IV, pt. 2, 451, and *Add. MSS,* 33,060, ff. 42-43
(Oct. 27, 1715).

[63] *Add. MSS,* 33,060, f. 54.

[64] Boyer, *op. cit.,* 441-444.

at the beginning of November, and continued sporadically for the best part of the ensuing year.[65]   As in the case of the commotion of the spring and summer, there was no adequate machinery of a public character to cope with the situation, and for a time the most effective counter-measures seem to have been of a private nature.

Sometime during the last unquiet days of Queen Anne, certain substantial and well-affected citizens had begun to meet at the "Roebuck" by St. Mary-le-Bow, in Cheapside, to express their loyalty to the Hanoverian succession and to be ready to suppress disorder.   In the course of the following months a number of these Loyal Societies sprang up in the and about London, the most notable being those which met in public-houses in Longacre, in Salisbury Court near Fleet Street, in St. John's, Clerkenwell, in Tavistock Square near Covent Garden, and in Southwark Park.   From the vessel in which they pledged their loyalty, these establishments were known as "mug-houses," and they seem to have been for a while the principal agencies in opposing and intimidating the disaffected.[66]

The first outbreak occurred on the evening before Guy Fawkes Day, when the mob, carrying an effigy in a black wig to represent William of Orange, was put to rout by the loyalists.[67]

The rioting was renewed on the 17th in the St. Martin-le-Grand district.   The loyalists met their adversaries as they swarmed into Newgate Street, crying "Highchurch, Ormonde, and King James!"   After a scuffle in which a score or more of the Jacobites were knocked down, they beat a retreat down Cheapside, where they attacked the "Roebuck" mug-house with

[65] Unless otherwise confirmed, the *Stuart Correspondence,* upon which part of our knowledge of the disorders rests, must be used with caution, as its authors naturally exaggerated their importance.

[66] Boyer, *Pol. State,* XII, 127-128.   Also *ibid.,* X, 588, and Tindal, *Hist. of Eng.,* IV, 502 and 503 note.   In 1713, Macky, referred to the Mug House Club in Longacre, composed of gentlemen, lawyers and tradesmen, which met on Wednesdays and Saturdays (*Journey,* 189).

[67] Boyer, *Pol. State,* X, 588.

great fury. The defenders within fired upon them, at first with powder and then with ball, which killed two and wounded a number of other rioters. Further bloodshed was prevented by the timely appearance of the Lord Mayor, with a body of officers and citizens, whereupon the mob took to flight.[68]

Many years later, the story was told of an exciting adventure of the perfervid young Duke of Newcastle in connection with what may well have been this very tumult, during the course of which his career was nearly terminated then and there. "Heading a party with Capt". Bell, they went into a Mug House in Cheapside, now occupied by Capt". Clark of the City Militia, where the opposite mob followed; and the Riot was so great that two men were shot dead in the passage, and Mr. Pelham escaped over the houses contiguous to the market & entered the top of Mr. Bethel's house, a cheesemonger, in Honey Lane Alley, now occupied by Mr. Taggart. Mr. Bethel being applied to by a gentleman in distress let him out at his shop door; but declared had he known who he was he should have gone back the way he came: so violent were party matters at that time."[69]

However contrary it may be to the time-honored view of the Duke of Newcastle as a timorous, fluttering politician, it cannot be gainsaid that he took a robust zest in his self-appointed rôle of demagogue, which even old age could not still. For, in 1768, when the sands of life had but a few more weeks to run, he was reported as declaring: "I love a mob. I headed a mob once myself. We owe the Hanoverian Succession to a mob!"[70]

---

[68] *Ibid.,* 591-592.

[69] *Add. MSS,* 5,832, f. 114b, from the *Cambridge Chronicle* of November 26, 1768. The circumstantial detail in which this very interesting incident is narrated lends credence to the source, although it is not confirmed elsewhere. The date is vaguely given as "in the year 1715," and it is possible that the affair took place at a time other than that assigned above; but the similarity as to place and circumstances in Boyer and the news-sheet is very close. The officer referred to was probably Capt. Joseph Bell, of the Blue Regiment of London Militia (Chamberlayne, *Present State,* 661). See also *Appendix B.*

[70] *London Magazine,* June, 1768, 329.

Following this stirring affair, there seems to have been no serious outbreak during the winter of 1715-16, and the next demonstration reported took place on St. George's Day, April 23, 1716.[71]

In the meantime, the rebellion had collapsed with the surrender of the kilted invaders at Preston, the defeat of Mar at Sheriff Muir, and the inglorious flight of the Pretender. By April, anxiety was at an end, and tranquility was once more restored throughout both kingdoms, so far as any armed insurgence is concerned; but the miserable Jacobite rabble of London remained steadfast to a forlorn cause, and to a prince who had deserted them.

The King's birthday and the day following were marked by outbursts greatly inferior in vehemence to those of the year before.[72] It was evident that the government, with troops released from the field, was getting the upper hand, and on the Pretender's birthday, June 10th, his supporters had to content themselves with cautiously wearing white roses, while troops mounted and on foot patrolled the streets day and night.[73]

Once again Newcastle appears as the organizer of a Whig mob, a rôle so out of keeping with his later history. In reporting the events just mentioned, one of the Jacobite correspondents in London refers to "Lord Pelham's mob, who distinguished themselves yesterday by wearing farthing warmingpans, his Grace's cunning contrivance, which aggravated the people like fire."[74] This device, referring of course, to the insulting Whig version of the parentage of the self-styled James III, had appeared on an earlier occasion in the streets of London, when it was carried in derision before the prisoners taken at Preston.[75] Whether or not the duke was really the first to

---

[71] *Stuart Papers,* II, 141 (Thomas to Inese).

[72] Tindal, *op. cit.,* IV, 500; *Stuart Papers,* II, 266; Boyer, *Pol. State,* XI, 643-644.

[73] Boyer, *op. cit.,* 743; *Stuart Papers,* II, 227 (Thomas to Inese), and 228-229 (Menzies to Inese).

[74] *Stuart Papers,* II, 227.

[75] *Lady Cowper's Diary,* 62 (Dec. 9, 1715).

put warming-pans to this ingenious public use it is naturally impossible to say.

Tumults still continued throughout June and July,[76] but with diminishing violence; and thereafter the populace seems to have subsided to its normal feelings. The disturbances were suppressed as soon as the streets were adequately policed by armed and organized bodies of men, rather than by irregulars, however zealous. Nevertheless, Newcastle must be given considerable credit for his contributions in money and leadership in the work of checking the spread of disaffection at a time when the least success might have encouraged Ormonde to make a descent upon the capital itself. Horace Walpole probably expressed the sentiments of many when he wrote Newcastle from the Hague, referring with approval to his labors "in ye service of the nation" and expressing for him "ye respect that every Englishman that loves his country must show you."[77]

Meanwhile, Parliament had been sitting since January, and it was on the first day of the new session that Newcastle delivered his maiden speech in the House of Lords. The first efforts of men who later rise to greatness as a rule go unrecorded, so it is not remarkable that we know so little of Pelham's words when those of Fox have been forgotten. As soon as the King and Commons had withdrawn, the duke rose and spoke on the present state of affairs, closing his remarks with a motion for the Address of Thanks. He was seconded by Dorset, and was then made chairman of the committee to draw it up. If he did not, like Burke or the younger Pitt, make his mark by his first speech, the loyal Whig Oldmixon declares that it left an impression of "its good sense and eloquence."[78]

There can be no doubt that Newcastle supported Townshend

---

[76] Tindal, *Hist. of Eng.,* IV, pt. 2, 502-504n. Boyer, *Pol. State,* XII, 128-132. H.M.C. *Polwarth MSS,* I, 47 (Robethon to Polwarth). *Stuart Papers,* II, 353 (Menzies to Blackwell).

[77] *Add. MSS,* 32,686, f. 98 (Mar. 12, 1716).

[78] Boyer, *op. cit.,* XI, 99. *Parl. Hist.,* VII, 225-226. Oldmixon, *Hist. of Eng.,* III, 626.

and Walpole in their implacable demand for the impeachment and execution of the luckless Jacobite Lords, which was the principal business of the next few weeks, for it is known that in March he voted Wintoun guilty.[79]

Owing to the flight of Ormonde in August, 1715, the High Stewardship of Westminster, an office corresponding to that of Lord Mayor of London,[80] save that it was held for life, had fallen vacant. Dean Atterbury had nominated Charles Butler, Earl of Arran; but four of the Chapter had refused to vote, and a quorum was consequently lacking. The question came up again on February 28, 1716, with Newcastle as the Administration candidate. All twelve of the prebendaries were present and divided evenly between the two competitors, whereupon Atterbury, as might be expected, gave his casting vote in favor of the earl.[81] The significance of this affair lies in the interpretation which was placed upon it by the government, for Arran labored not only under the stigma of Toryism, but also that of being the brother of the outlawed Duke of Ormonde, and he had already been chosen by the defiant Oxford as its Chancellor.

Anxious to indict the Tories once again and to justify the dismissal of Nottingham from the place of Lord President,[82] the Ministry now declared the choice of Arran to be a sign of the persistence of an obstinate and dangerous spirit of disaffection, and made it a basis for a still more important project, the repeal of the Triennial Act itself.[83]

Arguments to this purpose were not wanting, nor were they without cogency. Although one rebellion was crushed, it was

---

[79] Boyer, op. cit., 362.

[80] For the government of Westminster and the nature of the Stewardship, see Miege, Present State, 133.

[81] Beeching, Atterbury, 204-207. Calamy, Account of My Own Life, II, 348-349.

[82] Shrewsbury had been dismissed some time before, and the dropping of Nottingham on February 28 left for the first time a purely party government.

[83] Torrens, Hist. of Cabinets, I, 121-122.

known to the government that the Jacobites were laying plans for a new one and had reason to believe that it would be supported by assistance from Sweden.   The Gyllenborg affair was later to confirm the suspicions of the Ministry.   Such being the situation at home, it would be like courting disaster to risk an election, while on the other hand a fresh lease of life for the sitting Parliament would stabilize the new dynasty both at home and abroad.   Other reasons there were, appealing to party and to private interests.   Newcastle's attitude toward the Septennial Bill was unquestionably determined, like that of the other peers, by considerations of its favorable effect upon his electioneering interests.

In accordance with the precedent of the Act of 1694, on the 10th of April the bill was introduced into the House of Lords. The second reading took place on the 14th,[84] and was the occasion of a long and heated debate, in which Newcastle figured rather prominently.   Lord Ferrers had urged that the Pensioners' Parliament had caused the Merry Monarch "to neglect the affections of his people," and concluded therefrom that the repeal of the Triennial Act would have the same effect.   Newcastle rose to reply, and pointed out that though the Cavalier Parliament had indeed been staunchly Royalist at first, it later became critical and hostile to the King.   "Then passing over less material objections, he urged that the present happy settlement could not be maintained without taking away the seeds of corruption: that no cause ever miscarried in so many instances as that of the rebels; but that notwithstanding their defeat at Preston and Dumblain (sic), their being driven out of Scotland with their king at their head, their disappointments in other parts, and the execution of some of their leaders, the Jacobites were as insolent as ever."   This was the reason why he had opposed lenity in a late debate.   " 'My lords,' he said with vehemence, 'you must now strengthen yourselves and disarm your enemies. It is not to be doubted but the late unnatural

---

[84] Not on the 16th, as stated in Leadam, *Pol. Hist. of Eng.,* IX, 269. See references to note 86.

and monstrous rebellion was raised and fomented by large contributions of a restless, popish faction: the same means, my lords, will be used to renew the rebellion as soon as a proper opportunity offers. Their emissaries are busy everywhere to keep up the spirits of the people for a year longer, and then they hope to retrieve all by a new election.' " He concluded by setting forth the confidence which the passage of the bill would inspire in the Allies, who had not yet forgotten their sad experience of being left in the lurch![85]

Again, according to the Jacobite accounts, when Lord Anglesea asserted that the repeal of the bill would inflame the people against the King, the duke retorted "that they did not care a pin for them, and that if they would not love him, they would make them fear him!"[86] If these high words are authentic (and there is little reason to reject them), the intemperance may be attributed to the nervousness of a young speaker; and the sentiments to a memory of his classical studies.[87]

The bill passed the Lords without much difficulty, and had an equally easy passage through the lower House. While the bill was still in the Commons, petitions against it poured in from boroughs all over England.[88] Among these were Midhurst, Hastings, and Horsham.[89] The petitioners of the second-named place at least could have been inspired by no higher motive than unwillingness to exchange their triennial harvest for a less frequent one. Newcastle, whose authority was thus flouted by a corporation which still preserved a measure of

---

[85] Boyer, *Pol. State*, XI, 441-442. *Parl. Hist.*, VII, 300-301.

[86] *Stuart Papers*, II, 124 (Thomas to Inese, Apr. 16/27, 1716). Similar expressions are attributed to Newcastle in a letter from Menzies to Inese of the same day (*ibid.*, 122), where they are said to have provoked the rebuke of Nottingham, as "a doctrine new in England, and not openly avowed at Constantinople itself."

[87] *Cf.* the words of the Emperor Tiberius: *"Oderint dum metuant"*; in Suetonius, *Vitae*, 59.

[88] *Stuart Papers*, II, 140 and 145.

[89] *Com. Journ.*, XVIII, 429-430.

independence, wrote to the magistrates and freemen, expostulating with them for their temerity.[90]

But if the constituencies protested, the members themselves showed nothing but complaisance, for reasons that are not hard to seek. In Sussex, which was probably typical of other counties, twelve members supported the measure to five who opposed it, while three failed to appear at the division. Five of the twelve were office-holders, and two more were directors in corporations closely connected with the government,—the Bank and the Company. The degree of Ministerial influence in the Cinque Ports in Sussex was demonstrated by the almost unanimous line-up for the bill. Seven members, of whom five were office-holders, and the other two relatives of Newcastle, gave their votes for the bill, and only one opposed it. A roll-call of the members for Nottinghamshire would reveal the same general docility.[91]

Newcastle had now served, it may be said, two years of apprenticeship in the service of the Whig party, and he was now about to be rewarded by being taken into partnership in the business of government. While wealth and influence had contributed their share to his advancement, as was inevitable in those days, these were not all. Patience and energy, as well as money, had been lavished in the campaign; he had borne the burden and heat of the day in the gloomy House of Lords, and, in bringing his country through a crisis, danger to life and limb had been encountered—all out of an honorable ambition to serve the State. It was not without reason that, at the beginning of 1716, his countrymen began to hail him as a patriot.

---

[90] Boyer, *Pol. State,* XXIII, 310.
[91] Data based on lists in *Parl. Hist.,* 367-374.

V

Newcastle and the Administration of Sunderland and Stanhope, 1716-1721

In the midst of these national alarms and political vicissitudes, events were taking place of a purely private nature, but of the very first consequence in the life of the new duke.

At the time of his uncle's death, it had been looked upon as a highly probable and natural thing that young Pelham would marry his pretty cousin and thus preserve the great Holles fortune intact.[1] What the sentiments of the Lady Harriet were is not known; but Pelham seems to have been quite ready to marry her, especially after the unpleasantness arose over the will. But the resentment of the duchess and the perseverence of the Harleys brought such plans to naught, as has been seen.[2]

Several years passed after this unromantic affair, and the unsuccessful suitor, thrown into the vortex of public storm and stress, seems to have devoted himself to politics rather than to the ladies. Very soon, however, pressure was brought to bear upon him from a new but very urgent source, which caused him to reflect seriously upon the subject of marriage.

In less than a year after his coming of age, Newcastle's reckless prodigality had outrun even his great fortune, and he was in a position where only the most radical action would remedy matters.[3] He had bought the thrill of victory in his first election at the price of a shower of gold, and now his

---

[1] H.M.C. *Portland MSS*, V, 53-54 and 65. *Whole Life and Noble Character of John, Duke of Newcastle*, 6.

[2] *Add. MSS*, 33,064, f. 5: "I dare scarce venture to mention Lady Herriott's name," he wrote his aunt, as late as June, 1713. "Could I be so happy as to be thought worthy of her, I can assure your Grace there is nothing in the world I would not do, either to make your Grace easy, or for her satisfaction; your Grace might in that case dispose of me and all that belongs to me." H.M.C. *Portland MSS*, V, 53.

[3] In April, 1716, Auditor Harley referred in a letter to his nephew to "how fast the Duke is galloping out of his estate." *Ibid.*, 522.

agents were presenting their bills for payment.   His fondness
for building was of royal proportions, and operations were
being carried on at three places at once.   Vanbrugh had been
given a free hand in modernizing Newcastle House: at Nottingham Castle were being laid out "the finest gardens in all
that part of England";[4] while Claremont, his new mansion in
Surrey, was springing up at a rate that was only equalled by
the impatience of its master.[5]

It is highly significant, that as early as May, 1715, old Archdeacon Bowers was able to get the small loan of £200 for his
Lordship only upon the strict understanding that it must be
repaid at Michaelmas.[6]   At the end of July he wrote again, in
tones of paternal affection, but with the most profound concern,
and painted a most alarming picture of the duke's affairs.
Evidently the latter had deliberately absented himself from
home, rather than face an expected visit and a lecture from his
old mentor.   Bowers reproached him and expressed his sorrow
for his "aversion to business, which must be of fatal consequences one time or another."   He reminded him of his recent
promise of retrenchment; but pointed out that every day's delay
in fulfilling it was dangerous, and that there was no way to pay
the vast debts "but by a frugal management."   "Pray, my Dear
Lord," he continued, "do not please your self with imposing
on us old fellows with promises & then laugh at us when ye
present turn is served.   Alas, ye injury will be principally to
your self, so your friends cannot help grieving for you.   I am
very sure your Ldp. cannot go on six months in ye way you
are in without plunging yourself into such difficulties as will
make you uneasy all your life time."[7]

But Newcastle was resolved neither to retrench nor be ruined.
There was another alternative, always open to improvident
young gentlemen with titles.   He now began to consider the

---

[4] Defoe, *Tour*, II, 548.
[5] *Add. MSS*, 33,064, ff. 122-123.
[6] *Ibid.*, f. 75.
[7] *Add. MSS*, 33,064, ff. 81-82.

offer of the fine match for which he had displayed such little enthusiasm some months before.[8]

In the meantime another offer had been made for the hand of Lady Harriet Godolphin by a family of great wealth and position, which the Duchess of Marlborough had declined, "to show that money is not the chief point," a reason that sounded strange from that source. New honors had also come to Newcastle, who now wore the strawberry leaves. The first step in the resumption of negotiations was taken by Newcastle himself, when late in the summer of 1716 he wrote Sir John Vanbrugh at Scarborough, announcing that he had "come to an absolute resolution of marrying somewhere before the winter was over," asking if he had any fresh intelligence concerning Lady Harriet, and making inquiries about her fortune.[9]

Although he professed to look upon matchmaking as "a damned trade," the knight wrote at once to the duchess, who had been spending the summer at Bath with the invalid duke and the young lady in question. Her ladyship, whose reputation was once summed up as the "stingy, penurious, griping duchess,"[10] replied coolly that she was no longer at liberty to provide a portion, as she had "other children that were so unhappy as to want her help": but she expressed her liking for the match, and promised to do all in her power to arouse the interest of her equally stingy lord. In other words, as Vanbrugh told Newcastle, she was "much disposed to persuade the Duke to part with his money, and was only for saving her own."[11] There was no reply to this, and while at Bath she

---

[8] At the same time, Newcastle began to mortgage large tracts of land in Sussex, and barely a year later fresh indentures were made, including the ancestral seat of Laughton itself. *Sussex Archaeol. Coll.*, XXXVII, 69-70.

[9] Vanbrugh to Godolphin, *Coxe MSS*, XLVI, 148, *apud* Thomson, *Memoirs*, 544.

[10] Said by Sir Godfrey Kneller (H.M.C. *Portland MSS*, V, 398). The duchess was reputed, about this time, to be worth at least £500,000. (*Stuart Papers*, III, 251).

[11] *Add. MSS*, 33,064, f. 115.

formed the acquaintance of Peter Walter,[12] Newcastle's steward, and enlisted his aid in the affair, much to the indignation and resentment of Vanbrugh, who was soon afterward dismissed from his employment at Blenheim by the duchess.

Nothing seems to have occurred until the fifth of November, when Vanbrugh had an interview with Newcastle at Claremont, upon the earnest request of the duke himself. The latter seems to have been genuinely impressed by Sir John's eulogies of Lady Harriet; but plied him for further particulars of her behavior at Bath, and for his impressions of her "person, sense, and temper" while on a recent visit to Blenheim.

Once again young Newcastle showed the same extraordinary thoughfulness and common sense in his attitude toward marriage which he had displayed upon the earlier occasion, a characteristic so remarkable for his time and station, and for which he has nowhere been given credit. He told Vanbrugh that it was "the greatest concern of his life," that he expected "some other satisfaction in it than many people troubled themselves about," and that he "might judge what a terrible disappointment he should be under if he found himself tied for life to a woman not capable of being a useful and faithful friend, as well as an agreeable companion."[13] Then, having received the warmest assurances from the knight, he came to an absolute resolution of treating.

The question now to be decided was that of the portion; and, owing to the Duke of Marlborough's apoplectic stroke in May and his relapse in November, negotiations had to be carried on altogether with the canny duchess. "I don't at all believe,

---

[12] Peter Walter (1662-1745), an attorney, and Clerk of the Peace for Middlesex, and M.P. for Bridport (Dorset), 1715-1722. He was Newcastle's steward for Dorset, Wilts, Herts, Kent, Suffolk, and Middlesex (*Add. MSS*, 33,320, f. 8a). He made a fortune, and was often able to help Newcastle out of difficulties. He was the original Peter Pounce, in Fielding's *Joseph Andrews*. *Vide* Pope, *Works*, III, 141 and 142n.

[13] Vanbrugh to Godolphin, *Coxe MSS*, XLVI, 148, in Thomson, *op. cit.*, 544; same to Ds. of Marlborough, *ibid.*, 535. *Athenaeum*, Aug., 1890, 289 (Vanbrugh to the duchess).

however, she's indifferent in the matter," wrote the resentful
Vanbrugh with characteristic energy, "for she is not a Fool,
though she's a—worse thing.   But as in all her other Traffick,
so in a Husband for her Grand Daughter, she would fain have
him good and cheap."[14] Newcastle had made rather large demands and was becoming impatient. Townshend, Walpole, and
Lord Godolphin, the young lady's father, were interviewed,
and all expressed not only their approval of the match but
their vexation that nothing could be done to hasten things
along.   They all intimated that the conqueror of Tallard and
Villeroy might, haply, soon cease to be, and in that case all
would be well, as Godolphin was willing to meet all of Newcastle's demands.[15]

The duchess came to London at the end of October, and
as negotiations took place thereafter by personal conversations,
the correspondence comes abruptly to an end.   Still no settlement was reached for several months, owing, apparently, to
the fact that Newcastle and his friends held out for a portion
of £30,000, which the Marlboroughs thought excessive. Bowers
told Newcastle he could not do with less than that sum, "besides presents to ye Lady, jewels, and charges of ye marriage.
*Vous savez bien qu'il faut avoir vingt mille livres sterling pour
mettre les Terres de Sussex en liberté & dix mille livres sterling
serent necessaire pour les autres occasions qui touchent votre
honneur et votre intérêt.*"[16]   By the end of March, 1717, a
settlement was finally reached.   The Duke of Marlborough
contracted to pay a portion of only £20,000, while Newcastle
agreed to provide an annuity of £1,400 for his prospective
duchess.[17]

---

[14] *Add. MSS*, 33,064, f. 114.

[15] *Ibid.*, Naylor to Newcastle, f. 118, and Vanbrugh to same, ff. 122-123.

[16] *Add MSS*, 33,064, f. 112 (Mar. 13, 1717).

[17] The marriage indenture is calendared in *Sussex Archaeol. Coll.*,
XXXVII, 70-71. In *Remarks* appended to Vanbrugh's letter to Godolphin
(*supra*, note 13), Lady Marlborough writes: "My Lady Harriot had
£22,000 to her portion, provided by the Duchess of Marlborough."

The wedding took place on April 2, 1717,[18] and whatever disappointments there were in her dowry seem to have been compensated for by the sixteen-year-old bride herself.   The pair were genuinely devoted to each other, and even in the midst of a Sussex campaign Newcastle was never too tired at the end of a day of canvassing to thank his "dearest" for her letters, give her an account of his doings, and close with some tender expression.[19]   Thus, too, had Marlborough written his devoted Sarah from the plateau of Blenheim.   In an age when marital infidelity was fashionable, and the Court itself set an example of license, even his greatest detractors weer unable to bring charges of this character against Newcastle, who seems to have been, from first to last, a model of the conjugal virtues.[20]

The Duchess of Newcastle appears very rarely in contemporary writings and seems never to have been a leading figure in the world of fashion.   Perhaps she inherited her disposition as well as her plain countenance from her grandfather, the Treasurer, of whom Burnet wrote: "He was, perhaps, the most silent and most modest man that was ever bred at a court."   In spite of early expectations,[21] the marriage proved to be childless, a circumstance of considerable political importance in bringing the duke and his brother closer together.[22]

[18] See Lawrence Eusden's epithalamium, *"A Poem on the marriage of . . . the D. of N. to Lady H. G.,"* an allegory in which the bridegroom is referred to as a great patriot.

[19] *E.g. Add. MSS,* 33,073, ff. 9-11.   In 1766, near the close of his life, he referred feelingly to the duchess as one "who has been the best friend and best wife to me for . . . forty-nine years." *Add. MSS,* 33,003, f. 80b, quoted in Bateson, *op. cit.,* 91.

[20] Horace Walpole (*Reminiscences,* 80) relates that Newcastle for political reasons, "affected to be in love with" Princess Amelia, one of George I's unmarried daughters, described by Saussure as "a handsome blonde, with charming features." *Cf.* Charteris, *Early Life of Cumberland,* 50-51.

[21] *Add. MSS,* 33,064, f. 133 (Bowers to Newcastle, Oct. 13, 1717); *Athenaeum,* Aug., 1890, 290 (Vanbrugh to same, Oct. 9, 1717) ; and H.M.C. *Portland MSS,* V, 535, can be interpreted in no other way.

[22] *Add. MSS,* 32,686, f. 255.

Whatever financial relief the marriage effected was only partial and temporary, and Newcastle, like Disraeli, was destined to go through life harrassed by the want of money. Six months after, Bowers was obliged to write another long letter of advice and remonstrance,[23] in which he complained that he had been scheming for two years to no effect, because of the duke's "continuing still to have the same inclinations." He again urged a "regulation," and pointed out that in four years "there will be a new Parliament, & then, though we should be better managers than we were last time, yet a considerable sum must be expended in a just and honourable way, for I know your Grace would not let your interest sink." But once more relief was sought, not in economy, but in further mortgages.[24]

Disinterestedness and absolute honesty as a servant of the Crown are qualities which are universally admitted in the duke's favor, even by his most bitter critics.[25] Yet this means comparatively little, as long as he is regarded as a Midas who could afford to be honest. It must be realized that in spite of the most acute, lifelong embarrassment in money matters Newcastle never sacrificed his integrity by enriching himself at the public expense, a circumstance all the more remarkable for the age of Bolingbroke and the first Lord Holland.

The political results of the Newcastle-Godolphin match were of considerable importance, for through his wife Newcastle was brought into immediate family relationship with the great Duke of Marlborough and a score of peers claiming descent

---

[23] *Add. MSS*, 33,064, ff. 131-133.

[24] *Sussex Archaeol. Coll.*, XXXVII, 71.

[25] *E.g.* Bradshaw, *Chesterfield's Letters*, III, 1425; Maty, *Chesterfield's Works*, III, 419. It was Lord Shelburne's opinion that Newcastle "was at bottom an honester man" than Chatham (Fitzmaurice, *Life*, I, 84). When the duke resigned in 1762, and the King offered to compensate him for his vast expenditures in the Crown service, the old man answered loftily: "that in office he had never consider'd the profit of employment, that out of office he could not bear the thought of being a farthin's charge on the crown: that if his fortune had suffer'd by his loyalty, it was his pleasure, his glory, and his pride, and that he desired no reward but his majesty's approbation." Barrington to Mitchell, *Add. MSS*, 6,834, f. 37.

from or alliance with him by marriage. Among these was
Sunderland himself, whose second wife, Lady Anne Churchhill
(1682-1716), was the aunt of the new Duchess of Newcastle.
The duke's prestige was tremendously augmented by being
thus identified more closely than ever with the innermost circle
of the patrician oligarchy that was the government.

The marriage was particularly important for bringing him
into closer relationship with the powerful Marlborough-Sunder-
land faction of the Whig party at the very time it was successfully outmaneuvering the Administration leaders. Unfortunately, the sources are practically silent on the details of
Newcastle's relations with the two coteries at this critical juncture; but it has been seen that Sunderland and Stanhope were
not mentioned in the marriage negotiations, while the "brother
ministers" were in consultation with the young duke and did
everything in their power to further the match, although the
relations between the two Ministerial groups were already at
the breaking-point. The explanation for this is difficult to see.

The dissensions which had raged within the Whig ranks ever
since 1714 had been permitted to smolder for a season in the
presence of the common enemy; but no sooner was the Jacobite danger past, and the continued existence of Parliament
assured, than the flames burst out with greater intensity than
ever.[26] The events of the past year and a half had not only
led to several dismissals from the ranks of the Ministry, and
consequent additions to the opposition, but also to the development of fresh rivalries.

Walpole and Townshend had earned the bitter enmity of the
Hanoverian faction by thwarting their interference in English
affairs and by their repeated refusals to satisfy their venality
and their craving for peerages. The King's reigning favorite,
the Baroness von der Schulenburg, who was created Duchess
of Munster, was angry at not being made an English duchess,
and laid the blame on Townshend.[27]

---

[26] *Stuart Papers*, II, 75 (Southcott to Paterson), and 158 (Brinsden
to same).

[27] Coxe, *Walpole*, III, 58 (Walpole to Stanhope).

Sunderland's restless ambition had not been slaked by his succession to the Privy Seal upon the death of Wharton; and as for Marlborough, he had not missed the significance of the fact that instead of himself his old enemy, the Duke of Argyle, had been sent against the Pretender.

Nevertheless, the power of the Marlborough faction was demonstrated by a series of events which now took place. After the flight of the Pretender, Argyle had failed to pursue his discomfited countrymen with the ruthlessness that was thought proper; and as a result he was superseded by General William Cadogan, a partisan of Marlborough's and his favorite officer. Now Argyle was the particular confidant and adviser of the Prince of Wales, in whose household he served as Groom of the Stole; and should the King make his proposed visit to his German dominions, leaving the prince as Regent, the head of the Campbells would be in a position to ruin the Marlboroughs. While Argyle used all his influence to get the consent of Parliament to the proposed visit, Marlborough advised the King to divide the prince's authority as Regent with a council.[28]

At this juncture, the Marlborough faction suffered a blow that was as distressing as it was unexpected, when the old duke sank before a stroke of apoplexy on the 28th of May. Although he did not succumb, he was incapacitated for months to come and never fully recovered in health or understanding. The active leadership passed at once to Sunderland, while Cadogan, now a baron, was expected to succeed to the post of Captain-General,[29] although both Stanhope and Argyle were his superiors. There was a bright side of the calamity, however, as the Duchess Sarah was much more willing to spend her lord's money in the services of the intrigue than he would have been himself.[30]

Meanwhile, the jealously between Argyle and Cadogan had been inflamed almost to the point of a duel, when the latter,

---

[28] *Stuart Papers*, II, 200 (Thomas to Inese, May 21, 1716).

[29] *Ibid.*, 252 (Magny to James III, July 5, 1716).

[30] *Lady Cowper's Diary*, 120 and 123.

disdaining the official services of his rival, presented himself one day directly to the prince.[31] This incident provided the excuse that the King and the Marlborough faction desired. The prince had resisted any limitations upon his regency with characteristic determination and only yielded at the solicitation of Argyle; whereupon the jealous monarch had told him that no one should be about his son who had more interest than he.[32] Accordingly, on the day following the affair above related, both Argyle and Islay, his brother, were turned out of all their employments, and the prince was directed to dismiss them from his service also.

The outcome of this contest was generally recognized as a demonstration of the ascendency of the Marlboroughs, and the triumph was signalized by the appointment of Cadogan as plenipotentiary to the States-General, and of Sunderland to the lucrative post of Vice-Treasurer of Ireland.[33]

The disappointed greed and baffled meddling of the one, and the newly whetted but unsatisfied ambition of the other, now brought the Hanoverians and the partisans of Marlborough together in a scheme to reconstruct the Ministry. But for the haste of the King's departure, it was declared, the scheme was to have been executed in the summer of 1716. Walpole, who had proved to be too scrupulous a Chancellor of the Exchequer, was to be removed. Stanhope was to be restored to the army. Just what would be done with Townshend was not certain.[34] Sunderland was to use his influence to bring about the repeal of the obnoxious clause in the Act of Settlement disqualifying foreigners from the peerage of the United Kingdom.[35] It

---

[31] *Stuart Papers,* II, 278 (Menzies to Inese). The incident occurred June 28.

[32] *Stuart Papers,* II, 316 (Walkinshaw to Mar, July 29).

[33] *Ibid.,* 305 (Murray to Mar, July 12); 338 (Oglethorpe to Mar, Aug. 11); 412 (Menzies to Inese, Aug. 27).

[34] Coxe, *Walpole,* III, 58-59 (Walpole to Stanhope, July 30); and 119 (Townshend to Stanhope, Oct. 16). H.M.C. *Townshend MSS,* 102. *Cf. Lady Cowper's Diary,* 118-120.

[35] Coxe, *Walpole,* I, 162.

was even proposed, probably by Sunderland,[36] that a coalition Administration be established, which would include Carnarvon at the Treasury, and Nottingham, Carleton, and other Tories in good standing at Marlborough House in important posts.[37]

Whatever sweeping alterations might have been contemplated or desired, the time was not yet ripe for their consummation, and on July 6th the King set out joyfully for his electorate, without making any but the most necessary changes, all of them agreeable to the "brother ministers." Nevertheless, the events of the next five months were to bring about almost all that the intriguers wished.

The circumstances that led to the famous Whig schism of 1716 were four in number, and the first of these was the characteristic Hanoverian jealously and suspicion on the part of the King for his son and heir, of which more anon. The prince chafed under the restrictions placed upon his authority as Regent, and in retaliation he endeavored to set up an interest of his own in Parliament, independent of the King's. Magnificent entertainments were provided at Hampton Court, where Tories and "disgusted" Whigs alike were welcomed, and where the prince exerted himself to be agreeable, in palpable contrast with the usual aloofness and reserve of his father. Although the prince had been compelled to dismiss the Duke of Argyle from his service, the latter remained in constant attendance and enjoyed as much favor and influence as ever. On the contrary, Townshend and Walpole were received with nothing more than civility.[38] Their embarrassment was acute, for not only were they obliged to preserve cordial relationships with

[36] *"Er hat . . . oft daran gedacht, ein aus beiden Parteien gemischtes Ministerium zu bilden. Diejenigen, die statt eines Whig-oder-Tory Kabinetts eine schlechthin Englische Regierung wünschten, mussten in Sunderland ihren Mann sehen."* (Michael, *Eng. Geschichte,* II, 38). It will be remembered that neither was Marlborough a party man.

[37] *Stuart Papers,* II, 345 (Menzies to Inese, Aug. 2); 379 (Murray to Mar, Aug. 15); also vol. III, 145 (Guthrie to Mar, Oct. 27, 1716). *Lady Cowper's Diary,* 121-122.

[38] Coxe, *Walpole,* III, 60 (Walpole to Stanhope, July 30), and II, 64 (same to same, Aug. 20).

the son's court, in order to transact the business of government, but also to demean themselves so that this conduct could not be misrepresented to the father as double dealing. It was in this dilemma that Walpole wrote Stanhope, who had accompanied the King to Hanover: "We are here chained to the oare, and working like slaves, and are looked upon as no other, for not only the behaviour and conduct of the prince are a weight upon us, but the industrious representations that are made of our being last with the king reduces our creditt to nothing."[39]

The second cause of friction was the disagreement in the Ministry with regard to a proposed treaty with France, negotiations for which King George, on account of the pressure of affairs in the North, was impatient to complete. Townshend, who disapproved of anything that increased the land-tax or made a war in defense of Hanover likely, deliberately delayed the signature, under the pretext of unwillingness to make any engagement independent of the Dutch.[40] Meantime, Stanhope and Sunderland had been converted to the treaty, and the attitude of His Majesty was set forth in a letter from the earl to Townshend. "Never," he wrote pointedly, "had he seen the King resent any thing so much as this affair, in which he thinks not only Mr. Stanhope, but himself not well used."[41]

The third source of irritation was a personal misunderstanding between Walpole and the King over the payment of certain German mercenaries,[42] contracted for by the King with the consent of the Council. His Majesty contended that before he left England Walpole had promised to find the money somehow, but that instead, he, the King, had been obliged to pay the subsidies out of his own pocket. As Walpole protested

---

[39] *Ibid.*, 64 (Walpole to Stanhope, Aug. 9/20, and *Stuart Papers*, II, 378 (Murray to Mar, Aug. 15).

[40] See corres. in *Coxe*, III, esp. pp. 86, 99, 112-113, 126-127, and 134 (Sept.-Nov.).

[41] H.M.C. *Townshend MSS*, 103 (Nov. 11, 1716).

[42] On this subject, see *Coxe*, III, 109 (Stanhope to Townshend) ; 117 and 119 (Townshend to Stanhope) ; 125 (Stanhope to Townshend) ; and 134 (Walpole to Stanhope).

warmly that he had made no such promise, the same alignment took place once more, Townshend siding with his brother-in-law and the absentee Ministers with the King.

These differences would hardly have been the cause of the disruption of the Ministry, however, had it not been for the mischief-making intrigues of Sunderland, that kept alive these "heats and divisions" and finally precipitated a crisis. On the plea of ill-health, and professing the utmost loyalty to his colleagues whom he left in England, he had set out for Aix late in August. The waters did not detain him long, however, and he had turned up in Hanover in the middle of October, where he soon brought Stanhope and the King under his influence. He inflamed the King's misgivings by insinuating that Townshend and Walpole were caballing with the prince and Argyle, and convinced them that they were obstructing the French treaty and stultifying him in the matter of the subsidies. The Hanoverians added their innuendoes to the earl's, and their master's worst suspicions seemed to be confirmed when Townshend agreed to his request to stay abroad and, at the same time, asked for fuller powers for the prince.[43]

So exasperated was the King that on December 11, 1716, in a sudden burst of jealousy and resentment, he dismissed Townshend from his secretaryship and replaced him with Stanhope. Still, for a time, the Whigs seemed to act in accord, and Townshend was prevailed upon to remain in the Cabinet as Lord Lieutenant of Ireland. But this cordiality was more apparent than real, and in a short time relations between the Ministerial factions became so strained that it was impossible to go on. Upon Stanhope's motion for supply, to provide against the threat of Swedish aggression revealed by the Gyllenborg disclosures, Walpole's persuasive voice was significantly faint, and his adherents in the Commons voted with the opposition, so that the resolution escaped defeat by the bare majority of four

---

[43] Coxe, *op. cit.,* I, 169-175; H.M.C. *Onslow MSS,* 508-509; *Stuart Papers,* III, 353-354 (Menzies to Inese).

votes.[44]   On the same day, April 9, 1717, Townshend was summarily relieved of his lieutenancy, and the day following, to the great dismay of his royal master, Walpole gave up his seals.   About the same time, Devonshire, Orford, Methuen, and Pulteney followed his example.

The conduct and sympathies of Newcastle during this period are among the mysteries of his early career.   At all events, with Stanhope heading the Administration, the duke had been chosen to move the Address of Thanks at the opening of the second session of Parliament, on February 20, 1717.[45]   Again, on March 25, he is found defending the Mutiny Bill in Committee of the Whole, by the side of Lord Sunderland,[46] which meant that he endorsed Stanhope's principle of a large standing army and a spirited foreign policy against the convictions of Townshend—the elder Whig tradition against the new.   Apparently then, some time before the "brother ministers" laid down, Newcastle was already in the camp of their opponents, and ten days after this event he is found at a small dinner party with Sunderland, Stanhope, and Robethon, drinking confusion, no doubt, to the enemy.[47]

His failure to follow Walpole and Townshend into opposition was the first count in the charge of consistent treachery made against him by Horace Walpole and other political adversaries of the following generation,[48] but there are several factors which may be set forth here in explanation of his action.   To begin with, it must be remembered that party discipline at the beginning of the eighteenth century was almost nonexistent, and that after all Townshend and Walpole headed only one division of the Whigs.   Furthermore, Walpole himself was later to advise his young men to eliminate "always" from their political

---

[44] Coxe, *op. cit.,* I, 178-184, and H.M.C. *Polwarth MSS,* I, 213.

[45] Boyer, *Pol. State,* XIII, 221 and 223. (Same in *Parl. Hist.,* VII, 421-422.)

[46] Boyer, *op. cit.,* 346, and *Parl. Hist.,* VII, 429.

[47] H.M.C. *Polwarth MSS,* I, 219.

[48] Walpole, *Memoirs of George II,* I, 142, also his *Reminiscences,* 39. Hanbury-Williams, *Works,* "The Duke of Newcastle, a Fable," I, 1-13.

vocabularies. Newcastle's own conscience was clear. In 1739 he wrote Lord Hardwicke: "I can never charge myself with ever having been wanting essentially towards those I professed a friendship for in my whole life."[49] If it is urged that personal and family obligations would dictate his resignation, it must also be borne in mind that the duke was closely connected with Sunderland, and that the marriage negotiations were bringing him in closer contact with the Marlborough faction at this very time. As early as June, 1716, he was acting in the most confidential fashion for Sunderland in the House of Lords.[50]

There is no reason for believing otherwise than that Newcastle came to be genuinely out of sympathy with the behavior and foreign policy of his old friends, and that he was further weaned away from them by the offer of a place in the new Administration. His defection may be dated at some time during the uneasy period of Ministerial estrangement—between the end of November, when Townshend and Walpole were seen working for his marriage, and the following February, when Parliament convened.

It was during these same months that Sunderland was preoccupied with the labor of forming a new government, a task in which he was reduced to all sorts of shifts. "He bought all men as he could get them," wrote Speaker Onslow later, "some by places, others by promises, and many by more secret ways, as it was generally said and believed, and with unbounded profusion. Men set their own price and had it, as he and they knew their value, because the numbers in Parliament ran so near as to make any one person considerable enough to be had at any rate. I never knew so corrupt a time; and which laid such a foundation for the continuance of it that God only knows when it will have an end."[51]

---

[49] *Add. MSS*, 35,406, f. 167 (Oct. 14, 1739).

[50] *Add. MSS*, 32,686 f. 127 (Sunderland to Newcastle, June 6, 1716). This *MS* is dated only "Wednesday noon," and is wrongly calendared among the *MSS* for 1718. Internal evidence supplies the correct date.

[51] H.M.C. *Onslow MSS*, 509.

Fortunate it was for Sunderland that the resignations had not come in December, as he would have been unable to get a majority. By April, however, as a result of the transactions Speaker Onslow describes, everything was ready. Only four of the original Cabinet of October, 1714, remained. Stanhope took Walpole's offices of First Lord and Chancellor of the Exchequer, but could not take his place. Sunderland then succeeded the former in Townshend's old post at the Northern Department, the one he had coveted so long. Men now spoke of the "triumvirate" of Stanhope, Sunderland, and Cadogan.[52]

The Hanoverians, who had helped to bring about these alterations, were well pleased with the way things had turned out. "The present servants of the Crown are of a nature much more tractable than we could hope to find those who so insolently left our service," wrote Bothmer in May, "nor can His Majesty or Madam the Duchess ever expect a cabinet less troublesome than they now have."[53]

While Stanhope was the ostensible head of the new Administration, he was soon eclipsed in influence in domestic affairs by Sunderland,[54] who was "never at heart's ease whiles he beheld a greater than himself." The earl put a high estimate upon his talents, and many of his contemporaries accepted him at this valuation; but he possessed neither the political sagacity nor the consistent principles of Robert Walpole—the solidest foundations of political power in any age. Nevertheless, he was not without parts. A man of learning and a lover of books, of which he had a magnificent collection, he was very skilful in parliamentary practice and could claim an impressive knowledge of foreign affairs.[55] As for the rest of the Administra-

---

[52] Michael, *Eng. Geschichte,* II, 37 and 556.

[53] *Stuart Papers,* IV, 251 (Bothmer to Schütz). *Cf.* Michael, *op. cit.,* II, 554, and 556-557.

[54] *Stuart Papers,* III, 429 (Menzies to Inese), and V, 568 (Jacobite Memorial, Aug. 1, 1717). *Lady Cowper's Diary,* 169.

[55] Michael, *op. cit.,* II, 38, who thinks Sunderland was *"von den Zeitgenossen sehr überschätzt worden."*

tion, while purely Whig it was hardly the equal of the old one.[56] Its greatest weakness lay in the lack of a first-rate financier. Stanhope was primarily a foreign minister, and Sunderland's grasp of business matters was equally defective.

The Duke of Newcastle may have been among those included in the Ministry either because of Sunderland's necessity or his desire for colleagues dependent upon himself: or, it may be that Newcastle's solid services and influence would have designated him for a place in any alternate Whig government. On the duke's part, it was probably the offer of Ministerial rank that led him to part company with his old associates. It would seem that Townshend had not found this necessary to secure his adherence, although at one time, in October 1716, it appeared that he would obtain official employment, when it was rumored that he was to succeed the Duke of Somerset in the important Household post of Master of the Horse.[57] For some reason, however, the appointment did not materialize, and instead the office was put temporarily in commission.[58]

The position in which he was now installed, at the age of twenty-three, was that of Lord Chamberlain of His Majesty's Household; the first step in his lifelong career as a servant of the Crown. The oath of office was taken April 13, 1717,[59] and the next morning, for the first time, he waited upon the King, white staff in hand, and wearing the gold key of his office. After kissing hands, he went next to the apartments of the Prince of Wales, where he was accompanied, significantly, by his Grace of Marlborough,[60] who left his sickbed to assist at

---

[56] See Speaker Onslow's excellent estimate, *op. cit.*, 508-510, and that of Dubois in Michael, *op. cit.*, II, 634-635.

[57] Oldmixon, *History of England*, III, 640. *Lady Cowper's Diary*, 53. Somerset was dismissed Oct. 25, through the instrumentality of Walpole and Townshend, when he came to the support of his Tory son-in-law, Windham.

[58] Boyer, *Pol. State*, X, 336. *Cf.* Mahon, *Hist. of England*, I, 213, and Ward, *Electress Sophia*, 250-251.

[59] *L. C. Registers*, Appointment Books, series II, vol. 63, p. 171.

[60] Boyer, *Pol. State*, XIII, 490.

this ceremony.   Two days later he was sworn of the Privy
Council.[61]

Of all the great offices, that of Chamberlain involved the
least amount of direct political responsibility; but it gave the
holder constant access to the King's private ear, and as a result
its potentialities were considerable, as Newcastle was after-
wards to demonstrate.   As was the custom with the great
Household officers in the eighteenth century, it included a seat
in the Cabinet, where, as later events will disclose, Newcastle
was by no means a figurehead.

As Chamberlain, Newcastle had an army of noblemen and
flunkies under his supervision, from Lords of the Bedchamber
to Ratcatcher, to the number of nearly five hundred,[62] and the
patronage at his disposal was correspondingly large.[63]   Thus
was provided another source of electioneering influence, by the
judicious distribution of offices among the county families.
Next to the Lord Steward, Newcastle was the highest civil
officer in the Royal Household, and in the House of Lords he
enjoyed precedence over all other dukes.   The last, but not the
least of the benefits of the place, when the state of the duke's
finances is considered, was the stipend of £1200 that went with
it.

The duties of the Chamberlain were extensive, but save on
ceremonial occasions they were probably performed by Coke,
the veteran Vice-Chamberlain.   He had "the oversight of all
offices belonging to the King's Chamber, except the precinct of
the King's Bedchamber, which is wholly under the Groom of
the Stole; and all above stairs, who are all sworn by him (or
his warrant to the Gentleman Ushers) to the King.   He hath
also the oversight of the officers of the Wardrobe at all His
Majesty's houses and of the Removing Wardrobe, or of beds,

---

[61] L. C. Registers, supra, vol. 86, p. 11.

[62] Lists in Chamberlayne, Present State, 540-547, also L. C. Registers,
vol. 8.

[63] For examples see L. C. Registers, vol. 63, 177-195; H.M.C. Coke MSS,
118; and Add. MSS, 32,686, f. 173, and Add. MSS, 33,079, f. 2.

tents, revels, music, comedians, hunting, messengers, trumpeters, drummers, handicrafts and artisans retained in the King's service. Moreover, he hath the oversight of the Serjeant at Arms, of all the physicians, apothecaries, surgeons, barbers, etc. To him also belongeth the oversight of the chaplains, though he himself is a layman."[64]

Newcastle's family influence in the Cabinet was early strengthened by the marriage of Henry, seventh Earl of Lincoln, with his sister Lucy, in May, 1717.[65] His new connection had succeeded Walpole at the Pay-Office in October, 1715, and was lord of a large estate in the fen country.

The new Chamberlain had not been in office many months when another schism, of which he was the immediate instrument, broke out in the Palace itself, which shook the Court to its foundations and proved to be of the first political importance. Reference has already been made to the coolness and misunderstanding which prevailed between the meagre-souled monarch and the heir apparent. The origin of the quarrel goes back to their Hanoverian days, and is best attributed to the grudge the King bore for his son on account of the delinquency of his mother, the prisoner of Ahlden.[66] At all events, their estrangement had been apparent to all when they arrived in England,[67] and it was not diminished by the prince's complete exclusion from any active share in government. The Argyle affair and his impotent Regency in 1716 were not forgotten.

Such being the state of affairs, the various discontented ele-

---

[64] Chamberlayne, *op. cit.*, 100. *Cf.* Giuseppi, *Guide*, II, 44. Perhaps the most interesting side of Newcastle's tenure of the office of Chamberlain is his long controversy with Steele, which arose almost at once over a theatre patent, and was not settled until 1721. The affair is fully treated in Stevens, *Party Politics and English Journalism, 1702-1742.*

[65] As Newcastle had no issue, all the later dukes of this title, including the present (eighth) duke, are descended from this pair.

[66] See Ward, *Electress Sophia*, 284 and note. According to some, the King doubted his son's paternity: (Walpole, *Reminiscences,* 32; St. Simon's *Mémoires* (ed. 1829), XVIII, 197; Glenbervie, *Diary,* II, 98).

[67] See Bonet's report, and Schulenburg to Leibnitz, in Michael, *Eng. Geschichte,* I, 862.

ments, both Whig and Tory, naturally gravitated about the heir. As early as August, 1716, a Jacobite observer informed the Duke of Mar that "Young Hopeful is making a party of his own, in opposition to the present managers";[68] and, after the events of April, this faction received a powerful accession in Townshend and Walpole and their friends,[69] who, from this time until 1720, were in strong opposition.

So evenly divided were the two conflicting wings of the Whigs that the new Administration was never wholly out of danger in the House of Commons, and both sides were reduced to courting the Tories, who held the balance of power.[70] The instability of this political equilibrium was demonstrated almost at once, by an assault that nearly ended in ruin for the new government. Cadogan was accused in the Commons of peculation in the transportation of Dutch troops to England during the Rising of 'Fifteen, and he was acquitted by the very close vote of 204 to 194. Had the opposition successfully maintained its charge, the fall of the Ministry could hardly have been averted.[71]

With Townshend and Walpole at the head of the opposition, it was the object of that body to pursue the leader's old policy of reducing the standing army and preventing foreign war. The third session of Parliament opened on November 21, 1717, and two weeks later, upon Walpole's motion that the army be reduced to twelve-thousand men, the government was able to muster a majority of only fifty at the division.[72] The opposition Whigs, however, soon found the Tories were unstable and unreliable allies; and by the middle of December the government had carried the appropriations and retained the army and fleet

---

[68] *Stuart Papers*, II, 396.

[69] *Ibid.*, IV, 143-144 (Mar to James III, Mar. 27 1717).

[70] *Stuart Papers*, IV, 291-292 (Mar to Erskine, May 31, 1717), and 331 (Menzies to Mar, June 8).

[71] For the whole subject, see: Boyer, *Pol. State*, XIII, 702-705; *Parl. Hist.*, VII, 466-468; Michael, *Eng. Geschichte*, II, 42-43; and *Annals of Stair*, II, 20-22 (Addison to Stair).

[72] *Stuart Papers*, V, 301 (Guthrie to Inese, Dec. 10, 1717).

upon its actual footing. On the day this was voted, the Tories stayed in bed.[73]

It was confidently asserted at that time, and is hardly to be gainsaid now, that the rupture between the King and the Prince of Wales, to be narrated presently, was deliberately provoked by the Ministry. Sunderland had been instrumental in bringing about the dismissal of Argyle, and in curtailing the prince's authority as Regent; and later, while in Hanover, he had misrepresented the latter's behavior to the King. As a result, upon every possible occasion the prince had treated Sunderland, Cadogan, and even Marlborough with the greatest contumely.[74] It has been seen already how the prince's faction in Parliament had succeeded in embarrassing the Administration; and if the King again went abroad as he planned, in the spring of 1718, leaving his son Regent as before, the Ministry would indeed be in a serious predicament.

The birth of a second son to the Prince and Princess of Wales on November 2 provided the opportunity the artful Sunderland desired. His plan was to bait and provoke the choleric prince into some desperate act of insubordination against his exasperated parent's express authority, and so bring about an irreparable breach between the royal pair.

It was the custom for the King of England to stand as godfather to his grandsons, and to associate with himself some great peer, usually the Lord Chamberlain, in the ceremony of baptism.[75] Whether Newcastle received this honor as a matter of course, or whether he demanded it at the instance of Lord Sunderland[76] as some asserted and as the prince believed, can-

[73] *Stuart Papers*, V, 307 (Menzies to Inese, Dec. 12).

[74] *Ibid.*, 610 (Atterbury's Memorial of Dec., 1717): Brosch, *Lord Bolingbroke*, 330-331; Michael, *op. cit.*, II, 635 (Abbe Dubois *Mémoire* in *Archives du Ministère des Affaires Etrangères*), and 51 (the Imperial Resident's anecdote).

[75] *Add. MSS*, 35,838, f. 407.

[76] Walpole, *Reminiscences*, 105; Michael, *op. cit.*, II, 53, says: *"Newcastle hatte dies als ein Vorrecht seines Amtes für sich gefordert,"* but *cf.* the *MSS* cited above and *Egerton MSS*, 921, f. 84.

not now be determined. At any rate, without consulting his son, the King designated the duke as godfather, along with Diana, Duchess of St. Albans, the first Lady of Honor to the Princess of Wales. The prince was so furious that he was unable to sleep that night, for it had been his desire that his uncle, Ernest Augustus, Bishop of Osnabrück and Duke of York and Albany, and his sister, the Queen of Prussia, should act in this capacity.

There are numerous accounts of the dramatic events[77]—half serious, half ludicrous—which followed, testifying to their sensational interest and importance. The ceremony of christening the infant took place the evening of November 28, in the bedchamber of the Princess of Wales. According to the account given to Horace Walpole many years later by Lady Suffolk, who as Lady of the Bedchamber was an eye-witness of what occurred, the sponsors stood at one side of the bed, and the prince and Ladies of Honor on the other. The ceremonies finished, and the King at some distance with his back turned, the little prince was no longer able to contain his rage. Striding in front of the bed, and stepping on the Duke of Newcastle's toes, he whispered fiercely in his Grace's ear, "You rascal, I will find you!"

His Royal Highness's English was none too good, and the astonished duke thought he was being challenged with the words "I will fight you." At once he left the Palace, going straight to Stanhope, Sunderland, and Bernstorff with the story,[78] and their satisfaction at the way the prince had fallen into a trap may be imagined. King George was advised of his offspring's latest contumacy, and in his rage took what was for

---

[77] *Add. MSS,* 35,838, f. 407; *L. C. Records, Miscellanea,* vol. III, 38-39 (extracts from Dormer's Note Books of Ceremony) ; H.M.C. *Polwarth MSS,* I, 404-405 (Tilson to Lord Polwarth) ; *Stuart Papers,* V, 273-274; Boyer, *Pol. State,* XIV, 613-615, being a reprint from the *Critick,* a weekly of Jan. 13, 1718; Walpole, *Reminiscences,* 40; *etc. Cf.* the account in Michael, II, 52-54.

[78] Michael, *op. cit.,* II, 53.

him the extraordinary step of calling a Cabinet meeting. His
choler had not abated by the next morning when the Ministers
assembled, and he assured them that had he been in Hanover
he would know what to do.[79] Less violent measures were fixed
upon, however, and it was decided to send the Dukes of Roxburghe, Kent, and Kingston to the prince for an explanation.
Although his Royal Highness was unsparing in his denuncia-
tions of Newcastle, he denied that he had challenged him. With
his usual clumsiness, he then made matters worse by insulting
Roxburghe, when the latter assured him that Newcastle had
acted unwillingly and only at His Majesty's request.[80] As a
result of this fresh contumely, he was confined to his apartments, and the two letters he despatched to his father on Saturday and Sunday[81] were insufficient to allay the storm. On
Monday afternoon, December 2, another meeting of the Cabinet
was held, at which Marlborough was present, when it was decided to order the prince to leave the Palace at once.

Leaving their four children behind, in accordance with the
King's command, the prince and princess and their people took
their departure from St. James's that night, finding temporary
refuge with Lord Grantham, in Albemarle Street. Two months
after, the princely court was set up permanently at Leicester
House, which by an odd coincidence had been built and named
for Newcastle's great-grandfather in the halcyon days of
Charles the First.

The King's resentment did not stop with the disgrace of the
prince. On Tuesday, Sunderland had the satisfaction of order-
ing the prince's guard of honor withdrawn, and of notifying
all the foreign Ministers that if they visited the son's court that
of the father would be barred to them. Furthermore, all office-
holders and their wives were commanded to resign any employ-

---

[79] *Stuart Papers,* V, 275 (Hamilton to Mar, Dec. 2, 1717).

[80] Reports of interview in *Egerton MSS,* 921, f. 84; and *Add. MSS,*
35,838, f. 407b.

[81] Given in French and English in *Egerton MSS,* 921, f. 84b, *Add. MSS,*
35,838, ff. 408-409, and in Michael, *op. cit.,* II, 625-626.

ments they might enjoy in his household; and it was even proposed to deprive him of the annual pension of £100,000 which
had been settled upon him.[82]

Of more permanent importance than these unseemly acts of
persecution was the hatred which the prince ever after manifested for those whom he held responsible for his humiliation.
He swore a thousand times that he would never forgive Newcastle,[83] and long after, as George II, the duke was to find him
always contrary, and ever inclined to look upon him as one of
the necessary evils of the country he disliked.

Sunderland's vaulting victory had again o'erleapt itself, and
now he had to reckon with the ever-present danger of the demise
of the Crown and the accession of the prince, in which event
he had nothing to expect but ruin. It was this apprehension,
which was shared by the Ministry as a whole, that inspired still
another scheme, which proved to be one of the most noteworthy
consequences of the quarrel. This was the Peerage Bill of
1719.[84]

However ill-disposed the prince might be, and however
threatening the distant future, for Newcastle personally the
present held nothing but contentment and the smiling favor
of his sovereign. A few days before Christmas he was seen
at the play, sharing a box with His Majesty and the Duke of
Marlborough.[85]

The third session of Parliament, which had been under way
for a month, was not remarkable in anything in particular,
and as early as December 23, Stanhope was able to tell Dubois
that everything was "going according to the wishes of the
King, who would have no further embarrassment in money
matters for the rest of the session."[86] Nevertheless, the insecurity of the government was being continually demonstrated by

---

[82] *Stuart Papers,* VI, 607, and H.M.C. *Portland MSS,* V, 549.

[83] Hervey, *Memoirs,* I, 38-39.

[84] H.M.C. *Onslow MSS,* 509.

[85] H.M.C. *Portland MSS,* V, 550 (newsletter).

[86] *Hardwicke Papers,* quoted in Mahon, *History of England,* I, 296, n.

the smallness of its majorities and the efforts needed to obtain them.[87]

The most notable event and the sharpest contest of the session centered about the Mutiny Bill, which passed the Commons 186 to 105, when Walpole, after exerting himself to the utmost to defeat the measure, finally went over to the Ministerial side, with the declaration that he would rather have mutiny and desertion punished by martial law than not at all. The bill came up for a second reading in a very full House of Lords on February 19, 1718. It was a remarkable demonstration of the factiousness of the opposition to hear a soldier like Argyle and a sailor like Orford declaiming against a bill the necessity of which no one in reason could deny. After a great debate, the bill was consigned on the 20th to a Committee of the Whole, when the opposition again sought to stave it off before it went into Committee, where proxies would not be allowed. Newcastle shared the burden of the debate which followed, shoulder to shoulder with Stanhope, Sunderland, and Cadogan.[88] After some further hostilities on the 24th, the Court came off victorious, by a vote of 88 to 61. The opposition stuck to its guns, however, and the bill for rebuilding the church of St. Giles, introduced by Newcastle himself, passed the Lords March 8th by the slender majority of 70 to 63, while three days later the Forfeited Estates Bill only escaped defeat by a margin of twelve votes.[89]

Unscathed but panting after this series of narrow escapes, the Ministry must have breathed easier when Parliament rose on the 21st of March. On the other hand, the spirits of their enemies must have drooped at the failure of their most heroic exertions.

---

[87] H.M.C. *Portland MSS,* V, 554 (Edw. to Abigail Harley, Feb. 6, 1718); 556 (Newsletter, Feb. 19); 557 (Edw. to Abigail Harley, Mar. 9); *Stuart Papers,* V, 524 (Menzies to Inese, Feb. 17); 526 (Murray to Dillon, Feb. 17); VI, 106 (Hamilton to Inese, Feb. 24); 176 (Count Gazola to Nairn, Mar. 21); and H.M.C. *Stair MSS,* 189.

[88] For the Mutiny Bill see *Parl. Hist.,* VII, 536-548. Newcastle's speech is given on p. 540, also in Boyer, *Pol. State,* XV, 200.

[89] *Parl. Hist.,* VII, 552 and 553, also H.M.C. *Portland MSS,* V, 557.

The choleric Townshend had been so transported at the discomfiture of the opposition over the Mutiny Bill "that he gushed out floods of tears in the middle of his speech."[90] Both sides were in a mood to come to some terms with each other, if possible.

Before any lasting accommodation could be made, however, it was necessary to bring about a reconciliation between the King and his son, and as early as December there were rumors that this was about to be effected.[91] The prince himself had fits of despondency, at which times he was anxious to make his submission. Townshend and Walpole had soon discovered the unwisdom of putting trust in princes, and they laid the blame for their ill success partly at the door of his mean-spiritedness and pusillanimity.[92] Even Argyle, the head of the prince's personal following, came to share the general contempt and soon ceased to have any communication with him.[93] It was these conditions that led Walpole to labor for the restoration of the prince to favor, providing agreeable terms could be obtained for his own followers.[94] While the negotiations were pending, the fire of the opposition was not relaxed, as has been noticed, and its fury may be interpreted as designed to hurry them along. The Ministry, who had never desired to part with Walpole in the first place, was not loath to regain a much-needed financier and at the same time deprive the opposition of its boldest leader. But all negotiations came to nothing, due probably to the loyalty of Walpole to his friends and the obstinate insistence of the prince upon the dismissal of Sunderland and Cadogan.[95]

A week before Parliament was prorogued, several altera-

---

[90] *Stuart Papers,* VI, 106 (Hamilton to Inese, Feb. 24).

[91] H.M.C. *Portland MSS,* V, 545 and 546.

[92] *Stuart Papers,* V, 159, 328, 612-613; and VI, 164, 165, 556, 607; also Hervey, *Answer to one Part of a Late Infamous Libel,* 55.

[93] *Stuart Papers,* V, 448 (Hamilton to Mar), and 432 (Mar to Ormonde).

[94] *Ibid.,* V, 524-525 (Menzies to Inese, Feb. 17), and 447-448 (Hamilton to Mar, Jan. 28).

[95] *Ibid.,* VI, 146-147 (Menzies to Inese, Mar. 3, 1718), and 505 (May 22).

tions were made in the Administration—alterations which were
not designed to heal the schism, but to correct the weaknesses
which the last two sessions had made manifest. Stanhope was
obviously out of place at the head of the Treasury Bench, and in
view of the delicate state of affairs on the Continent, he again
assumed the more congenial post of Secretary of State for the
Northern Department, where his real talents were soon to bring
about the Quadruple Alliance. A month after the exchange,
he was promoted to an earldom.

Considering the situation on the Continent and the immin-
ence of Spanish aggression, the presence of Walpole was urgently required at the Exchequer; but in his absence, no better
man could be found than the Yorkshire squire, John Aislabie,
Treasurer of the Navy since 1714. As events were afterward
to prove, a more disastrous choice could scarcely have been
made. Unhappily for himself, Sunderland now undertook the
onerous and unfamiliar duties of the First Lord of the Treasury, and for a time the dignity of Lord President besides.
The younger Craggs, the protégé and creature of the Marlboroughs left the War-Office, where he had succeeded Pulteney
upon the Whig schism, to become Secretary for the Southern Department. His place was taken by Viscount Castlecomer, another brother-in-law of Newcastle by his marriage
with the duke's older sister, Frances; but in less than three
months, through illness or incapacity,[96] he was obliged to give
it up. Lord Cowper, the upright and independent-spirited
Chancellor, retired in favor of the able but more obsequious
Chief Justice, Lord Parker. No further proof was needed
of the complete ascendency of the Lord of Althorp than the
row of nobodies, however efficient, that now filled the most
responsible offices. Aside from Stanhope, there was no one
in the Cabinet who could challenge his supremacy.

While these changes were still new, and before the fountain

---

[96] Cf. Torrens, *Hist. of Cabinets,* I, 186, and Tindal, *Hist. of England,*
IV, Appendix, Summary, 212. Christopher Wandesford was the grandson
of Strafford's successor in Ireland. He died in June, 1719.

of honor ran dry, Newcastle received his share of rewards by being made a Knight of the Garter. His election and investiture with the Garter and George took place on March 31, and the solemn installation at Windsor a month later.[97] There is reason for believing that the dignity was not obtained without a price. Duke John was alleged to have paid six thousand guineas for *his* Garter in 1698,[98] and it is probable that the rapacious Duchess of Munster profited handsomely by this transaction.[99]

At this juncture, it seems proper to pause in the narration of domestic politics, in which the Duke of Newcastle still bore but a subordinate part, to survey a scene in which he played a more brilliant and no less congenial rôle.

The first opportunity after the close of the session to indulge his taste for the pleasures of society was provided by the King's birthday. In the morning, when he went to offer congratulations to his sovereign, he "exceeded all ye nobility" in the magnificence and splendor of his equipage. "His Coach was preceded by all his Domestics and also by twelve Watermen in new Cloathes, who also walked on foot, two & two."[100] That night there was a great entertainment for His Majesty at Newcastle House,[101] ordered, no doubt, on an equally magnificent scale. Public business again intervened for a season, but at the end of July it was happily concluded, so that he could celebrate his own twenty-fifth birthday at Halland. From that time until Parliament assembled in November, he remained in the country.

Reference has been made already to his fondness for the countryside, a devotion which he shared with Robert Walpole,

---

[97] Boyer, *Pol. State*, XV, 373 and 450.

[98] H.M.C. *Frankland-Russell-Astley MSS*, 92-93. *Cf. Lady Cowper's Diary*, 113, and Michael, *op. cit.*, 577-578.

[99] *Stuart Papers*, IV, 251 (Bothmer to Schutz). The editor has blundered into making the reference to "the duchess" apply to Lady Newcastle.

[100] Lady Newton, *Lyme Letters*, 268.

[101] Boyer, *Pol. State*, XV, 549.

to the despair of their colleagues.   There, in the well-known
words of Pope, they could enjoy a

> happier hour
> Of social pleasure, ill-exchanged for power;

and for a season

> Smile without art, and win without a bribe.

In 1717 and again in 1718 the younger Craggs, who could
presume to such familiarities, wrote to reproach him for his
prolonged stay in the country[102] and threatened to deprive him
of the news as the only way to get him out.   Seven years later,
as Secretary of State, he was rebuked by Lord Townshend
with the words: "I can't help imagining that Claremont and
Norfolk take up a large share of your Grace's and my brother
Walpole's thoughts."[103]   In spite of his uncle's disaster, Newcastle was a devotee of the chase, and the upkeep of his stables
alone amounted to over £2,000 a year.[104]   Thus it was that
the effects of over-indulgence in the pleasures of the table and
the bottle were worked off, and a good old age promoted.

In 1718, the ancestral seats in Sussex and Nottinghamshire
were completely eclipsed by the great new edifice known as
Claremont.   It is a melancholy reflection that of this massive
fabric, constructed and maintained at such a ruinous sacrifice,
there is not a stone left standing.   It stood a mile south of
Esher, in Surrey, and formed one of the many noble mansions
that clustered about "royal Hampton's pile," three miles away.
Begun by Vanbrugh in 1710, it was almost complete in 1715,
when Garth paid it a lengthy tribute in one of his best-known

---

[102] *Add. MSS*, 32,686, f. 100 (Sept. 12, 1717), and f. 118 (Aug. 23, 1718).
[103] *Add. MSS*, 32,687, f. 87 (June 18, 1725).   The reply forms f. 101b
(June 30, 1725).
[104] H.M.C. *Coke MSS*, 118 (Newcastle to Coke, Sept. 5, 1717).   *Add.
MSS*, 33,064, f. 257 (Newcastle to Lady Lincoln, n.d. 1725 or 1726).   Stable
accounts in *Add. MSS*, 33,137.   See *Appendix D*.   These would seem to
refute the statements to the contrary in Yorke, *Hardwicke*.

minor poems.[105] Building was carried on, however, until 1724, the drains not having been laid until the year before.[106]

With the good-natured geniality and love of company that were among the duke's most striking characteristics, it was not remarkable that Claremont was the scene of many a brilliant gathering and noble dinner, served on the as yet unpawned Cavendish plate. And when the King honored it with his presence, as was the case in October, 1717, there was the standard to maintain set by the "English Crassus," when another ruler had been his guest at Welbeck.

Fortunately an account of the cost of maintaining all this splendor has survived among the all too scanty manuscripts of this period. In 1732, in a periodic fit of economy, a *Scheme of Regulation* based upon an annual budget of £12,000 was drawn up at the duke's request,[107] from which it is possible to arrive at what must have been regarded as a reasonable or minimum expenditure. Household supplies of all kinds absorbed £4,652, the wages and livery of all domestics, including a French *confiseur* and *chef,* added another £1,222, while the upkeep of the house, woods, and orchard, and the vegetable and flower gardens came to another £1,000, making a total of £6,874. These sums are, of course, exclusive of the expenses of the stables, already mentioned.

Claremont was noted for no gallery of paintings like those which graced the walls of Houghton, and no such wealth of precious tomes as those which formed the pride and ornament of Harley's seat at Wimpole and of Sunderland's Piccadilly

---

[105] A more exact, if less poetic description of the house, garden, and park, is provided in *Add. MSS,* 33,137, ff. 383-387. There is a contemporary view in the *Vitruvius Britannicus,* vol. III, and in Vanbrugh's *Works,* vol. IV, p. 112.

[106] Lovegrove, *Vanbrugh,* 15. Vanbrugh had previously built Castle Howard, in Yorkshire, for the Earl of Carlisle; Kneller Hall, near Hounslow; a theatre in the Haymarket; and most important of all, Blenheim.

[107] *Add. MSS,* 33,137, ff. 365-372. See this and other accounts in *Appendix D.*

mansion.[108]   The Age of Addison and Swift was passing.
Already the "alliance of authors and statesmen" was breaking
up, and the aristocratic patron was beginning to give way to
the rising class of booksellers.   Still, his obligations as an
aristocrat to the arts were not altogether neglected by Newcastle in his early years.   While he was never, as Pope said of
Halifax, "fed with dedications," Steele had once hailed him
as the friend of men of letters in the dedication of his *Political
Writings*.   Two years after this, in 1717, Congreve dedicated
an edition of Dryden's *Plays* to him.[109]   More important still,
it could hardly have been without some hope of success that
Horace Walpole appealed to him to take the great Voltaire
under his protection in 1726, upon his historic sojourn in England.[110]

Beginning in 1717, Newcastle began to demonstrate the
liveliest interest in foreign affairs, into the sources of which
interest it is profitable to enquire.   The arena of domestic
politics, with its struggle between Sunderland and Walpole,
provided slender prospects for ambitious men of less prodigious
mould.   The broader field of foreign politics, however, fur-
nished no such obstacles to a young aspirant like Newcastle, and
the vigor of the Continental policy of his principals in the Administration seems to have stimulated his imagination and
ambition, Stanhope in particular exciting his enthusiastic admiration.[111]

At any rate, from the first of October Newcastle was kept
in constant touch with the course of events in Europe by the
letters he received from Sunderland.[112]   It can hardly be without
significance that on the 19th, Abbé Dubois, the confidential agent

---

[108] However, many years later, Cradock spoke of the "great library" at
Claremont. (*Literary and Miscellaneous Memoirs*, 1828), I, 22.

[109] Pope, *Works*, VI, 16, note.

[110] *Add. MSS*, 32,685, f. 57.

[111] *Add. MSS*, 32,686, f. 145 (H. Pelham to Newcastle, Sept. 10, 1719),
and same to Hardwicke (Nov. 14, 1748), quoted in Yorke, *Hardwicke*,
II, 12.

[112] *Add. MSS*, 32,686, f. 108 *et sqq.*

of the French Regent, was among the guests at Claremont; and it is probable that it was about this time that the duke made the acquaintance of the Hanoverian Marshal, C. U. von Hardenberg, then on a visit to England, with whom he afterward carried on a friendly correspondence.[113] In June, 1718, when Stanhope was suddenly called to Paris, Newcastle applied to the earl's private secretary, Charles Stanhope, for the explanation of his departure, however secret, promising not to disclose the information to anyone alive.[114] Again, in July, 1720, when the amateur diplomatist was in Nottingham, he directed that "the news that came last from France" be sent to him at once.[115] From this time on, he may be said to have been absorbed in foreign politics and diplomacy as a sort of hobby, with the hope, no doubt, of eventually exchanging the Chamberlain's gold key for the white wand of a Secretary of State.

His first opportunity to act in a public capacity in relation to diplomacy came on July 22, 1718 (O.S.) when along with nine other Privy Councillors he affixed his signature to the tripartite treaty with France and the Emperor;[116] which, upon the tardy accession of the Dutch in December, became the Quadruple Alliance.

What proved to be one of the most notable sessions in the Administration of Sunderland and Stanhope was opened November 11, 1718. Weeks before Parliament assembled, both the Ministry and the opposition began to muster their forces for a renewal of the conflict. Walpole opened the debate with a vigorous onslaught on the measures of the Court party, and upon the recent treaties in particular. But, for the nonce, the Ministry was prepared, and its measures were approved in the Commons by a vote of 215 to 155. There is reason for

---

[113] Boyer, *Pol. State*, XIV, 351. Although constant reference is made to their correspondence, not a line has been preserved in the Newcastle Papers.

[114] Torrens, *Hist. of Cabinets*, I, 228, quoting *MS* source.

[115] *S. P. Dom., George I*, bundle xxii (P. Forbes, Newcastle's private secretary, to ?).

[116] Boyer, *Pol. State*, XVI, 50-51 and XVII, 82-98.

believing, however, that the strength of the Administration was more apparent than real, and that its initial success was obtained by unfair means. It was asserted that false reports of the date of assembly were circulated to delay the arrival of the Tories.[117] Furthermore, it was contended that Chancellor Parker secretly entered twenty-five proxies for the government before prayers, and then, for fear the Tories would likewise enter some, called prayers half an hour early, after which time they could not be entered, according to the rules. By this artifice, the Court obtained the small majority of fourteen in the Lords, and "the Tories taunted the Court that it couldn't raise five more votes, as they had forced everyone up upon pain of forfeiture of employment and pensions."[118] On the other hand, had the Tories turned out in force, the results might have been different, but many of them persisted in their policy of non-coöperation with the Whig opposition.[119]

Ever since the accession of the new dynasty the Dissenters had been led to expect some measure of relief from the party which had always professed its sympathy for them. The King himself was well disposed from the outset and so were some of the bishops, but the government made no move until 1717. At last, in November of that year, it had proposed "to consider the most effective way of strengthening the Protestant interest," but in the presence of the united opposition of the Tories and the followers of Walpole, the motion had been abandoned.[120]

But now, in 1718, the Administration was a year older, and its prestige had recently been stiffened by the Quadruple Alliance

---

[117] *Stuart Papers,* VII, 569 (Menzies to Dillon, Nov. 13).

[118] *Ibid.,* 567-568 (Thomas to Mar, Nov. 13), and H.M.C. *Portland MSS,* V, 570.

[119] There are numerous complaints of this apathy in the Jacobite Correspondence, *e.g. Stuart Papers,* VI, 238; VII, 162, 314, 569, 574, 593, 646. 663; and H.M.C. *Carlisle MSS,* 23. This solves Lord Mahon's quandary "that the seceding do not appear to have gained ground by their open juncture with the Tories" (*Hist. of England,* I, 296).

[120] Michael, *Eng. Geschichte,* II, 106-107; *Parl. Hist.,* VII, 502-504; *Commons Journals,* XVIII, 630; *Annals of Stair,* II, 38 (Craggs to Stair, Sept. 5, 1717).

and the defeat of the Spanish fleet off Cape Passaro. While
it is true that Stanhope had opposed the Schism Act when it
was passed in 1714, an enlightened statesmanship and a desire
to redeem old promises were not the only causes of the project
to relieve the Dissenters. With the time for a general election
drawing nearer, the Administration became more and more
uneasy, as the proposal to repeal the Septennial Act would presently reveal. Furthermore, the disabilities under which the
Nonconformists labored enabled the Tories to capture certain
borough corporations.[121] It would be a master stroke to emancipate the Dissenters and bind them to the government by ties
of gratitude.

It was with mixed motives, then, that Stanhope suddenly,
on December 13th, laid before the Lords his "bill for strengthening the Protestant Interest." The political motives also help
to explain the strength of the attack, in the face of which the
Ministry abandoned the clauses relating to the modification of
the Test and Corporation Acts. The Schism and Occasional
Conformity Acts were then swept away by safe majorities in
both Houses.

Although Newcastle's orthodoxy and devotion to the Established Church have been asserted,[122] there is no evidence
from the sources for this period at least that he had more
religion, as Voltaire put it, than the minimum which was required for party purposes. At all events, he supported the
bill in debate, along with his principals, which ended in its
commitment.[123] Fortunately, we are in possession of the Commons' division lists, from which it is manifest that of the
duke's borough nominees, although two failed somehow to
vote, only one cast his vote against the measure.[124]

---

[121] Clarke, *Hist. of Eng. Nonconformity,* I, 184-185.

[122] See *Add. MSS,* 5,832, f. 114b; H.M.C. *Portland MSS,* V, 571 (newsletter of Nov. 18, 1718) ; Gomme, *Gentleman's Mag.,* Eng. Topog., part
xii, 77.

[123] Boyer, *Pol. State,* XVI, 625.

[124] See lists in *Parl. Hist.,* VII, 585-588. Brigadier Sutton, M.P. for Newark, was the offender.

Having achieved this partial success with a measure of considerable moment, the Ministry now resolved to risk another,
one of the most far-reaching constitutional significance. With
all the politician's eagerness to perpetuate his power, Sunderland beheld the perennial prospect of the prince's accession to
the throne as a sword of Damocles above his head. Failure had
attended every scheme of reconciliation, and the petty persecu-
tions of the heir, so utterly un-royal, had been aggravated
rather than diminished.[125] The result was the famous Peerage
Bill, designated at once to muzzle the Prerogative by preventing for all time a repetition of the famous Tory peer-making of
1711-12, and to consolidate the power of Sunderland and Stanhope.

The King's spitefulness and his ignorance of the effect on his
prerogative combined to secure for the measure his consent, and
it was likewise calculated to appeal to the self-interest of every
peer. The bill was brought into the Lords on February 28th,
and proposed in brief "that the number of the English peers
should not be enlarged beyond six above the present number,
which, upon failure of male issue, might be supplied by new
creations; that instead of the sixteen elective peers in Scotland,
twenty-five to be made hereditary on the part of that kingdom,
whose number, upon failure of heirs male, should be supplied
by some other Scotch peers."[126] As was anticipated, the bill
passed its first and second readings without difficulty in a body
which hoped thereby to become an irresponsible, close corporation and a hereditary caste. In the lower Chamber, however,
and among the middle and upper classes generally, the antagon-
ism which the Peerage Bill aroused was overwhelming; and
apart from the sixteen representative peers, neither were the
Scotch nobility beguiled by the bait thrown out to lure their ac-
quiescence. The chorus was taken up by the newspapers and
pamphlets, and stay-at-home Members began to pour into the

---

[125] H.M.C. *Portland MSS*, V, 559 (Edw. to Abigail Harley, Apr. 13,
1718), and 560 (same to same, May 6, 1718).
[126] Duke of Somerset's outline plan in *Lords' Journals*, XXI, 83.

capital, while even the impecunious prince spent money right and left. The uproar assumed such proportions that when the bill came up for the third time on April 14, Lord Stanhope, like the good general he was, postponed it for a fortnight rather than risk defeat in the Commons. Four days later Parliament was prorogued. Thus the Peerage Bill was allowed to retire in good order, but only that it might be freshened to renew the charge.

At the same time that the Ministers were carrying on this public conflict in Parliament and in the prints, another one was going on behind the scenes, which bade fair to end in undoing them as it had their predecessors. So clandestine was the conflict that it seems to have escaped all but the most initiated contemporaries, and has been neglected if not ignored by modern writers.

The conflict in question was the result of what has been aptly termed the dual control of the King's business by his English and Hanoverian Ministers.[127] The King's German dominions were governed from London, to which place his Electoral court and certain Ministers had followed him. Being, as "honest" Shippen had once asserted to his cost, "a stranger to the English language and constitution," George I leaned heavily upon these familiar advisers, particularly Bernstorff, but also upon Bothmer and Robethon—the so-called Hanoverian Junta.[128] The sphere of activity and influence of the German Ministers was never clearly defined, and they saw no reason why their voice in English concerns should not be at least as great as that of Schomberg, Bentinck, or Van Keppel under the Dutch King.

[127] *"Doppelregiment,"* the expression of Professor Michael, upon whose quotations from the reports of foreign ambassadors this and the three following paragraphs are largely based. The diplomatic reports, with the *Stuart Papers* and Lady Cowper's incomplete *Diary,* are the only only considerable sources for this important topic. Ward's *Great Britain and Hanover,* 67-79, is an excellent secondary account.

[128] For Jean de Robethon see the article of J. F. Chance in the *Eng. Hist. Rev.,* XVIII 55-70. For characterizations of the other two see Abbé Dubois' *Instructions* to Senneterre in Michael, *Eng. Geschichte,* II, 635-636.

As might be anticipated, their interest in the affairs of northern Europe was immense, and it was in this direction that their influence or coöperation was particularly potent and particularly obnoxious.

The three were the objects of all the detestation that Englishmen are wont to harbor for the alien advisers of their sovereign; but as has been seen, this had not prevented Stanhope and Sunderland from joining with them for the overthrow of Townshend and Walpole. Under the regime which followed, the influence of Bernstorff was greater than ever, and as Bonet wrote, "through the great credit that he had with the King he held the Ministers in dependence."

This state of things went on well enough for about a year, but early in 1718 there were unmistakable indications that the two sets of Ministers were beginning to fall foul of each other.[129] Still the authority of the gruff old Bernstorff remained unshaken. Then on January 5, 1719 came the conclusion of the Treaty of Vienna between Hanover, Saxony, and the Emperor, which ran directly counter to the Anglo-French entente that Stanhope had so diligently nurtured; and after this the English seem to have resolved to shake off the Hanoverian incubus.[130]

Of the three "Triumvirs," Cadogan was the one most closely attached to the Junta,[131] and there was a bitter rivalry between this burly Irish officer and Lord Stanhope for the reversion of the Captain-General's baton.[132] For some time he had been gathering a party about him and he even had opposed the Peerage Bill. With the support of the Germans and the favor of his King, Cadogan put no limit to his ambition and even aspired to be *premier ministre*.[133] For these reasons Stanhope

---

[129] *Stuart Papers*, V, 432, and VII, 375-376 (Munster-Pigbore letters, May 30-31, 1718).

[130] Michael, *op. cit.*, II, 557-558.

[131] *Ibid.*, II, 636 (Dubois' *Instructions*).

[132] H.M.C. *Portland MSS*, V, 559 (Edw. to Abigail Harley, Apr. 1, 1718), and *Stuart Papers*, VII, 102 (Flint to Mar, Aug. 1, 1718), and V, 536.

[133] *Annals of Stair*, II, 103-104 (Craggs to Stair, Mar. 10, 1719), and 106 (same to same, Mar. 31).

and Craggs determined to strike at the Germans through the disgrace of Cadogan, in which scheme they were ultimately joined by Sunderland. In order to discredit him with the King, he was charged with bungling the negotiations with the Dutch; and in February his old rival, the Duke of Argyle, was restored to favor and taken into the government as Lord Steward.[134] Two months later he was made an English duke. This intrigue, which provides an excellent illustration of eighteenth-century government by faction and personal rivalries, failed to achieve its objects, and for another year the English and Hanoverians faced each other like two hostile camps, their relations constantly embittered by fresh provocations.

While matters stood thus in Parliament and in his counsels, on May 11, 1719, King George was able to get a belated start upon his second journey to his cherished fatherland. This time there had been no question of making the Prince of Wales Regent under any conditions, and instead the functions were exercised by a commission of thirteen Lords Justices, of which Newcastle was one.[135]

This was the first of the numerous occasions on which the duke was to hold this high office, and its importance on this occasion must be sought in the first-hand experience in foreign affairs which it gave him. Already he was able to exchange opinions with his principals on weighty problems on an authoritative footing. "Lord Sunderland goes from hence on Thursday sennight, & it will be very necessary for y(our) g(race) to come and assist those who are left behind," wrote Secretary Craggs from Battersea to Newcastle on the 10th of August. "He is now here with me and gives me his most hearty and sincere services." After referring to Stanhope's negotia-

---

[134] Besides Michael, see also H.M.C. *Portland MSS,* V, 575 (Edw. to A. Harley, Jan. 8, 1719).

[135] Boyer, *Pol. State,* XVII, 494-496. For a discussion of the Lords Justices in the 18th century see Turner in the *Eng. Hist. Rev.,* XXIX, 453-476, where, it may be noted, the Secretary of the Justices is consistently given as Delasaye, instead of Delafaye.

tions in the north of Europe, Craggs continued: "He was of your mind, and so have Lord Sunderland and I (been) in relation to ye Muscovite stroak."[136] In the same spirit the duke's brother wrote him a month later, congratulating him upon the "good success of your negotiations abroad."[137]

The opening of the new session now loomed large upon the political horizon, and the Ministry began to concert its plans for the coming conflict. From the Electoral hunting-seat of Göhrde near the river Elbe, Sunderland wrote Newcastle on October 11th: "Our affairs in all parts go as well as can be wished. After that, our winter campaign can't fail, especially since the King is more determined than ever to persist with vigor in all the measures you and yr friends wish. He is resolved to push the peerage bill, the university bill, and the repeal of the septennial bill. If this won't unite the Wigs, nothing will."[138] The last and most extraordinary of these projects was nothing less than a scheme to seduce the House of Commons into compliance with the Peerage Bill by an offer to make that ancient Chamber immortal!

Nothing could better demonstrate the extent of Newcastle's weight and authority in the Cabinet than the fact that it was due to him, at least in part, that this unparalleled proposal was nipped in the bud. His opposition was no less a tribute to his political sagacity, which saw the practical unwisdom of a project that had the approbation of his older and more experienced principals.

From Claremont he wrote Lord Stanhope in the middle of October, rejoicing over the latter's successes and the projected early return of the King. "I am very glad to find by my friend Craggs yt Ld. Sunderland and yourself are entirely of opinion for pushing the peerage bill," he continued. "I must own I can never think our constitution settled, or ye king entirely safe till it be passed. · · · · I must own, my dear Stanhope, I am not

---

[136] *Add.* MSS, 32,686, ff. 137-138.
[137] *Ibid.*, f. 145.
[138] *Ibid.*, f. 149.

of ye same opinion as to ye repeal of ye Septennial Bill, for
I think we shall evidently lose much more by it than we can
profitably get.   In ye first place, I am far from thinking it will
make ye Peerage bill go down ye better.   Some, I am sure, who
are very good friends to ye latter, will strenuously oppose the
former, and though I own we have but a small chance for any
lords (?) yett yt undoubtedly w'd make 'em ye more determined, & I took ye liberty to tell Ld. Sun., when he dropt
something of ye kind at Mr Comptroller's, yt I found it had
displeased some of our friends.   Besides, I must own I cannot
apprehend we have any reason to fear coming to a new election,
provided this parliam^t sits out its time, for then ye party can
by no means pretend to be disobliged.   Should this parliam^t
be continued, it would shew a great distrust of ye King's interest in England, & look as if our past conduct would not be
approved of, when, on ye contrary, we have all ye reason to
think that before this parliam^t ends, ye King's affairs will be
upon so glorious a foot that it will (be) almost impossible
to oppose him. · · · · Towards ye close of ye last session, there
was a great many ill humours stirring, & should this parliam^t
be continued beyond its time, nobody knows in what shape it
may appear. · · · · Give me leave only to suggest one thing—that
this point may be undetermined when we have the happiness
of seeing you on our side ye water, yt then we may take our
lists & see where we shall mend and where otherwise, & then
I dare say ye advantage will appear so great on our side yt
you will be of my opinion."[139]

Two weeks after these lines were penned, Stanhope was
inditing his reply in Hanover.   What with the success of
England's foreign policy and the unity of the King and his
Ministers, he wrote, never would the prospects for carrying
both the mooted bills be more auspicious.   He confessed that
he decidedly favored the repeal of the Septennial Act on its
own merits and for the interests of the country, and that

---

[139] *Add. MSS*, 32,686, ff. 151-153 (Oct. 14, 1719).

he had little hope for the success of the Peerage Bill without it.   But if Newcastle thought there would be too much opposition to the repeal in the Commons, and that the Peerage Bill might be carried "without the assistance of so strong an argument *ad hominem*," he was willing to submit to the opinion of their friends.   "They must govern us," he wrote, "& especially our friends of the house of commons.   If what is designed as a service to the house of commons and to the Whigg party be taken otherwise by them, it must undoubtedly be dropped."[140]

This is the last that is heard of the proposed repeal, and it is probable that upon the return of the King and Lord Stanhope it was determined to abandon it.   Nevertheless, in spite of this check, the Ministry persevered in the principal point at issue.   Parliament was opened on November 23, and two days later the Peerage Bill was re-introduced and got its first reading.   The history of the bill has been written many times,[141] and it would be to no purpose to detail it here again.   Sufficient it is to say that it passed the Lords on the 30th, practically without opposition, and was sent to the Commons where all indications pointed to its success, in spite of the storm of disapproval outside Parliament.   After all, the bill was in harmony with the Whig principle of limitation of the prerogative, and many felt it to be the surest way of safeguarding the Whig ascendency against Tory encroachments. At this point, however, there stood forth one who understood *quicquid agunt homines* better than any other leader of his time.   He spoke, and the bill was stopped in full career.   The man was Robert Walpole, and he invoked a principle more universal than either of the above when he appealed to the hope and ambition of every commoner to win a peerage for himself. Upon the second reading the bill was overwhelmingly rejected.

---

[140] *Ibid.*, ff. 155-156 (Oct. 27, 1719).   Given in part in Torrens, Hist. of *Cabinets*, I, 238.

[141] See especially the excellent article of E. R. Turner in the *Eng. Hist. Rev.*, XXVIII, 243-259.

The potency of his appeal was nowhere better manifested than in the way Newcastle's own nominees broke their leash for once and voted as their interests seemed to dictate. In Sussex, the three Pelhams, indeed, remained constant, but every other member there who owed his seat to the duke was found among the missing or on the side of the majority at the division. They had hearkened unto Walpole's ringing exordium, for they hoped some day to enter the Temple of Fame, of which he spoke, through the Temple of Virtue; and was it not true, as he averred, that if the bill passed "one of the most powerful incentives to virtue would be taken away"? In Nottinghamshire, either the loyalty of the ducal nominees was greater or their ambition less, and five of the eight remained steadfast; but of the four members from Yorkshire, including Sir Richard Steele, only one voted with the Court.[142]

The Ministry did not resign as it would be bound to do today. Besides the Lords' support, they still had the confidence of the King, and in the eighteenth century that was enough, as Pitt was one day to demonstrate to Fox. Nevertheless, with the triumph of the opposition, their position was fast becoming untenable, and there was no telling how soon the Germans might succeed in discrediting them with the King as they had Townshend.

One more avenue of escape remained. Sunderland's leaning toward a bi-partisan Ministry has already been noticed, and on several occasions since the schism began negotiations had been carried on with the Tories.[143] For a time it appeared that Bolingbroke's attainder might be reversed, and that he would be recalled. For Sunderland this would be like playing with fire, for it is inconceivable that any Ministry could long survive

---

[142] Based upon the lists in *Parl. Hist.*, VII, 624-627.

[143] H.M.C. *Portland MSS*, V, 535 (newsletter, Nov. 7, 1717); 565 (newsletter, Oct. 10, 1718); 573 (Edw. to A. Harley, Dec. 2, 1718); 575 (same to same); 576 (same to same, Jan. 11, 1719); and VII, 267 (Dec. 24, 1718). *Annals of Stair*, II, 24 (Addison to Stair, Sept. 2, 1717).

the presence of two men like himself and Bolingbroke. But according to Pentenriedter, the Imperial envoy, even the King had declared that he would throw himself into the arms of the Tories rather than join with the renegade Whigs again![144]

Now, following the defeat of the Peerage Bill, the Ministry began to approach the Tories once more. The details of the negotiations are very obscure, but there seems to have been a number of schemes on foot to promote the desired object. "In short, there was not a rogue in town that wasn't engaged in some scheme and project to undo his country," wrote Lady Cowper in her diary.[145]

Meanwhile the Hanoverians had been carrying on an intrigue of their own. For some time they had been working for the overthrow of the Administration and for the reconciliation of the King with the prince. Among other things, they represented to His Majesty that the present Ministers were "more masters than himself, and were resolved to continue so, and live on the spoil, and let none come in for a share with 'em, and at long run serve him as they did King James II."[146] The apparent decline of their influence late in 1719[147] and the defection of the Duchess of Munster through

---

[144] Michael, *Eng. Geschichte,* II, 607, quoting *Vienna State Papers.*

[145] *Lady Cowper's Diary,* 144.

[146] *Stuart Papers,* VII, 651 (Father Plunkett to James III, Dec. 8, 1718), and 375-376 (Munster-Pigbore letters, May, 1718).

[147] On October 27, 1719, Stanhope wrote Newcastle: "I cannot promise that the old man (*i.e.* Bernstorff) will be left behind; but I may safely assure your Grace that though he should come, the King will doe whatever shall be proposed to him, so make everybody sensible that he is not to meddle in English business. He is extremely piqued and mortified at his declining credit, and has taken a very slight occasion to vent his spleen and resentment against poor Robethon, whom he has cruelly offended without rhyme or reason. Robethon being his immediate subordinate in the German chancery may be insulted with impunity, the rather because whilst we are excluding the Germans avowedly from meddling in English business, we cannot openly support him. However, we shall hope to disengage him by the assistance of our good duchess" (*Add. MSS,* 32,686, f. 156). (The Duchess of Munster had been gratified with an English peerage as Duchess of Kendal in March, 1719.) See also Mahon, *Hist. of England,* II, *App.,* p. 80 (Stanhope to Craggs).

the bestowal of an English peerage served to stimulate their efforts to arouse the King's suspicion and resentment.

Early in April 1720, the scheme which they had hatched came unexpectedly to light, when Lord Sunderland was presented with a most astounding document.[148] It revealed that the Germans had perfected a plan to overthrow the present Administration and to bring in the leaders of the opposition Whigs, together with half a dozen Tories, in their room. To his dismay the earl saw that the Germans and the "disgusted" Whigs had stolen his own thunder and that the King, apparently, had come into their plans—how far he could not fathom. Something had to be done quickly. For three days Sunderland, Stanhope, and Craggs consulted with one another and then they had an audience with the King. After reproaching him for his bad faith, they laid before him their own hastily altered plan, which now provided not for the admission of the Tories, but for the reunion of the Whigs. There were hasty negotiations with the leaders of the Whig opposition, and Robert Walpole was foremost in the rôle of peacemaker. But, of all this, Bernstorff was kept utterly in the dark. The King was reconciled to everything but the notion of the restoration of the prince and demanded: "Can't the Whigs come back without him?" Sunderland too would have preferred to leave the heir in disgrace,[149] but Walpole was obdurate: no reconciliation, no *rapprochement*. At one time in the course of the negotiations it was rumored that the Ministry would have to submit to certain sacrifices, and that the Duke of Newcastle, among others repugnant to the

---

[148] H.M.C. *Portland MSS*, V, 594-596. Two other slightly variant versions of the original project sent to Count Zinzendorff at Vienna by Bernstorff are to be found in H.M.C. *Townshend MSS*, 104-106, and a French translation in *Archives des Affaires Etrangères*. Many writers have based their accounts of this mysterious affair upon the inadequate and misleading explanation in Coxe's *Walpole*, I, 229-230. Even Leadam blunders on the date of the "Project" (*Hist. of England*, IX, 297). Unfortunately the *Stuart Papers* have not been calendared beyond 1719.

[149] Coxe, *Walpole*, I, 229. This is what Walpole afterward told Etough.

prince, would be turned out;[150] but afterward nothing more
was heard of this.

By St. George's Day, April 23, 1720, everything was
ready; but so secretly had the whole affair been managed that
even William Pulteney, himself no cipher, was convinced that
not ten men in all England, including the prince, knew anything of it.[151] The latter was induced to write a submissive
letter which was delivered to the King that day at noon.
Secretary Craggs was promptly sent to Leicester House with
the royal invitation to come to Court. At three o'clock the
prince's chair was set down at St. James's Palace and there
was an audience of a very few minutes in the King's closet.
When the prince emerged the waiting courtiers were made
happy with the word that the wretched quarrel was officially at
an end.[152] It was a testimony to Newcastle's consequence that
he was one of the very few who were privy to the whole proceedings. As the prince withdrew from the presence the duke
put himself in his way, and it was ominous that his future
sovereign vouchsafed him not a word.

Although everybody was surprised and mystified, that did
not prevent an orgy of hugs and kisses and general rejoicing.
But old Baron Bernstorff did not rejoice, and Lady Cowper
describes a curious scene in which Stanhope broke the news
to him. The happy ending of the schism was signalized by
certain alterations in the Ministry, the most important being
the restoration of Townshend to the King's counsels as Lord
President and of Walpole to his old place at the Pay-Office.
Their opposition was at an end, but not for long would they
be contented with subordinate employment.

On June 11 the session ended, and for a brief season Wal-

---

[150] *Lady Cowper's Diary,* 130-131.

[151] Coxe, *op. cit.,* III, 186 (William to Daniel Pulteney, May 7, 1720).

[152] For a description of the incident, see *Marchmont Papers,* I, 409-410;
L. C. Records, Miscellanea (Master of the Ceremonies), vol. iii, 42; H.M.C.
Portland MSS, V, 596; *Lady Cowper's Diary,* 142; and Boyer, *Pol. State,*
XIX, 450-451.

pole retired from the scene to rusticate in his cherished Norfolk. As for Townshend, he was made one of the fifteen Lords Justices whom the King left behind upon his departure for Hanover a few days later. Newcastle was also one of their number. Baron Bernstorff accompanied his master home, never to return to England, and there was an end to the dual control. The stage was prepared for new issues and new rôles, with Squire Walpole as the hero of the piece and Newcastle as his *aide de camp*.

VI

Newcastle Becomes Walpole's Lieutenant

"I have heard but one sound these three months in this place, viz.: that of South Sea, which has got the better of men's politics and ladies' fashions, and has entirely engrossed all conversation." In this wise did a correspondent of the Earl of Oxford describe the London scene in the spring of 1720.[1] It is not the purpose here to write the history of the South Sea Bubble; but the enormous influence which it had on men and affairs, and not least upon the career of the Duke of Newcastle, necessitates a brief recapitulation here.[2]

The joint-stock enterprise known as the "Governor and Company of Merchants trading to the South Sea and other parts of America" had been conceived by Harley and incorporated by Parliament in 1711, with a view to restoring public credit and funding the national debt. By that year a large public indebtedness had been created for which the Bank of England was unwilling to provide, and as the limit of taxation had been reached, the government was anxious to discover some security still unpledged. It was observed that as yet no English company enjoyed an exclusive monopoly of trading privileges with the "South Seas," although the commercial and mineral profits to be had there were reputed to be large. The result was the incorporation of the South Seas Company, by which the government obtained a single creditor for debts amounting to almost nine and a half millions sterling. The holders of existing bonds exchange them for stock in the Company, with interest at six *per cent* secured by certain duties.

Although the South Sea Company had £10,000,000 in capital at its command—much more than any other company—

---

[1] H.M.C. *Portland MSS*, V, 594.

[2] Scott, *Joint Stock Companies to 1720*, III, 288-353, is the authority for the following account.

only a small portion ever was or could be actually employed. As long as the War of the Spanish Succession continued, expeditions to the Pacific were hazardous, and the Treaty of Utrecht and the *Asiento* agreement were disappointing in failing to provide the expected commercial opportunities. Then came the new Whig government which had favored the Bank of England instead of Harley's enterprise, and finally, in 1718, hostilities with Spain had broken out afresh. In 1719, after eight years of existence, actual trading operations were insignificant.

This situation tempted the Company to employ its capital and energies in other directions than the exploitation of the Pacific trade, and the sphere of activity was not far to seek. During the wars of Marlborough, the State had borrowed at rates of interest varying from 6¼ to 8 *per cent* on the basis of long-term annuities. After the war, the money market was easier, but in 1719, with capital available at four or five *per cent,* the Treasury was still paying the former high rates of interest. Agitation for conversion was begun as early as 1714 by financial experts like Archibald Hutchinson, and the success of Law's activities in France gave the movement strong support. Accordingly, in 1719 the government agreed to the conversion of the Lottery Loan of 1710 into South Sea stock, and the transaction proved so advantageous to all concerned that in November of that year the Company secretly proposed nothing less than the funding of the whole of England's indebtedness, both the redeemable loans and those issued on securities, which, exclusive of the debt due the Bank of England and the East India Company totalled almost £31,000,000. The public proposal was made in January, 1720, and in spite of the warnings of Walpole and others the Ministry was induced to recommend the scheme, so that it became law on April 7, 1720.

The danger lay in accepting the Company's proposals without any limitation as to the terms upon which stock was to be offered to holders of the debt. Furthermore, the facts of the inner history of the Company were concealed from the investors, and even the most thoughtful could not see that what was intended was not a legitimate business development but only a manipulation of the market, and were induced to buy upon the basis of what later proved to be partial evidence. So golden did the prospects of profit seem that all over England men and women vied with one another for the tempting shares. Each day the price mounted higher, until on June 24th £100 of stock was sold for £1,050—the highest point. The rage for stock-jobbing, which had been gradually growing for the last few years now burst all bounds, and there were all sorts of rival schemes brewing, some of them genuine and rational enough, but others, the so-called bubbles, hopelessly speculative and chimerical.

The echo of the feverish excitement that stirred even the little market-town of Lewes was heard in far-off Galata, when Lucy Pelham wrote her brother, the Turkey merchant, there. "There is nothing talked of here but South Sea (her letter ran), which has made a great many peple very rich; but known of our frends ar so much improve of there fortune as Coll. Pelham, who is now they say is worth 50 thousand pound."[3] Her illustrious cousin of Newcastle, who was spending the summer at Nottingham, was not altogether immune to the enthusiasm that infected the rest of mankind; but from a letter which he wrote to Craggs he seems to have been more interested in the preliminaries of the coming canvass than in the "subscriptions." With his usual good nature, however, he exerted his influence in the interests of his friends.[4]

The success of the South Sea Company's enterprise depended largely on the rise of stock, and all sorts of artificial means were adopted to this end. But inflation likewise launched the numerous unauthorized ventures and made it

---

[3] *Add. MSS,* 33,085, f. 30 (June 4, 1720).

[4] *Add. MSS,* 32,686, f. 163 (C. Stanhope to Newcastle, July 28, 1720); *Ibid.,* f. 166 (J. Craggs to Newcastle, Aug. 2, 1720) ; and *Stowe MSS,* 247, f. 166 (Newcastle to Craggs, Aug. 6, 1720).

difficult for the Company to get the cash from the subscribers
to its four issues of stock, and the scarcity of money would drive
up interest rates. Finally in self defense the Company turned
upon the "bubbles" and on August 18 writs of *scire facias* were
issued.

The panic which ensued shook down the flimsy fabric of the
bubbles, and gradually the South Sea Company itself slid down
into the general ruin, while the thousands who had been lured
by the hope of riches were pinched or even beggared. "We
are all here in a confusion on the fall of South sea stock," wrote
old Henry Pelham to his son in Turkey. "I think I may say
it is quite destroyed. Wee have abundance of bankrupts in
the City. I wish your old master holds it. Many familys are
undone. I thank God ours does pretty well, though some losses
we have all."[5] The Duke of Newcastle did not consider himself a great sufferer by the catastrophe,[6] but however small his
loss, he could ill afford it. According to a pamphlet which was
circulated not long after, bearing the significant sub-title *for
the use of Freeholders of Counties,* he lost £2,000 on the second subscription and both he and the duchess lost a like sum
on the third.[7]

The extent of the ruin to trade and industry and the widespread cry for retribution that arose when the worst was known
may be measured by the swarm of petitions from counties and
boroughs to the House of Commons in the spring of 1721.
Gibbon, the historian, tells how Lord Molesworth expressed his
satisfaction at the notion of meting out the ancient Roman
penalty for parricide to the authors of the South Sea ruin;
while Speaker Onslow marveled afterward that the calamity did
not "produce some convulsion in the state," so bitter was the
rage against the Ministry and the foreign King, whose son and
mistresses were known to have made fortunes.

---

[5] *Add. MSS,* 33,085, f. 35 (Oct. 16, 1720).
[6] *Add. MSS,* 32,686, f. 168 (Stanhope at Göhrde to Newcastle, Oct. 8,
1720).
[7] *Index Rerum et Vocabulorum.*

Parliament finally assembled on December 8th, and action was at once begun against the directors of the South Sea Company. In the course of the investigations by the Secret Committee, it was revealed that the passage of the enabling Act had been promoted by means of bribes, which took the form of stock given to Aislabie, Chancellor of the Exchequer, to the elder Craggs, Postmaster-General, and to his son, the Secretary of State. These three had divided with the King's mistresses, with Charles Stanhope (one of the Commissioners of the Treasury and a cousin of the Minister), and with the Earl of Sunderland.[8]

Like Cincinnatus from his farm, Walpole had been summoned from Norfolk in September, to rescue his beleaguered colleagues. His hour of destiny had come. Almost from that moment may be dated his long reign of twenty-one years. It is interesting, if fruitless, to speculate upon what would have been the history of the Ministry had there been no bubble, and had Walpole and the Lord of Althorp been left to continue their inevitable struggle for supremacy in the ordinary course of affairs. The rôle which Walpole now assumed is suggested in the name of "Screen," which he earned as a result. Much of the "inside" history of the South Sea Company remained a secret from that day to this, and whether Newcastle was cognizant of the corrupt dealings of his colleagues or whether he was involved in their obliquity is unknown; but there is not a shred of evidence that he was either.

But there were two members of the Ministry who were not destined to have need of the services of Walpole. On Friday, the third of February, there took place at Newcastle House what Lord Harley called a "great debauch," but which the prints subdued to "merry meeting." Stanhope, Craggs, and some other "great men" were present and "they drank excessively of New Tokay, Champagne, Visney, and Barba Water,

[8] *Parl. Hist.*, VII, 711-739 (*First Report of the Committee of Secrecy*); H.M.C. *Portland MSS*, V, 614 (Harley to Oxford, Feb. 16, 1721), and 615 (T. Harley to Oxford, Feb. 17).

thirteen hours, as it is said."[9]   It is impossible not to connect
this affair with the tragedy of the following day, when Lord
Stanhope was seized while replying to an attack in the House
of Lords, which ended in his death on Sunday night.   Ten days
later Craggs was dead from the smallpox.   Two other lords,
unnamed, who had partaken of the same lethal beverages, were
seriously ill and one of them had a very narrow escape.
Whether or not this was the young host himself will always
be unknown.

Aislabie was too deeply involved in the corruption and had to
be sacrificed to the universal outcry for a victim; while Charles
Stanhope was got off by the narrow margin of three votes.
The Earl of Sunderland's case was next to be considered by the
House of Commons.   There was less evidence against him, owing to the fact that he had connived at the escape of Robert
Knight, the former cashier of the Company, after the latter had
been arrested on the Continent; and on the plea that his con-
viction would result in the overthrow of the Whig government
and the triumph of the Tories, Walpole obtained his vindication by a majority of sixty-one.[10]

Nevertheless, public opinion made it impossible for Sunderland to continue at the Treasury.[11]   As early as February 2,
the King promised Walpole that he should be First Lord and
Chancellor of the Exchequer at the end of the session,[12] and
in the meanwhile he was practically in authority there.   The
burning question was whether Sunderland could hold his power
at all, especially after the death of Stanhope, the delivery of
whose seals to Townshend he was unable to prevent.   Had he
lived, Stanhope would undoubtedly have returned to the army

---

[9] H.M.C. *Portland MSS*, V, 616 (Lord Harley to Oxford, Feb. 18, 1721) ;
Oldmixon, *History of England*, III, 710; Boyer, *Pol. State*, XXI, 182-183.
One is reminded of another "merry meeting"—that of Shakespeare, Dray-
ton, and Ben Jonson—and of its fatal outcome.

[10] H.M.C. *Onslow MSS*, 508, and H.M.C. *Clements MSS*, 308 (Onslow
to Molesworth, May 6, 1721).

[11] H.M.C. *Carlisle MSS*, 30 (Lady Irwin to Lord Carlisle, Feb. 11, 1721).

[12] *Ibid.*, 28-29 (Vanbrugh to Lord Carlisle, Feb. 2 and 7, 1721).

in the room of Marlborough, whose resignation had been demanded by the King.

Sunderland's influence with the King and the Duchess of Kendal was still very great; and though he was forced to submit to these blows, he still hoped to retain a strong following in the Cabinet, where he remained as Groom of the Stole.[13] These facts, and the need for at least the appearance of unity in the Whig ranks at this critical time, led to the inclusion of two Sunderland men in the new Ministry, Carleton being made Lord President and Carteret Secretary of State for the Southern Department.

In these changes that took place in the spring of 1721, as a result of the South Sea scandals and the mortality of Ministers, the Duke of Newcastle had no share. As a loyal supporter of Sunderland, he might have hoped to succeed Craggs at Whitehall, and it is quite likely that the appointment of Carteret was a keen disappointment. However, if he himself obtained no advancement at this time, his brother, Henry Pelham, took his first step in a career as financial understudy to Walpole, whom he was one day to succeed. Upon the reconciliation of the King and the prince the year before, he had been made Treasurer of the Chamber; and now, on April 3, 1721, he became one of the three junior Lords of the Treasury, at the same time that Walpole assumed the first place at that board.

After a prolonged and momentous session, full of unusual travail, Parliament rose on the 10th of August, and Newcastle retired to Halland for rest and recreation. Again the veil is lifted from the obscurity in which so much of his earlier career lies, and from this time onward, the manuscript materials for his personal activities and opinions become more and more profuse. For some time before this date, however, the Ministry had been rent by the inevitable clash between the Walpole and the Sunderland Whigs. Instead of losing his preëminence by his labors in restoring the national credit, as the earl had

---

[13] H.M.C. *Portland MSS*, V, 615-616 (Harley to Oxford, Feb. 18, 1721); *Carlisle MSS*, 30-31 (Vanbrugh to Carlisle, Feb. 18 and 28, 1721).

hoped,[14] Walpole's ascendency increased daily. In describing the situation to a friend, Newcastle wrote that "Ministers are drove to doing the most cruel barbarities and greatest injustice in the world, or running the risk of bringing the greatest misfortunes on the public."[15]

The duke was still loyal to Sunderland, in spite of his adversities, and made no effort to hail the rising sun of the Norfolk squire. Nevertheless, he felt considerable uneasiness, as the following letter shows, and also displayed his characteristic tendency to lean upon a sturdier nature for support. "I have not one thought in ye world but for ye interest of ye king, ye Whigg cause, & if you will allow me to say so, your lordship, to which I shall ever be bound by the strongest tyes imaginable," he wrote. · · · · "It appears our good master is determin'd to shew all the world that he has the same regard to your Lordship that he always had, and all honest men must wish him to have. · · · · For God's sake, my dear lord, give me leave for to hope for ye sake of ye king and all your faithful servants, that you will continue at ye head of ye king's affairs, yᵗ ye source and direction shall come from you, & and that all others should act in ye manner ye king intends they shou'd, & since they are now convinced of that point, I verily believe they will. You know I neither love their persons nor court their interest." He then closes with the appeal: "Let me have the pleasure of hearing from you, that you think things in a good way, & that you are determined to protect us all."[16]

Sometime during the early part of August there was a project on foot sponsored by the Sunderland faction, which was constantly referred to in correspondence with Newcastle merely as "the Scheme." Carteret's boast[17] that the whole affair had

---

[14] Hervey, *Memoirs,* I, 43.

[15] Newcastle to Jordan (July 18, 1721), quoted from *MS* by Torrens, *Hist. of Cabinets,* I, 304.

[16] *Add. MSS,* 32,686, ff. 189-190 (Newcastle to Sunderland, Aug. 26, 1721).

[17] *Ibid.,* f. 185 (Carteret to Newcastle, Aug. 22, 1721).

been "well managed," and that "not the least particular of our whole scheme has ever come out," was certainly justified by the mystery which still surrounds it. Whatever this intrigue may have been, it was evident that it boded no good for Walpole and his friends. Luckily for them, Lord Townshend succeeded in effecting a reconciliation, which at least ended the open discord for some time to come. The purport of it seems to have been to restrain Walpole from exerting influence outside of his department. In spite of all that he had since done to salvage the credit of his kingdom and the honor of his dynasty, the dull, vindictive George I. was loath to forgive the man who, for three years, had been the mainstay of the opposition, and who had consorted with his hated heir. "The King is resolved that Walpole shall not govern; but it is hard to be prevented," wrote Carteret.[18] Neither of the first two Hanoverians ever escaped from this dilemma!

The next subject which occupied the attention of the Ministers was that of ecclesiastical appointments, and for the first time Newcastle is seen influencing the make-up of the episcopal bench. Particular care had to be taken in this matter, in view of the election now but a few months in the distance. The death of the Bishop of Durham caused a series of promotions, and Hoadly was translated from the see of Bangor to that of Hereford. At the suggestion of Newcastle, his old friend Archdeacon Bowers was considered in connection with the vacancy at Bangor, but it was regarded as not worthy of his acceptance.[19] "I hope these promotions will not be disapproved off by y^r Grace," wrote Sunderland in one of his few surviving letters. "We shall now have 19 Wig bishops out of the 26, which is a pretty reasonable proportion."[20] A week later Carteret wrote in a still more flattering vein: "I dare say y^t yr Grace is pleased with ye distribution of ye Church preferments. You foresaw better than we did. No ground has been lost since yr absence

---

[18] *Ibid.*, f. 193 (same to same, Aug. 27, 1721).

[19] *Ibid.*, also ff. 197-198 (same to same, Sept. 9, 1721).

[20] *Add. MSS*, 32,686, f. 204 (Sept. 21, 1721).

& we shall be very glad to be reinforced by you soon."[21] However courtly these phrases, the modest share which Newcastle
bore on this occasion stands in striking contrast with his later
influence, when half the higher clergy were his appointees.[22]

After a short recess of a little over two months, Parliament
came together the 19th of October, for a session which in spite
of the hopes of many to the contrary proved to be the final one
of the first septennial Parliament. Its history need not detain
us here; and it is sufficient to remark that Newcastle bore his
full share of the burden of debate,[23] against an opposition that
was reduced to a noisy but almost complete impotence.

The general election which now ensued was scarcely less
critical and important than the last. Despite its eight years of
de facto rule, and despite the failure of the Rising of 'Fifteen,
the Hanoverian dynasty was still unsettled and unpopular, and
the South Sea disaster had shaken it to its foundation. "If · · · ·
some bold men had taken advantage of the general disorder
men's minds were in to provoke them to insurrection, the rage
against the Government was such for having, as they thought,
drawn them into this ruin, that I am almost persuaded, the King
being at that time abroad, that could the Pretender then have
landed at the Tower, he might have rode to St. James's with
very few hands held up against him." So wrote Speaker Onslow, an eyewitness to the rage and desperation of those
times.[24] The hopes and plots of the Jacobites were revived,
as the government well knew, and the conspiracy of Atterbury
would soon disclose its strength. The English Tories were by
no means few or powerless, although they were deprived of
office and preferment. The Septennial Act and the subsequent
effort to repeal it had demonstrated the unwillingness of the
Whigs to face a fair election, and now that Walpole was once

---

[21] *Ibid.*, ff. 206-207 (Sept. 28, 1721).
[22] Bateson in *Eng. Hist. Rev.*, VII, 685-696 ("Clerical Preferment under
the Duke of Newcastle").
[23] *E.g., Parl. Hist.*, VII, 927, 931, 935, 969.
[24] H.M.C. *Onslow MSS*, 504.

more in power, even he urged that the sitting Parliament be indefinitely continued, because he had no hope of getting another one as tractable.[25]   Many patrons and candidates were inclined to agree, for had not the opponents of the Septennial Act predicted that the price of votes would increase?[26]

Whether it was for this reason, or on account of the need and determination of the Whigs to retain their monopoly, the election of 1722 proved to be one of the most corrupt that had yet taken place.   Hoffmann, the Austrian Resident, reported to his government that "money-bribes to procure election were never so large and so manifest as on this occasion.   Everyone who has a vote seeks to sell it on the highest market, under the pretext that just as it has become common for the members to sell their votes in Parliament to the Court for places, pensions, and ready money, it was reasonable that they should sell their own also."[27]   Certain it is that in 1726, John Bristowe, Newcastle's estate agent for part of Notts, claimed £820, 13s, 5d as election expenses still unpaid;[28] and although this is slightly below the sum laid out in 1715, it can hardly represent the total amount expended in the campaign of 1722.

As early as the summer of 1720 the duke began to make active preparations for the coming contest at Nottingham, and from thence he had written to Craggs: "All our views must be turned to next Parliam'.   I hope I shall do my part."   His activities there are best described in the same long, rambling letter, in handwriting rather worse than usual and partly illegible, for reasons that will be manifest.   "You must now allow me to be pretty full of my new Countrey entertainm', & perhaps before I end be more vain than my good friend will approve of.   In short, we have here a most delightful place, & a countrey as well disposed as possible, & I don't doubt but we shall have ye good effects of it.   I have scarce been sober since I came, &

---

[25] Coxe, *Walpole*, III, 217.

[26] For an instance of this assertion see *Parl. Hist.*, VII, 355.

[27] Michael, *Walpole als Premier-Minister*, 528-529.

[28] *Add. MSS*, 33,320, f. 5.

did not go to bed till six this morning. So you must allow that as an excuse for my rambling. Ye glorious first of August was solemnised by ye whole Countrey. Man, woman & children being so easy in their affairs y^t ye men had like to have broke their necks, & ye women lost all y^t is dear to them. A more loyal corporation is not in ye world than Nottingham & I believe I may say we shall have no opposition there, for ye Tories themselves seem desirous of coming in. · · · · I had yesterday Judges, grandjury, &c to dinner. They will all do w^t I wd. have them. · · · · Levintz & several Tories have been here, very civil but cruelly dejected. · · · · I have already taken by Storm ye most Tory Town in ye whole county & intend to go on till all is over. In short, my dear friend, allow me to be a little vain & say I have already done some service. Newark will do w^t I wd. have them. Retford I have not yet been at, but don't doubt I shall give a good acct. of it. · · · · We keep open house every Tuesday & Friday, wch. if our strength holds out, will do ye business." In conclusion the duke wrote: "Believe me, I do not lead a pleasant life here; but for ye reasons you know will very readily undergoe it, & ye longer I can stay I fancy ye better. The Ds. of Newcle. & all y^t belong to me are exceedingly your servts & desire their complim^{ts}. Harry beggs in a particular manner his, & is as good as Heart can wish.[29]

Turning now to Sussex, the situation there was hardly less propitious, although there were several factors that were troublesome. As has been seen, the duke spent August and September in that county, at which time he entertained the voters generously, and late in November or early in December he seems to have planned to go down again but was dissuaded by Archdeacon Bowers. "There is not likely to be any opposition for the county at the next election, and so no need for much application or expense," wrote the old man, who never missed a chance to instil the principle of retrenchment.[30]

[29] *Stowe MSS*, 247, ff. 164-166.
[30] *Add. MSS*, 33,064, f. 214 (n.d., but probably the time mentioned).

The contest in Sussex centered in Hastings, where Sir William Ashburnham, a relative of the duke by marriage, and John Pulteney stood in the Pelham interest against Archibald Hutchinson, who may be best described as an independent Whig.[31] Fortunately, our knowledge of this particular contest is very full and marked by circumstances of peculiar interest. Late in November Sir William and Captain James Pelham, Newcastle's cousin and confidential agent, appeared at Hastings and requested that an assembly of the Corporation be called, in order that the duke's letter recommending Ashburnham might be read to them. About the same time Pulteney put himself in nomination by means of a letter.

The baronet and "cousin Jemmy" went again to Hastings on the 7th of December, and on the following day the latter wrote a report on the results of their visit.[32] The mayor having been away, they had a talk with John Collier, a local politician of great consequence. Born in 1685, and educated in the law, he had become town clerk of Hastings in 1707, and mayor in 1719, in the meanwhile building up such a degree of influence that even the Duke of Newcastle, the great local magnate, had perforce to bargain with him.[33] He seemed desirous of accepting the duke's proposal to come under his protection, but he expected a place as tide-waiter at the Customs House worth £100 a year. In return, Collier promised to keep everything quiet in the town and to discourage any opposition to Sir William and Pulteney. Pelham discovered a number of freemen who proved to be obstinate, but he also "found out ways to come at some of them, if there be occasion. 'Tis hardly possible to get promises from those ordinary fellows," he wrote, "and since we are likely to gain the only power that can oppose us, I am not much for pressing to far, to avoid the number of requests that would be made to your grace."

---

[31] He was not a Tory, as Michael (*Eng. Geschichte,* I, 612) asserts.
[32] *Add. MSS,* 32,686, f. 209.
[33] Crake, *Collier Correspondence,* where he is incorrectly said to have sat in Parliament under Anne and George I.

Surprisingly enough, in view of his earlier connection with the borough,[34] Pulteney proved to be more of a liability than an asset to the duke's cause, and displayed none of the *savoir faire* needed on such occasions. "He now writes two or three simple letters every post, to know how his interest stands before he quits his place. Tells them 'tis against act of parliament to treat the town whilst he is in the customs house, or even to offer his service, and hopes his publick letter was understood only as an intention to be a candidate when he had quitted his place." Every vote was being mustered; and Pelham expressed great concern lest one Captain Gilliard should die of his consumption, and so create a disturbance about his place; and also about old Perrigo, whose son was lost at sea after he had been promised a place in the Admiralty.

Archibald Hutchinson, the opponent who caused all this perturbation, was one of the most singular figures of his day, although he has been utterly neglected by modern writers. Born in Ireland in 1665, of Protestant parents, he seems to have resided for the most part in Westminster, where he had a considerable estate. In 1715 he married one Mary Gayer, of Stepney, a lady of fortune, from whom he was separated. He sat in Parliament in 1713-15, and, as he was an authority upon financial matters, upon the accession of George I. he was made a Commissioner of Trade and Plantations. It has already been seen how he was chosen for Hastings in 1715. Being a staunch friend of the Duke of Ormonde, he had opposed his impeachment and as a consequence had lost his place, after holding it for only eight months. Following this he had gone over to the opposition, and afterward became a member of the Prince of Wales' party. He now won the reputation of being a determined opponent of the Administration on all occasions, now attacking the Septennial Bill or the management of the army, now the financial policy of the government or the South Sea

---

[34] John Pulteney (died 1726), uncle of the famous Earl of Bath (1684-1764), was a Customs Commissioner and had sat for Hastings in 1695, 1698, 1700, 1701, and 1702.

bill; but first and last he was a relentless foe of parliamentary bribery and corruption.[35] After some demur, upon what seems today the absurd ground of the "infirmities of an advanced age" (he was then fifty-six), he had, on November 25, 1721, announced his intention to stand for re-election, in a letter to the mayor, jurats, and freemen of Hastings. It was against this stormy petrel, then, that the duke and his henchmen pitted their efforts.

Outside of Hastings the results of the election were nowhere in doubt. At Seaford, Sir William Gage, Bart., and Sir Philip Yorke stood in the Pelham interest, at the unanimous request of the bailiff, jurats and freemen—fifty-two in all.[36] Sir Philip was the young Dover attorney who had first entered Parliament in April, 1719, for Lewes, under the auspices of Newcastle. This marked the beginning of a connection which grew into a deep and lifelong friendship between the duke and the man who was to become Earl of Hardwicke and one of England's ablest Chancellors. It also marked an important stage in the history of the family of Yorke, which has been likened to the rise and fall of César Birotteau, the perfumer.[37]

When Parliament was prorogued on March 7th and three days later dissolved, the electoral canvass of 1722 began in earnest. This was the signal for the general scattering of the Lords and Commoners to the various quarters in which their parliamentary interests lay. Newcastle had anticipated the dissolution by appearing at Hastings on the 5th, "attended in the manner which became his high quality." After personally recommending the choice of Ashburnham and expressing his good opinion and wishes for Pulteney before an assembly of electors, the great man proceeded to go about to the homes of the freemen, soliciting their votes. Hutchinson had completed

---

[35] See esp. Hutchinson's own *Collection*, 4-6 and 15-17; also *Stuart Papers*, V, 524; and VII, 299, 314, 526. Coxe, *Walpole*, III, 73 (Poyntz to Stanhope). Oldmixon, *History of England*, III, 722.

[36] *Add. MSS*, 35,584, f. 249 (Mar. 10, 1722).

[37] Williams, "The Eclipse of the Yorkes," in Royal Hist. Soc. *Transactions*, 1908, 129.

his canvass before the arrival of his Grace and he now contented himself with inditing a long epistle to the magistrates and freemen of the port, which afterward was published in the *Freeholder's Journal* and in Boyer's *Political State*.[38] In this missive he proceeded to denounce the interference of a peer and an officer of the Crown in a local election, in utter contempt of the standing order of the House of Commons; and he also reminded them that the duke had been one of the warmest champions of the Septennial Bill, for which they had shown their disapproval on several occasions.

Forty out of approximately three-score voters had already promised their support to Hutchinson, which rendered his election certain. As a consequence, in the efforts of the duke's agents to retrieve these votes, no quarter was given. Five years before, old Richard Caswell had been turned out of an employment of £60 a year; but now, about a week before the election, he was suddenly remembered, and had a pension bestowed upon him as a superannuated officer. On March 20th, two days before the election, Geoffrey Glyd, another old fellow, was told that his daughter was dying. Hastily he took horse and rode ten miles to where she lived, only to find that he had been hoaxed; and upon his return to Hastings he took pains to preclude further attempts upon him by staying with a relative. Other voters in straightened circumstances felt that their integrity was not proof against importunity and asked that they be guarded the night before the election. All these were among those who had promised their votes to the doughty, plainspoken Irishman.

Leaving Pulteney at Hastings, the duke had already set out upon a tour of the rest of his preserves. Our knowledge of his itinerary, with its vicissitudes and temptations, is based upon a series of ten letters[39] written to the duchess in the course of the month's campaign. In the first of these, dated from Bishopstone, he wrote in part: "Our hands are so full from one place

---

[38] Boyer, *Pol. State,* XXIII, 308-310. *Cf.* Hutchinson's pamphlet.
[39] *Add. MSS,* 33,073, ff. 9 to 18, March 11 to April 6, 1722.

to another y^t we hardly know how to turn ourselves. · · · · I can assure my dear I have thoroughly kept my word with you, for I have been perfectly sober ever since I left you. We scarce ever drink a Drop & indeed I have quite left it off. This, I am sure, will be good news to you, who have such a concern to me."

On the 16th he was at Halland, where there was "a great deal of company." This convivial gathering proved too much for the genial duke, and he was obliged to confess that he had "transgressed" for the first time since he came into the county. "I was a little sick this Morning & wanted prodigiously my dear Nurse," he wrote disconsolately. Whether it was due to contrition inspired by this experience or to an incipient *taedium vitae,* the next letter, written from East Grinstead, announced: "I am thoroughly tired wth all these diversions I used to love in Elections."

The bulletins from the scene of action now came thick and fast, announcing the results of all these labors. On the 20th Gage and Yorke were triumphantly returned for Seaford, "to ye great satisfaction of Every Man in Town." But at Hastings the duke's worst fears were realized, when two days later Pulteney was defeated by a single vote. The results showed: Ashburnham, 56; Hutchinson, 33; and Pulteney, 32. The defeat was due to the fact that Newcastle had failed somehow to come to terms with Collier, and as a result the latter had, at the last minute, won over two of the freemen whose votes had been promised to the ducal candidates. According to Hutchinson, eleven of those who did vote for Ashburnham and Pulteney were officers in the service or pay of the Customs House, while seven others were relatives of those so employed. As if to compensate for this "mortification," Henry Pelham, junior, and Thomas Pelham were returned for Lewes, "by ye greatest majority that ever was known."

The election for the county members took place at Lewes on the 5th of April; and as there was no contest, Speaker Compton was triumphantly re-elected, with the duke's brother as his col-

league. The number of freeholders who appeared for the poll
was said to be the largest in history, the duke himself bringing
about twelve hundred with him from Halland. Fortunately,
the particulars of this affair have been preserved and are worth
reproducing for the picture they present of an election day two
hundred years ago.

"This being the day for county election, about 11 in the
forenoon the Rt. Hon. Spencer Compton, Esq., came to the
top of Glindbourn Hill, some small distance from this town,
accompany'd by his Grace the Duke of Dorset and a very
great number of clergy, gentlemen, and freeholders; here they
were met by the high sheriff. Some little time after, the other
candidate, the Hon. Henry Pelham, Esq., came to the same
place, accompany'd by his Grace the Duke of Newcastle and
a very great appearance likewise of clergy, gentlemen and freeholders. Here these two gentlemen join'd and receiv'd each
other with mutual acclamations of joy. They proceeded together to this town in the following order: first the servants
belonging to the gentlemen; then the high sheriff's men, with
pikes in their hands; and then the musick. Then came the
clergy in a body which consisted of a greater number than has
been known on the like occasion. Next came the high sheriff,
attended by six running footmen. Then came the candidates,
supported on each side by the two noble peers before mentioned,
and followed by the gentlemen and freeholders. Thus they
marched quite through the town to the top of the hill which
leads to the western parts of the county, where they were met
by Mr. Butler, late knight of the shire, and a great body of
gentlemen and substantial freeholders from those parts. After
this, they returned through the town to the court house,[40]
where the high sheriff was placed in a balcony. There they
made a stand, and a proclamation being made for silence, His
Majesty's writ was read, after which Compton and Pelham,
being cry'd up by the unanimous voice of the county, those two

---

[40] There is a picture of old Lewes Town Hall in Horsfield's *Lewes*, I,
opposite page 210.

worthy gentlemen were declared duly elected to represent the
County of Sussex in the ensuing parliament."[41]

The results outside of Sussex are best described in Newcastle's own letter to his lady. "I conclude you have heard of
our Sweep att Newark, Nottingham, & in ye Yorkshire Bur-
roughs. We were very hard run att Nottingham, wch is a
great surprise to me. I thank God I have hitherto succeeded
in all my Elections, Mr. Pulteney's at Hastings not properly
to be called mine."[42]   But the county election was won only
after a very close contest with the powerful Tory opposition, so
close that the duke himself was uncertain of the outcome. Viscount Howe and Sir Robert Sutton were his Grace's candidates,
and out of a total of 2,624, there were only 92 votes between
Sutton, the highest, and Francis Willoughby, the lowest candidate.[43]

These triumphs won under the auspices of Newcastle were
typical of the results throughout the country. "It must be a
great mortification to the Tories," wrote Vanbrugh, "to find
that even in this juncture, when so great discontents are stirring,
a Whig Parliament of no small majority can be got."[44]   Out
of 558 members the Whigs had a majority of over 200, and
the number of Tories declined to about 170.[45]   Once again
Newcastle had demonstrated his ability to deliver the grist to the
Administration mill, and the good effects of this may be seen
in the developments of the next few years.

Hardly had the poll-books been closed and the last returns
despatched, when the end came for one who must have watched
the results with the keenest interest and attention. After a brief
illness, the Earl of Sunderland died of pleurisy on the 19th of
April, 1722. To paraphrase the words of Swift, twice had he
seen the fruit of power turn rotten at the very moment it grew

---

[41] Boyer, *Pol. State,* XXIII, 504.
[42] *Add. MSS,* 33,073, f. 17 (Mar. 31, 1722).
[43] Bailey, *Annals,* III, 1135.
[44] H.M.C. *Carlisle MSS,* 37 (Apr. 6, 1722).
[45] H.M.C. *Sutherland MSS,* 190 (May 1, 1722).

ripe—first in 1710 and again in 1720; but until the very last
he never ceased to hope for ultimate mastery. As Walpole's
sway extended over an increasing number of Whigs, Sunderland had sought to heighten the King's lingering distrust of the
"brother ministers,"[46] and to win his consent to a mixed Administration, composed of the earl's own following of Whigs,
together with the Tories. In these efforts he had been unsuccessful; and (on Walpole's own authority), the King was said
to have replied to these importunities on one occasion by declaring that he had parted with Walpole once against his will and
that he would never do so again as long as he was willing to
serve him. What secret and more audacious plans Lord Sunderland may have had are unfortunately obscure, owing to the
destruction of his private papers soon after his death. But it
was generally believed that he had made overtures to the
Jacobite Bishop of Rochester and even to the Pretender himself.[47]

The importance of the personal factor in eighteenth-century
politics again becomes apparent when it is realized that the death
of Sunderland, following hard upon that of Stanhope and of
Craggs, removed one of the last remaining obstacles in Walpole's path to supremacy. The same unforeseen event must also
be regarded as of decisive importance in the career of Newcastle. Nothing is known of his sentiments toward Sunderland
and the schemes that stirred his restless spirit in the last few
months of life; but it is certain that Newcastle was too staunch
a Whig to sympathise with any plan to introduce Tories into
the government, and he would have shared the general aversion
to any dealings with the Court of St. Germain. The way was
now open for him, along with many other Whigs who had been

---

[46] *Marchmont Papers*, II, 3.

[47] For Sunderland's intrigues see: H.M.C. *Onslow MSS*, 510; H.M.C.
Carlisle MSS, 37-38 (Vanbrugh to Carlisle, Apr. 24, and May 5, 1722);
H.M.C. *Bagot MSS*, 345 (Johnston to Graham, May 12, 1722); Coxe,
Walpole, I, 286-288. Lord Mahon, who examined the uncalendared por-
tion of the *Stuart Papers*, exonerates him of the worst charges (*Hist. of
Eng.*, II, 27 and *App.*).

left leaderless by the death of Sunderland, to make his peace
with and resume his former allegiance to his old friends and
kinsmen, Walpole and Townshend. Despite Newcastle's failure
to join them in opposition in 1717 and his political estrangement covering a period of five years, he was presently on terms
of greater intimacy with them than ever.

Walpole was now in a position of almost unrivaled authority.
Although at first the King was rendered very apprehensive
by the loss of one of his most trusted counsellors in Sunderland,[48] he soon learned to put his confidence in the "brother
ministers." Walpole's power was also deeply rooted in the
influence which he had obtained over the Duchess of Kendal,
"as much Queen of England as ever woman was," and over
the Princess of Wales. Until 1730 he shared his supremacy
with his brother-in-law, who had charge of foreign affairs;
but their partnership was fast becoming Walpole and Townshend, instead of Townshend and Walpole.

"He laboured all he could to unite those to him who had
been peculiarly dependent on my lord Sunderland, some he succeeded with, but not all."[49] The most important of these last
were Carteret, who regarded himself as the heir and successor
of Stanhope and Sunderland, and Cadogan, Commander-in-
Chief and Master-General of the Ordnance, who felt that the
mantle of Marlborough had fallen about his shoulders. For the
present, both these men were too useful or influential to permit
their dismissal; but in the end, both were to learn that their
choice lay between submission and proscription.

Unlike his late rival, Walpole would have no dealings with
the Tories, for he was resolved to establish his power on a
purely Whig basis. Nevertheless, he recognized the fact that
as long as the Tory party flourished it was always possible
for some disaffected Whigs to join with them, as he had once
done himself, and embarrass if not overthrow the Administration. With a directness characteristic of the man, Walpole

[48] H.M.C. *Carlisle MSS*, 37-38 (Vanbrugh to Carlisle, Apr. 24, 1722).
[49] H.M.C. *Onslow MSS*, 465.

made overtures in person to Bishop Atterbury,[50] at once the
most brilliant and the most dangerous of the Tories. The prelate refused his offers, for even then the plot which goes by his
name was being fast matured. But he was a marked man, and
his refusal was the signal for the government to strike. For
some time the Ministry had been aware of the existence of a
plot; and now, on May 19th, the first move was made against
the conspirators by the arrest of George Kelley, a Non-Juror
and agent of the Pretender.[51] Later, for want of proof, he
was discharged on bail; but on July 28 he was re-arrested as
he was about to embark, and on the 24th of August Atterbury
himself was seized and sent to the Tower. Although the
evidence against him was not conclusive, Walpole showed no
mercy to the bishop, who was tried, deprived, and banished
from England. The plot was a wild, harebrained affair, but
Walpole purposely exaggerated its significance in order to further his own credit and to taint all Tories with the name of
Jacobite.

In order not to provide his opponents with political capital,
as well as for reasons that were less partisan, Walpole pursued
his former policy of peace and retrenchment. Neither he nor
Townshend had shared in Stanhope's policy of alliances, and
they had even fought it; but they now enjoyed the fruit of his
exertions. To prevent the breakdown of the latter's Anglo-
French alliance, a new tripartite agreement was signed with
France and Spain on June 2, 1721; and on the death of Sunderland, Carteret hastened to assure the French[52] that *"les ministres
du Roy sont entièrement d'accord; et que nonobstant les dis-
putes et contrariétéz qu'il y a eües entre nous, c'est la ferme
intention de touts de suivre les maximes des Comtes de Sunderland et Stanhope par rapport à la France et au Cardinal, et que*

---

[50] Beeching, *Atterbury*, 274 and 278-279. The interview took place in
May, 1721.

[51] Details in *Add. MSS*, 32,686, f. 227 (Stephen Poyntz to Newcastle,
July 28, 1722).

[52] *British Diplomatic Instructions*, 30-31 (Carteret to Schaub, April 25,
1722, *Add. MSS*, 22,517, f. 48).

le Roy ne veut jamais s'en departir." The influence of the foreign situation upon domestic policy at this time is well illustrated in the correspondence among the three Ministers in 1723. Walpole expressed his dread of the consequences of a promise he had made the King to raise £150,000 on the land tax between Michaelmas and Christmas.[53] In a letter written the following day, Newcastle declared: "If an opposition be made by sending a fleet or granting a subsidy, that may create ill humour amongst our friends, especially those that do not in every respect mean well, which may be improved to the advantage of the Jacobites."[54] These sentiments were echoed in a despatch from Townshend of the same period. "I am satisfied," he wrote, "that the surest way to continue things there on the present good foot, and to putt our credit with the king past all danger of competition or accidents, will be to form a good scheme for the next session, by falling on some new expedients for the ease of the nation and the benefit of trade and credit, which points his majesty has so much at heart that the succeeding in them will infallibly rivet us in his esteem and give us greater advantage over our adversarys than can be hoped for from carrying any particular point against any of them.   For this reason, I beg of you to turn your thoughts as early as you can towards bringing the supplys of the next year within two shillings in the pound and the malt, and I submit it to your consideration whether the uniting the South Sea and East India companys and the easing our East India trade in some such manner as I hinted in my last would not be very popular, and at the same time divert any ill-humour which may be stirring in the Parliam'."[55] A month later, Walpole wrote: "My politics are in a narrow compasse. If we keep perfectly well with France & the Czar, I am under no apprehensions of foreign disturbances, wch. alone can confound us here."[56]   Tran-

---

[53] *Add. MSS,* 32,686, ff. 284-285 (July 25, 1723).

[54] *Ibid.,* f. 286, and *Stowe MSS,* 251, f. 16 (July 26).

[55] *S. P. Dom. Regencies* (Hanover), vol. iv, no. 2 (Townshend to Walpole, July 17, 1723).

[56] *Add. MSS,* 32,686, ff. 320-321 (Aug. 31, 1723).

quillity was at once the indispensable foundation of the material prosperity of the nation and the security of the dynasty. This achieved, Walpole knew his personal power was assured.

It is now time to turn to an examination of the share which the Duke of Newcastle had in carrying out this vital if uninspiring policy. On June 3, 1723 the King embarked upon his third journey to Hanover, where he remained until early in the following January. Both Secretaries of State accompanied His Majesty abroad, one reason being, doubtless, that Townshend had no mind to have his bitter experience of 1716 repeated. Before his departure, the King had designated a commission of fifteen Lords Justices, of which Newcastle was again a member, to carry on the government in his absence.

It is from correspondence which now ensued between the Ministers abroad and those at home that it is possible to reconstruct the duke's activities. In spite of the fact that he held only the passive post of Chamberlain, when the correspondence begins on June 28, Newcastle is already seen in the position of third member of the government, or, to put it in another way, junior partner in the firm of Walpole and Townshend. There was no other member of the Administration who enjoyed anything like his confidence and credit with the duumvirs. While the explanation of this fact may be sought to some extent in his parliamentary influence (for Walpole, like Chatham, sometimes found it necessary to "borrow the Duke of Newcastle's majority"), it may be attributed to a much greater degree to the duke's temperament.

On account of his alleged jealously of power, Walpole has often been accused of surrounding himself with mediocrities, and among these Newcastle is sometimes numbered; but however that may be, the latter was invaluable to him at a time when, for both political and economic reasons, unruffled discipline and order in the State were indispensable. Genuine ability, without egotism, and capacity for steady and faithful service, if not brilliant parts, were qualities which the duke had demonstrated. Unlike men of the stamp of Carteret and

Pulteney, Newcastle was easy-going and willing to co-operate as a colleague with the "brother ministers" without striving to be first. His capacity for hard work needs no other testimony than the vast collection of manuscripts that he left behind—the *Newcastle Papers,* which are alike the joy and the despair of the historian.

His disinterestedness, another characteristic which made him so useful, was again demonstrated in a remarkable fashion at this time. By the middle of 1723, Newcastle was again in the narrowest financial straits, due in part to the expenses of the recent election. His old friend, Thomas Bowers, who had been elevated to the see of Chichester in the fall of 1722, wrote him[57] announcing that he and Peter Forbes, his Grace's private secretary, had stretched their credit in his behalf as far as it would go. Although the duke had set aside a portion of his estate to settle his obligations, he had exceeded his allowance by £4,000, and it was impossible to pay the sums due because the rest of the estate was saddled with the debts already contracted. In his anxiety the good bishop had finally taken the liberty of confiding in Lord Townshend, and intimated that since the cause of Newcastle's distress had proceeded from the vast sums expended in the service of the government, some relief might be expected from that quarter. He even went so far as to express his wish that the duke had "a more profitable place." Townshend agreed that his Grace "had indeed deserved well of the Government," and declared that the sum mentioned might be provided "without anybody's knowing it but a few particular friends y^t might be relyed on, & y^t he would farther consider of it & advise with Mr. Walpole about it."

Townshend was as good as his word and he begged Newcastle to give "Brother Walpole" leave to procure the money for him. The younger man's reactions were expressed in a letter to the prelate[58] and in sentiments which do him the greatest credit. "You know very well, my dear lord, the great back-

[57] *Add. MSS,* 33,064, ff. 218-223 (June 12, 1723).
[58] *Add. MSS,* 32,686, ff. 252-258 (June 6 and 7, 1723).

wardness I have always had to ask or receive any summ of money of ye king, how I detest it in others & consequently how unwilling I shall be to do ye like myself. But, however, if no other way can be found out (wch still I hope may, rather than ye innocent should suffer by long want of their money), I must overcome my own temper & submit to those things by necessity wch. other people have done by instigation; but in that case I think it much more honorable, as well as advisable, for me to accept an increase of salary, rather than accept of a present summ of money, wch. can only stop the gap, without removing ye occasion, wch. is my yearly exceeding my allowance."

Although the details are interesting, the way in which New-castle proposed to extricate himself from this difficulty must be dismissed in a breath. A marriage was to be arranged be-tween some great heiress and his impecunious brother, who would be invested with the duke's estates in Lincolnshire at once, in return for the immediate gift of £30,000. This ar-rangement was fair enough, as the duke had abandoned all hope of issue, and his brother, or any children he might have, would eventually get all. In October, 1726, Henry Pelham married Lady Catherine Manners, the daughter of the second Duke of Rutland; but whether this excellent scheme was ever carried out does not appear.[59]

In the debates in the House of Lords, Newcastle could also give a good account of himself. "Th' applause of list'ning sen-ates to command" was an art that suited the genius and aroused the admiration of the age, and undergraduates and statesmen alike devoted themselves to acquiring eloquence. But different ages have different tastes in oratory; and the lofty, ponderous rhetoric of a Bolingbroke or a Chatham, replete with classical tags, no longer excites the homage of a less stately and leisured epoch. Accordingly, when Earl Waldegrave, referring to the duke as a speaker, alleges that his manner was ungraceful, his

---

[59] *Ibid.*, ff. 255-258, and 33,064, ff. 218-223 (Bowers to Newcastle, June 12, 1723).

language barbarous, and his reasoning inconclusive,[60] it must in fairness be remembered that the canons of criticism were those of another age. If one may judge his speeches by his letters, the word barbarous may be right enough, for most of them are constructed badly and poorly expressed. His contemporaries agree, however, that he was bold, animated, and persistent in debate and never at a loss for words or argument. It speaks volumes that he appears so often in the pages of Boyer and of Cobbett. In the first session of the new Parliament, which sat from October 11, 1722 to May 27, 1723, he figured repeatedly in debates, with speakers of the highest flight.[61]

Finally, the choice of Newcastle as the third member of what was almost a triumvirate may be attributed to his interest and training in foreign affairs. He liked to refer modestly to himself, as "a great dabbler in foreign politicks."[62] While his equipment in this direction was by no means on a level with that of older and more experienced men, it was far from contemptible; and combined with the factors aforementioned gave him strong claims to preferment.

In the absence of his two colleagues, Walpole exercised their functions in addition to his own, and when he succumbed to the lure of Norfolk, Newcastle took his place. Once in a letter addressed to Walpole at Houghton, Newcastle added a jesting postscript to his brother: "My love to Harry, and tell him a Secretary of State (though only deputed) never writes to his brothers except they are foreign ministers, plenipos, &c."[63] On one occasion at least, while Walpole, Devonshire, and Godolphin were fox- and hare-hunting, Newcastle was left alone in full charge.[64]   Among other things, he would read all corre-

---

[60] Waldegrave, *Memoirs,* 12-13.

[61] Boyer, *Pol. State,* XXIV, 521; XXV, 52-53 and 661; Tindal, *Hist. of Eng.,* IV, pt. 2, 663, and Oldmixon, *Hist. of Eng.,* III, 720.

[62] *Stowe MSS,* 251, f. 17b; *S. P. Dom., Regencies,* no. iv, and *Add. MSS,* 32,686, f. 287.

[63] *Add. MSS,* 32,686, f. 358 (Oct. 22, 1723).

[64] *Ibid.,* ff. 357 and 362, Newcastle to Townshend and Townshend to Newcastle.

spondence, including intercepted letters, acknowledge the receipt of those from Townshend, despatch such as he thought important to Walpole and give necessary orders.[65]

The close intimacy of Newcastle and the duumvirs is apparent in the letters which he exchanged with them. Often when Townshend was too busy to write the duke personally, he would conclude despatches to Walpole that were marked "most secret" with such words as: "You know any hint of secrecy does not extend to his Grace of Newcastle," or "I earnestly recommend to you that my private letters · · · · may be imparted to no one living but the Duke of Newcastle."[66] Walpole's letters sometimes closed in an equally flattering vein. One of them ends with the words: "Yr Grace, I hope, is fully persuaded that 'tis impossible for any man to be more sincerely & affectionately than I am, my dear friend, yr Grace's most faithful and humble serv't."[67] After due allowance is made for the courtly style of the day, the feeling behind these words, coming as they do from the blunt and straightforward First Lord, seems genuine enough. Horace Walpole, in Paris, was also in *quasi*-official correspondence with the duke.

Newcastle's rôle was by no means confined to seconding the decisions of his two principals. Stanhope had once told him that he could "judge as well as anybody";[68] and, with all his ill-will, even Hervey had to confess that "to give him his due, (he) seldom slipped an occasion to manifest his good judgment."[69] On one occasion Walpole wrote: "I shall grow proud of my own way of reasoning, when I find it so agreeable to yr thoughts. Could Ld. Townshend see yr Grace's last letter to me & compare it with what I wrote to him upon ye

---

[65] *S. P. Dom., Regencies* (Hanover), vol. iv (Newcastle to Walpole, July 15, 1723), and *S. P. Dom., Regencies,* vol. 68 (Walpole to Townshend, Oct. 18, 1723).

[66] Letters of July 16 and Aug. 11, 1723. *Stowe MSS,* 251, ff. 9b and 23b.

[67] *Add. MSS,* 32,686, ff. 300-303 (Aug. 10, 1723); and *ibid.,* ff. 320-321 (Aug. 31).

[68] *Ibid.,* f. 156 (Stanhope to Newcastle, Oct. 27, 1719).

[69] Hervey, *Memoirs,* I, 261. *Cf.* Channing, *History of the U. S.,* II, 238.

same subject, he would never believe we did not confer notes."[70]
Walpole and Townshend both solicited his opinion on men
and affairs, and although Newcastle was usually in agreement
with them he never hesitated to express an opinion contrary
to their own.[71] In the events of the next two years, then, even
when Newcastle is not specifically mentioned, he must be conceived of as busily engaged behind the scenes in the interests of
the "brother ministers."

The beginning of the historic Opposition to the government
of Robert Walpole is usually associated with the period lying
just beyond the terminus of the present work. While it is true
that the Opposition did not begin to take shape and gather
strength for several years after this date, the elements which
composed it already existed in embryonic form within the body
politic, and its stirrings were noticeable as early as the period
now dealt with. These elements were of heterogeneous origin:
Jacobites, Tories, and Whigs, men in or out of office; and combined, as Burke said of the Bedfords and the Grenvilles, "for no
public purpose but only as a means of furthering with joint
strength their private and individual advantage."

In 1722 the Tories had been wandering in the wilderness
for eight long years, and although their hopes had repeatedly
been raised—most notably in 1720—they had been as often
dashed. With the death of Sunderland—the Moses who seemed
about to lead them to the Promised Land,—their latest prospects
had gone glimmering. The successor of Sunderland's policies
was Carteret; but it was becoming apparent to the Tories that
he had not succeeded to his power, and many of them had not
abandoned hope that Walpole might yet be brought to do something for them. But, as Newcastle told Townshend, "All sorts
of negotiations with the Tories is so useless that Walpole is
resolved to avoid it."[72] With the departure of Atterbury, their

---

[70] *Add. MSS,* 32,686, f. 326 (Sept. 6, 1723).
[71] *E.g. ibid.,* ff. 286-287 (Newcastle to Walpole, July 26, 1723), and ff.
316-318 (same to same, Aug. 25, 1723).
[72] *Ibid.,* f. 269 (July 5, 1723).

ablest leader, the active headship was exercised by several peers, most notably Bathurst, Gower, and Anglesea, while Sir William Windham still continued to lead the party in the Commons.

Unfortunately for Walpole, no sooner had he rid himself of Atterbury than a still more formidable opponent appeared again upon the scene of English politics. "I am exchanged," was the exiled bishop's exclamation, when he was told as he landed in Calais that Bolingbroke had just arrived there homeward bound. As early as 1716, the viscount had begun negotiations for his restoration, and in 1718 his pardon had appeared to be imminent again, owing to the favor of Sunderland and Stanhope and their hope of gaining his support against the opposition.[73] On both occasions, Walpole had succeeded in defeating the proposal; but now, in May of 1723, he was obliged to yield before the by no means disinterested influence of her Grace of Kendal. But until the Act of Attainder against him was repealed, Bolingbroke was left in an equivocal position, without estates or seat with the peers; and it was to secure these that he henceforth bent every effort. The Ministerial correspondence of the time presents a picture of a chastened man, distrusted by all but a few, but eager to earn confidence by the betrayal of the secrets of his former allies.

On June 28, soon after Bolingbroke arrived in England, Walpole waited upon him with the intention of talking to him "in a very right manner," as Newcastle told Lord Townshend.[74] Whatever happened in this interview is not known; but Walpole suceeded in keeping clear of all engagements with him, and he prepared to return to the Continent.[75] In the meantime he renewed some old friendships and connections, calling, among others, upon Lord Godolphin, the son of his old colleague and Newcastle's father-in-law. The duke himself was at his door but did not see him. Bolingbroke's affair was upon everybody's

[73] Michael, *Englische Geschichte,* II, 608-611.
[74] *Add. MSS,* 32,686, f. 266 (June 28).
[75] *Ibid.,* f. 270 (July 5).

lips; and although his own conduct was beyond reproach, some of his friends were led into indiscretions.

About the middle of July the viscount had another interview with Walpole. "He introduced the conversation with excusing himself for entering into any negotiation, which he would or would not proceed upon, as I should approve," the latter wrote to Townshend. "He told me he had held several conversations with Sir William Windham and Ld. Bathurst, who spoke to him in their own names and in the name of Ld. Gower. They declared themselves weary of the situation they were in and ready to enter any measures with your Lordship and your humble servant." A less sagacious man than Walpole might have seized what appeared to be the prospect of uniting the Whigs and the Hanoverian Tories and extinguishing the Opposition in a single stroke. Instead (to continue his letter), "I answered it was both impossible and inadvisable for me to enter into any such negotiation, and told him I thought he was doing a most imprudent thing, who was to expect his salvation from a Whig Parliament, to be negotiating to bring in a sett of Tories; that if this should be known his case would be desperate in Parliament, and desired and advised him to give this answer to his friends as from his own farther recollection."[76]

On August 9th there was a farewell dinner at Walpole's house in Arlington St., and the viscount got his ultimatum. The former talked in the same strain as before, civil but firm, telling him that what he asked was consistent neither with the King's service nor the humor of the Whig party. He advised him not to go from Aix to Hanover, in order to make his application to the King in person, "as it would do no good and just cause trouble." Two days later,[77] Bolingbroke set out for France, having accomplished none of the objects of his visit.

Other than this, the only difficulty experienced from the Tories by the Ministry was in the contested election of the two sheriffs of London and Middlesex, from which the Whigs

---

[76] *Stowe MSS,* 251, ff. 12-14b (Walpole to Townshend, July 23, 1723).
[77] *Add. MSS,* 32,686, f. 301 (Walpole to Newcastle, Aug. 10, 1723).

emerged victorious.[78] Early in October the Tory cause suffered another blow in the death of Lord Cowper, one of the few men in public life whose reputation had not fallen off through the transactions of the past ten years.

But the Tories were not the only opponents of the Ministry. There were many within the ranks of the Whig party itself who remained outside the Walpole machine,—disappointed place-hunters and "bitter-enders," who refused to take kindly to the new party discipline or yield to the blandishments of the "brother ministers." For nearly two years following the death of Sunderland, it appeared that all these elements that had a grievance against Walpole would find a leader in Lord Carteret.

John, Baron Carteret, was born in 1690 and succeeded to the title at the age of five. He had won a remarkable reputation at Oxford, from whence, as Swift declared and Chesterfield agreed, "he carried away more Greek, Latin and philosophy than properly became a person of his rank." Under the friendly patronage of Stanhope and Sunderland, he had made a brilliant reputation as a diplomatist in Sweden and Denmark, and as has been seen, in March, 1721, he had succeeded Craggs in the Southern Department. Possessing an arrogance and presumption which were lacking in Newcastle, he refused to acknowledge the leadership of Walpole in domestic affairs; and depending upon his favor in the eyes of the King and his German ministers and favorites, through his command of their native tongue, he set himself up as Walpole's rival. Certain failure awaited his ambitions, however, for he lacked the natural qualifications and disdained those methods which were the secret of Walpole's success. The details of election bored him, as they did Disraeli. He was all for glory. "He thought," wrote Speaker Onslow, "the business of consulting the interior interests and disposition of the people, the conduct of business in

---

[78] *S. P. Dom., Regencies* (Hanover), vol. iv (Walpole to Townshend, June 8 and July 4 and 19, 1723), and *Add. MSS,* 32,686, f. 276 (Newcastle to Townshend, July 12), *etc.*

Parliaments, and methods of raising money for the execution even of his own designs was a work below his applications."[79]

Such, in brief, was the history and character of the man who now sought to replace Walpole in the confidence of the King and to set up a party of his own in England. It was the task of Walpole and Townshend to circumvent his intrigues; but at the same time they could not, as yet, afford to break with him, for it was all important to reassure the Regent and Dubois that England would adhere to the close alliance which Stanhope had made with France.

Among the adherents upon whom he could more or less depend were several members of the Council and a strong minority of the Lords Justices, consisting of Lord Chancellor Parker, the Earl of Berkeley (First Lord of the Admiralty), the Duke of Roxburghe (Secretary for Scotland), and Earl Cadogan; while Viscount Harcourt, the converted Tory, was trimming as usual. Lechmere (the former Attorney-General), Carlisle, Montague, and other peers were also sitting on the fence.

Of the inchoate opposition in the Commons at this time, less is known, as Parliament was up; and in the brief, well-planned session of January-April, 1724, Walpole carried all before him. Apart from the Tory Windham, there was no outstanding leader, but the discontent which was already rankling in the breast of one of Walpole's oldest and ablest allies was soon to provide another. This man was William Pulteney, the future Earl of Bath. He had resigned his place as Secretary-at-War and had gone into opposition with Walpole in 1717; and upon the end of the Whig schism in 1720 the latter had offered him only a peerage, which he had refused. With the vindictiveness that Hervey attributes to him, Pulteney had gone at once to the Prince of Wales and babbled the contemptuous remarks that Walpole had made about the heir.[80] In the spring of 1723 he applied for the minor place of Cofferer of the House-

---

[79] H.M.C. *Onslow MSS*, 471.

[80] Hervey, *An Answer to One Part of a Late Infamous Libel*, 55.

hold,[81] which upon the resignation of Lord Goldolphin was finally bestowed upon him, May 28, 1723. He now began to come under the influence of his cousin, Daniel Pulteney, who had been one of Sunderland's closest adherents, and was now one of the irreconcilable opponents of Walpole.[82] About a month later there took place what Newcastle called "some remarkable passages" between William Pulteney and Walpole. "His whole discourse was thoroughly impertinent & seemed to hint at the great difficulties of next sessions, and that (the) Whiggs might bring the affair of Bolingbrook on in order to putt a negative upon it, & asked Mr Walpole what he would do in that case. Walpole told him he should always go with the Whiggs, but not call two or three the Whigg party."[83]

It was these elements which Carteret sought to rally to his standard. In order to do so, he industriously circulated stories of his superior credit with the King and the corresponding weakness of the "brother ministers." He claimed that "he had the King's heart and affection and that others were employed through the exigency of affairs."[84] In consonance with the policy of Sunderland and Stanhope, his preceptors, he planned to build his power upon a bi-partisan basis. Bolingbroke told Walpole that the Tories had been in measures and correspondence with Carteret all through the winter of 1722-1723, and that Carteret had often urged them to attack Walpole personally.[85]

In order to counteract Carteret's gasconnades and to make plain to the waverers and trimmers just where the power really lay, the Ministry decided to make an example of one of his principal partisans—General Lord Cadogan. On May 30, as Commander-in-Chief, the latter had issued orders to which Walpole had taken exception, and the King was brought to

---

[81] *Add. MSS*, 32,686, f. 200 (Carteret to Newcastle).

[82] H.M.C. *Onslow MSS*, 466; H.M.C. *Clements MSS*, 331 and 367; and *Add. MSS*, 32,686, f. 266 (Newcastle to Townshend, June 28).

[83] *Add. MSS*, 32,686, f. 270 (same to same, July 5).

[84] *Ibid.*, f. 268.

[85] *Stowe MSS*, 251, ff. 12-14b (Walpole to Townshend, July 23, 1723).

revoke them with the injunction that Cadogan should act only upon the instructions of the Lords Justices.[86] In spite of their representations to the contrary, many Whigs and Tories recognized the weakness of Carteret's party in their inability to avert this blow. Newcastle did his share in making matters plain by giving Lechmere and Carlisle a true account of the affair and cautiously insinuating that suitable employments were awaiting their complete submission.[87]

Newcastle also proved to be of great service to the duumvirs in their ecclesiastical policy. The majority of the clergy, including the two Archbishops, were Tories or even Jacobites, and Atterbury was their idol and martyr. The insecurity of the throne and the exigencies of party politics both showed the need of reconciling the Church and the dynasty. One cause of disaffection lay in the unintelligent method of distributing preferment. Promotions were too often conferred upon the favorites of politicians in payment of private obligations, irrespective of their attitude toward the government; while loyal men who felt entitled to recognition were passed over by their inferiors.[88] It was in this way that Thomas Bowers—Newcastle's "guide, philosopher, and friend"—had gained his mitre.

It was now proposed to adopt the principle that Thomas Fuller had long before laid down, of making the pulpit "of the same wood with the Council Board," by means of using the royal prerogative and Crown livings to create a bench and clergy attached to the government and to Whiggery. The unusual number of sees that fell vacant by death or promotion in 1723 provided a rare opportunity for the inauguration of this excellent policy. First of all, however, it was necessary to discover which of the episcopate were well affected toward Carteret and if possible to detach them; and secondly, to select some outstanding member of the bench of bishops upon whom the Ministers could rely as their ally and adviser.

---

[86] Torrens, *History of Cabinets,* I, 322-323.
[87] *Add. MSS,* 32,686, ff. 268 and 280.
[88] Sykes, *Edmund Gibson,* 108-109 and App. B.

Carteret had claimed that the bishops were devoted to him, especially Gibson of London and Willis of Salisbury; and although Newcastle had denied the truth of this to Lechmere, he admitted to Lord Townshend that he was not free from suspicion. Nevertheless, Edmund Gibson was the very man who was singled out to act as ecclesiastical director to the Ministry. On August 19 Gibson presented Walpole with a list of recommendations for promotion. "His lordship seemed in a very good humour," wrote the latter to Newcastle *(more suo)*, "& as long as we continue such good boys & obey our orders so punctually, I should hope our spiritual governours will not be much dissatisfied. But this is certainly the man among them & wth whom we ought to manage and cultivate & I promise you I act my part well." Somewhat later he wrote: "We grow well acquainted. He must be pope & would as willingly (be) *our* pope as any bodies."[89] With these sentiments the duke agreed: "He has more sense & I think more party zeal than any of them. . . . I intend very soon to take an opportunity of writing very largely to the Bp. of London, upon pretence of the several vacancies there are amongst the king's chaplains and shall endeavor to do what good I can."[90] Soon Carteret came to speak coldly and slightingly of Bishop Gibson, while in London every one of the vacancies, including the Primacy of Ireland, was being filled as the prelate proposed. Newcastle had done his share to bring about this state of affairs· "I have not been wanting in my endeavour to convince the Bp. of London how truly y^r lordship & Mr· Walpole are friends to him, and how desirous you are, in all ecclesiastical affairs, of being directed and advised by him," he wrote "I think it has had its effect and he both thinks of things and persons as we wish."[91] Walpole was well pleased with the way everything had turned out and was confident that the new fathers in God would value the King's grace to them "next to ye Holy Ghost."

[89] *Add. MSS,* 32,686, f. 312 (Aug. 22), and ff. 326-327 (Sept. 6, 1723).
[90] *Ibid.,* ff. 317-318 (Aug. 25).
[91] *Ibid.,* f. 386 (Newcastle to Townshend, Nov. 1).

Meanwhile Lord Townshend was writing triumphantly from Hanover: "I make no doubt but Lord Carteret and his emissarys have taken care to sett forth the church preferments as the effect of his superior interest here; but I do assure you that his credit with the King as well as that of his friend Bernstorff is fallen so low that unless some new mine should be sprung at the Göhrde (of which I see no probability), he is without resource on this side of the water."[92] His words were confirmed in November, when Bernstorff was finally driven altogether from public life to find solace in his orchard, his place in the Hanoverian Ministry being taken by Newcastle's old friend, Marshal Hardenberg. Furthermore, Carteret lost his usefulness in the eyes of the "brother ministers" when the death of Dubois in August and that of the Regent in December made way at Versailles for the Ministry of the Duc de Bourbon and the Comte de Morville, who hated the Orleans family and were no friends to the Stanhope tradition.

In the meanwhile, Carteret, unused to the Southern Department, and anxious to retrieve his position, was led into several intrigues, which cannot be considered here, save the one which may be said to have provided his own *coup de grâce*. Since the Duchess of Kendal was hand in glove with Walpole, Carteret had courted the support of the other royal favorites, the Countess of Darlington[93] and her sister-in-law, Madame Platen. Accordingly, as early as the spring of 1722, he undertook to further a match between Amalia, the daughter of the countess,

---

[92] *Stowe MSS,* 251, ff. 54b-55 (Townshend to Walpole, Oct. 5, 1723, N.S.).

[93] Sophia Charlotte von Platen-Hellermund, who in 1701 married the Hanoverian *Oberstallmeister,* Johann Adolf von Kielmannsegge, and was created Countess of Darlington, is usually described as a mistress of George I (*e.g.* Lady Montagu's *Account of the Court of George I at his Accession*). However Professor Ward, despite his earlier version in the *D.N.B., s.v.* Schulenburg, in his authoritative work on the Electress Sophia (pp. 250-251), and in the *Cambridge Modern History,* VI, 19, declares that her intimacy with the King must be ascribed to the fact that she was the child of his father, the Elector Ernst August, by the latter's mistress, Clara Elisabeth von Platen-Hellermund.

with the Comte St-Florentin, son of the Marquis de la Vril-
lière, one of the French Secretaries of State, whose assent was
to be requited by a dukedom. This scheme aroused the jealousy
of the "good duchess," and as it dragged on the intrigue became
a trial of strength not only of the rival charmers but of the
Ministers who lent their support to either side.

In the middle of October Horace Walpole was sent upon
a confidential mission to Paris, ostensibly to learn how matters
stood there, but actually to undermine the Ambassador, Sir
Luke Schaub, and to checkmate Carteret, his patron. The
fact that a close relative and ally of the "brother ministers"
should be sent to France—Carteret's own province—was in
itself a significant achievement. Both the old French Ministers
and their successors had resisted the aspirations of Lady Darlington, in spite of the open support of the King. Upon his
return to England, the latter abandoned the scheme as hopeless;
but Carteret and the sly, vain Schaub persevered in their designs and continued their representations as to their superior
credit at Court. The position of the rival envoys became awk-
ward and even ridiculous, and as a result of Horace Walpole's
repeated protestations,[94] the choice between the two was put
squarely before the King. The die was cast and Schaub was
removed.

This blow was the signal for the fall of Carteret himself.
On April 3 his place was taken by the Duke of Newcastle. The
reason for this choice is obvious enough in the light of the
duke's relations with the Ministers, and there is every reason
to believe that for the past two years he had been grooming for
the place. Less than a year before he had written the Bishop
of Chichester of "some prospect I have had of exchanging my
place for one infinitely more profitable."

Nevertheless, his elevation was a surprise and disappointment
to some of his contemporaries, and later writers have echoed
these sentiments in speculating why Newcastle was preferred

---

[94] Coxe, *Memoirs of Horatio, Lord Walpole*, I, 132-134, 143, and esp.
his letter of Mar. 22, 1724, pp. 144-145.

to William Pulteney. Pulteney himself was sanguine to the last, although he afterward denied that he had asked for the secretaryship and asserted that Walpole was the only person who had mentioned it to him, and that cursorily.[95] In view of the relations of Newcastle and Pulteney, respectively, to the Ministry, it is hardly likely that Walpole could have made this offer seriously, if at all; and whatever claims Pulteney may have had to his gratitude, he had done much to extinguish them by his conduct of the past year. According to Hervey, while the struggle between Walpole and Carteret was raging, "Mr. Pulteney thought by his dexterity so to manage his affairs that whoever was the sacrifice, he should be the successor: to this end he entered into a secret correspondence and treaty with Lord Carteret, of which Sir Robert Walpole got intelligence, and from that moment resolved since Mr. Pulteney had endeavoured to secure himself an entrance at this door in case it was opened, that at least he should never come in where he held the key."[96]

If any other reason for the choice be needed, it is supplied by the characters of the two men concerned. Walpole, that keen student of human nature, recognized in Pulteney an independence of spirit which would make him a dangerous rival in the House of Commons, while the younger man showed no inclination to set up in business for himself.

Opinion in diplomatic circles regarding the promotion of Newcastle was uniformly critical.[97] The tendency was to regard the appointment as merely temporary, and his dependence upon the "brother ministers" was generally recognized. Newcastle would have been the last to deny this relation, and his attitude to his position is brought out in a frank and modest letter to his old friend, Horace Walpole. Beginning with ex-

---

[95] Hervey, *An Answer to One Part of a late Infamous Libel,* 51-52.

[96] Hervey, *Memoirs,* I, 12.

[97] Brosch, *Bolingbroke,* 152, note (Venetian Envoy's comment); Coxe, *Walpole,* III, 301 and 302 (Letters of Broglio to Louis XV, July 10 and 20, 1724); Lucas, *George II and His Ministers,* 280-281 (Letter of Palm, the Imperial Resident, 1726); and H.M.C. *Clements MSS,* 383 (Lekeux to Molesworth, Jan. 28, 1725) and 391 (same to same, Apr. 12, 1725).

pressions of confidence and friendship, he begs him to put a favorable construction on what he does and to be generous with advice, which would be esteemed highly. "Though perhaps it may be unpolitick in a minister yet it is very pardonable in a friend freely to own to you that nothing but my dependence upon the friendship and great ability of my lord Townshend at home and the information and advice that I shall receive from you abroad could have induced me to undertake an office which at present must be so difficult to me. The obligations that I have to your relations must needs oblige me to do all that lies in my power for their service, and I hope you will from this time correspond with me with the intimacy and friendship of a brother. . . . . I shall in everything act in concert with My Ld. Townshend and according to the advice & instructions that I shall have the pleasure of receiving from him."[98]

A few days later, his duties actually begun, he wrote again in part: "I have sent you two long publick letters, which I believe you will not be displeased with, though I am not so vain as to desire you should think they are my own performance. My predecessor continues to give himself the air of great satisfaction and lavish professions, while my case is to be beloved by some & not very civilly treated by others; but all that I foresaw & therefore must and will despise it. The foreign ministers here approve or not, as they stand affected to my predecessor and his friends."[99]

By virtue of the office into which the duke was formally sworn on April 26th,[100] he became one of His Majesty's Principal Secretaries of State, with offices in the Cockpit, in Whitehall. The multifarious duties of the office included both foreign and domestic concerns and involved functions which today are distributed among numerous Ministers. Although either of the Secretaries was supposed to be prepared to exercise the functions of the other, in actual practise each of them was given

---

[98] *Add. MSS*, 32,738, ff. 178-179 (Apr. 2, 1724).
[99] *Ibid.*, f. 192 (Apr. 6, 1724).
[100] *Privy Council Register*, no. 88, Geo. I, iv, page 491.

direction over one of the two provinces into which foreign
countries were divided. As Secretary for the Southern Department, France, Switzerland, Italy, Spain, Portugal, and Turkey
belonged in Newcastle's department; while Townshend occupied
the other secretariat, regarded as the more important at this
period on account of the critical condition of Northern affairs.
The duties of the new Secretary consisted in corespondence with
the English diplomatic, military, and commercial representatives
abroad, drafting their instructions, receiving foreign envoys,
signing warrants and credentials, and in general complete direction of foreign policy.

His domestic functions were no less extensive, and involved
the consideration of petitions and memorials on all sorts of
subjects: the control of commitments, reprieves, and licenses;
intercourse with every department and board in the government;
and correspondence with the American colonies.[101] Since the
Union with Scotland, there had been a third Secretary for the
northern kingdom; but upon the triumph of Walpole, the Duke
of Roxburghe, one of Carteret's adherents, was dismissed from
that post and the functions of the office were permanently divided between the two remaining Secretaries.

At this point, in April, 1724, with Newcastle at the age of
thirty-one duly installed in the Southern Department, this history ends. He was now on the threshold of a new and wider
career, which was not to be ephemeral as his critics judged, but
to last for thirty years, and only to be exchanged for the Prime
Ministry itself. In but a short time, his position was so assured
that Lord Hervey was afterward enabled to declare that "Sir
Robert Walpole, his brother, Mr. Horace Walpole, Ambassador
to France, the Duke of Newcastle, and Lord Townshend . . . .
were, properly speaking, the whole old administration at the
death of the late King."[102]

---

[101] Miege, *Present State,* 239-240; Chamberlayne, *Present State,* 84-86;
and Andrews, *Guide to the Materials for American History,* I, 20 and note.
[102] *I.e.,* George I, Hervey, *Memoirs,* I, 38. On July 10, 1724, Count
Broglio wrote the King of France: "I am convinced that the government

In 1724 Newcastle looked out upon a different world from that in which he had been born, and he had done something to change it. The Sun-King, whose victories had accompanied his birth, was no more, and his place in a declining kingdom was taken by a weak voluptuary. Despite a host of baffled schemers and a France now prostrate, the duke had helped preserve the Revolution—for him the central event of history—to bring the Hanoverians to the throne, to nip a counter-revolution in the bud, and to make possible in some degree the ascendancy of the man with whose name the age is indissolubly connected—Robert Walpole. In these exertions he had never spared himself, and his services, his fortune, and his life itself had been offered in the interest of the State. Personally incorruptible, his name is synonymous to many with what the modern world is pleased to call corruption; but the unfairness of holding against him the political standards of another age must be apparent. The political ideals and practices of his day were not of his making; and after all the stream of corruption sprang not from above, but from the electorate.

Advancing years served to confirm certain eccentricities, such as his haste and his extreme anxiety for his health,[103] over which his critics, who mostly wrote during the later period of his life, made merry. But, as one shrewd contemporary declared, "even the defects and faults which might have appeared in his character were rather of service to him, as they often tended to soften resentments and helped to give that great power of which he was possessed an appearance less formidable."[104]

---

is entirely in the hands of Mr. Walpole, Lord Townshend, and the Duke of Newcastle." Coxe, *Walpole,* III, 301.

[103] As early as 1717 Bowers alluded to his "being in a continual hurry" (*Add. MSS,* 33,064, ff. 131-133), and in 1722 Newcastle himself reminded the duchess "You know what a hurry I am always in" (*Add. MSS,* 33,073, f. 11). In connection with his aversion to unaired beds, it is interesting to point out that the death of Sir William Jones, the Attorney-General, was attributed to that neglect (North, *Examen,* 509), and this circumstance may have gone to make up family tradition.

[104] *Annual Register,* V (1762), *History,* 46.

A true portrait of the real Newcastle cannot be drawn until the vast mine of manuscripts that he left behind has been thoroughly and impartially explored. That the Newcastle who will emerge will not be the Newcastle of the pages of Horace Walpole and Lord Hervey is demonstrated by the ever-growing number of students who have taken the trouble to dig even a little way in this huge collection.[105] Lacking the driving-force of Walpole or the vision of Chatham, he had indeed his shortcomings and his limitations; but he was sensible of them,[106] and, if he had taken his own measure, he would have judged himself like Roger North, the biographer: "though not of the prime of my rank, yet not contemptible."

---

[105] For revisionist estimates of Newcastle, see: Charteris, *Early Life of Cumberland,* 136-137 and 328-331; Charteris, *Cumberland and the Seven Years War,* I, 15-17 and 37-38; Michael, *Englische Geschichte,* II, *intro.,* vii, and the same author's estimate in the *Cambridge Modern History,* VI, 397; Turberville, *House of Lords,* 261; Tunstall, *Admiral Byng,* 15; Von Ruville, *Pitt,* I, 246-249; Winstanley, *Chatham and the Whig Opposition,* 13-15, 16-18 and 239-241; Winstanley, *University of Cambridge,* 35-36 and 145-146; and Yorke, *Hardwicke,* I, 284-288.

[106] *Add. MSS,* 35,406, ff. 165-167 (Newcastle to Hardwicke, Oct. 14, 1729).

Appendix B

A Tale of Two Tubs, or the B(rother)s in Querpo
Printed for A. Price, jun., near Ludgate, London, 1749.
55 pages. Price 1s.

(Beginning at page 5, line nine.)
Their Father was a good old Knight
Who hated Wrong & stood to Right;
Who lov'd his Country, kept the Peace,
And never dangl'd after Place.
A good Estate he had, not large,
Enough to bear out ev'ry Charge.
Two Sons he had, his Age to bless,
In whom he plac'd his Happiness.
TOM was the eldest of the Pair,
Him Fate ordain'd the Booby Heir;
Harry was youngest of the Twain,
The deftest Lad in all the Plain;
They both were early put to School,
Where soon was known which was the Fool.
TOM was the Dunce, his Comrades tell,
And scarce could learn to read or spell;
But then for Grammar and Syntaxis,
Poor Boy! it was enough to crack his
Undocible and Paper-Skull,
Who'd always been his Mother's Lull:
The Master took the utmost Pains,
But Masters cannot furnish Brains,
   At length deliver'd from the Rod,
To fructify the heavy Clod,
And to improve his Infant Knowledge,
Forthwith he's sent to learned College.
But TOM, it seems, had Sense enough
To know that all was idle Stuff,
That there was taught: To Arts & Science
Therefore he bids a full Defiance;
But yet resolves to shew his Parts
In learning much genteeler Arts.

[171]

By Midnight Candle who wou'd pore,
And read old musty Authors o're?
Who wou'd perplex his Brains to know
What's done two Thousand Years ago,
And so neglect the gayer Scene
Where Joy & Pleasure ever reign?
To rake and swagger, whore & drink,
For which he never wanted Chink,
Suited his more exalted Thought
Than all the learned Doctors taught.
    HARRY, meanwhile consider'd that
His Means were slender, small his 'State;
And therefore to make good the Ballance,
Resolves he will improve his Talents.
Closely to Study he applies,
In Hopes by this in Time to rise,
By Dint of Merit to a Station,
To be the Wonder of the Nation.
How he succeeded in his Plan—
Why, wou'd you know? Behold the Man.
    Old Dad, mean Time, is gone to rest,
And TOM of all is soon possess'd.
And now he seems kind Fortune's Minion,
While she, to gain his good Opinion,
Fresh Favours heaps upon his Head,
And splendid Scenes around him spread,
Titles & large Estates, God bless us!
He sees himself as rich as Croesus;
Enough to make a Wit run mad,
But that no such fine Wit he had;
For Wit to Madness is ally'd,
And thin the bounds that them divide,
As Poets say, and Poets know,
As their own Works do plainly shew.
    However, TOM will cut a Figure
And tho' he's great, wou'd still look bigger.
With this Intent, he brews a Store,
Till his large Cellars hold no more.
A stock of Brandy, Wine & Rum

By Cart-loads to his Storehouse come.
Then calls his neighbours, far & near,
To drink their Fill of humming Beer.
Plenty of Punch, full strong & stout,
Prepares to make his Banquet out,
Fills to the Brim capacious Bowls,
And thus regales their thirsty Souls;
Barons of Beef adorn the Board,
And who so great as now, my Lord?
  With Paunches stuff'd, & Heads all addled,
The Guests, of Sense and Limbs disabled,
Present a Scene so odd & new,
As Hogarth's Pencil never drew.
Parsons & Squires, & Knights & Clowns,
And spruce young Fops from neighbouring Towns,
All mingled in the motley Throng,
Not to be mimick'd in my Song.
Here some are singing, dancing, roaring,
Others in a Corner, snoring;
Some quarreling & others fighting,
Some spewing here and there some sh-----,
Hats, Wigs & Caps lie here & there,
And broken Glasses ev'ry where;
While Clouds of Smoke around 'em rise,
Enough to blind the D----'s Eyes.
  This Scene gave TOM a vast Delight,
No Prospect 'ere so pleas'd his Sight.
So very pat it hit his Taste,
That he resolves to make it last.
  When they had all well bung'd their eyes,
And pigg'd into their sev'ral Sties,
And slept and snor'd some Hours away,
Again he brings them into Play;
Begins anew the same Carouse,
Again he drenches them with Booze.
  The Country Volk were quite amaz'd,
And gap'd & swallow'd, spew'd & prais'd
Their gen'rous hospitable Donor,
And bow'd & scrap'd & thank'd his Honour.

Thus Tom grew popular amain,
Without the Labour of his Brain;
All that had Forty Shillings Land,
Were now his Servants at Command.
  Harry, the while with Envy ey'd
His Brother's Fame thus spreading wide,
While he, scarce known or thought on must
To his own little Fortune trust;
By which he ne'er could hope to rise
Above a Justice at Assize.
He thrumm'd his Wits, & beat his Pate,
To try if he could mend his Fate.
At length bethought himself, 'twas best
To crave his Brother's Interest;
By which in Time, he might be sent
To give his vote in Parliament.
So said, so done, and TOM agrees
His Brother's Humour so to please,
By help of Punch & good strong Bubb,
The Freeholders are brought to dubb
Him Knight o' the Shire, a Noble Station,
An Overseer of the Nation
  Staunch were his Principles, a Whig,
And still on Tories run his Rigg.
From Court he always took his Cue,
And still its Measures did pursue;
Boldly oppos'd what e're was done
To shake or undermine the Throne.
His active Merit was regarded,
Highly applauded & rewarded.
Commission'd he to Preston goes
To fight his King's & Country's Foes.
Success in that commended still
His forward & unshaking Zeal.
Thus having brought his Ship to Port,
Basks in the Sunshine of the Court;
Where we shall leave him till anon
His Mightiness we call upon.
  Just at this Time, or therabout,

High-Church & Tories made a Rout,
Abus'd the Low Church, Whigs & King,
And made the Town & Country ring;
In ev'ry Street made Mobs & Riot,
Nor let their Neighbours live in Quiet.
Our noble Tom, for so we call him,
Resolves, whate'er betide, to maul 'em.
His Emissaries out he sends,
To muster up his trusty Friends.
The Chimney-sweeps & not a few
Of fam'd St. Giles's lousy Crew,
From Kent-street sturdy Fellows come
With Crab-tree Sticks without their Broom,
From Spittlefields a num'rous Troop,
Of hungry weavers made a Group.
Tinkers & Pedlars from Hedge-Lane,
Are in the hardy Service ta'en,
Some from their Garrets downward rush,
Some from their Cellars upwards push;
All hasten to their Rendezvous,
In hopes of Plunder or of Booze.
With Clubs & Broomsticks all are arm'd,
And with their Noble Captain charm'd.
The goodly Sight his Heart expands;
To Heav'n he lifts his clumsy Hands,
And thanks the Powers above that he
So many hearty Friends cou'd see,
Ready to join his loyal Cause,
And fight for Liberty & Laws.
And then a Speech he splatter'd out,
Not heard by half the Revel-rout;
And told them how they shou'd behave,
Bid them be resolute & brave;
That ev'ry Man shou'd have his Pay,
No less than Half a Crown a Day;
Besides strong Beer & Cheese & Bread,
And Plaisters for each broken Head.
A loud Huzza, from rusty Throats,
Proceeds in harsh discordant Notes,

Then Tom, as Captain takes the Lead,
Fit Body to so fit a Head!
    And now, ye Jacobites, stand clear,
Nor longer think to domineer.
Ye Tories too, & High Church low'r
Your Topsails, or you'll rue the Hour,
That e'er you did presume t'oppose
Such daring, such intrepid Foes.
    Now Thumps & Blows, & lusty Knocks,
Are dealt between the hardy Blocks,
Wher'ere the Combatants do meet,
In narrow Lane or open Street,
Like Greeks & Trojans bold & stout,
Most furiously they lay about,
Now many Bruises on the Sconce,
And many Bangs across the Bones,
Were giv'n & took by either Side,
As each their vig'rous Arms apply'd.
But Tom's brave Fellows, better paid,
And, while in Arms, much better fed,
Stood to the Tack like Desperades,
Nor minded Bones, nor broken Heads;
No wonder then they were victorious,
Which made our Captain very glorious.
    These harried Frays & Mob-Commotions
Rais'd up by Whig & Tory Notions,
Increasing daily fast & thicker,
Exhausted much our Tom's Exchequer.
    His Ready-rino all was gone,
And then his Plate must go to Pawn.
Then he began to hang his Wings,
And ponder on the Sum of Things,
But han't he large Estates? Yes, sure;
And while they last, he can't be Poor.
Then, prithee, what should make you falter?
This instant send for P(eter) W(alter),
For he, I know, has Thousands lent
And asks no more than Ten per Cent.
Tom takes th'Advice, & dips his Lands

To Pay his Ragamuffin Bands.
  When all was past, & Peace restor'd,
He found himself a needy Lord.
His Lands were mortgaged, Rents diminish'd;
From splendid Grandeur almost finish'd,
Most melancholy Prospects rise,
Some far, some near, to blast his Eyes.
  His Prince, considering well his Merit,
His Service done, & noble Spirit,
His loyal Zeal of late express'd,
How many Nights he'ad broke his Rest,
How often he had run a-tilt
In Danger's Mouth; how often felt
The dreadful Thumps of Tory Crew,
The Marks of which, still black & blue,
Are visible his Body on,
Requires he should be look'd upon.
Besides the Fellow's foolish Zeal,
Stark mad has run him out at Heel.
Bankrupt & beggar'd for our Sake,
We must some Pity on him take.
And since he seems of so much Weight,
Let him be our first Sailer of State.
  Now Tom is more alert than ever,
Looks wond'rous big & cocks his Beaver,
To all his Friends he shews the Odds;
Talks Politicks with Shrugs & Nods.
With broken Hints & mystic Terms
His depth of Knowledge he confirms,
Not Machiavel himself cou'd seem
A Statesman cunninger than him.
Men wondered at the Transmutation,
And swore twas done by Inspiration,
Or else by Fortune he alone
Had got the Philosophic Stone,
And by some secret Art, untold,
Had chang'd his pond'rous Lead to Gold.
But TOM, unconscious of the Lie,
Was not oblig'd to give a Why.

He thus assumed Wisdom's Face,
And acted with so much Grimace.

   Soon after this, our Annals say,
The famous Bob came into Play,
A man so fam'd all over Europe,
That all were fond to hold his Stirrup;
And then his Skill in making Treaties
With foreign Courts, surprizing yet is.
In Schemes his Brain was still prolifick,
And all his Measures most pacifick;
Tho oft attack'd, no Ground he lost,
For twenty Years he rul'd the Roast.

   Tom closely stuck to this Comptroller,
As close as Louse to Beggar's Collar;
Learn't all his Maxims, wrote em down,
In future time to make his own;
Back'd ev'ry Scheme that Bob could frame,
And thus went Hand in Hand in Fame. *(etc.)*

Appendix C

(i) *Letter from Anthony Trumble to John Gyles,* January 17, 1714-15, *Add. MSS,* 33,064, f. 38. See pp. 47-48.

The letter begins by saying that Lord Clare was invited to Hastings some time ago to recommend a friend of his to stand for the next election. He arrived this day sevennight and was received in the most distinguished manner by the mayor, jurats, freemen and others. His lordship gave a "splendid and generous" entertainment in return. He met with no opposition but what comes from Gyles' uncle, Thomas Gyles, a strong supporter of Sir Joseph Martin. This same Thomas is also responsible for keeping another uncle of John Gyles, Thomas Lovell, and all the rest of that name on the same side.

"I continued at Hastings from Monday till Thursday Evening," the letter goes on, "and notwithstanding all the striving that your uncle Gyles can do I find he cannot near bring up his Interest to Ballance with that already made & engaged for my Lord Clare. I had an opportunity of haveing about an hour & ½ private discourse & argument with yor Uncle Gyles & as the truth is he says he cannot neither in Hon^r nor with honesty receed from makeing Interest for Sr Jos. Martin, because it was Sr Jos. that put you in one of the Ct. in the South Sea office & your Uncle says it is for that & no other reason y^t he is for supporting of Sr Jos. Interest at this time. Now I put the Case to you to Consider seriously with yor self how far it now lyes in Sr Jos. power to Assist & Support you any longer. I do not know how you stand in yourself in yor politicks, But you must be Sensible as things are Visibly seen now to all people we are & must be hereafter in a flourishing way. And I do not find that Sr Jos. inclinations Stands that way. Therefore you'l think that Sr Jos. can Assist you no further nor no higher. If so look back to my Lord Clare who is ye best of Men & delights to do good & promotes those that serve him: yor Uncle Gyles has now this moment ye fairest & certainest opportunity of promoting you to anything that is reasonable. And I am assured yor Capacity deserves better, & depend on it none shall be forwarder in using my best endeavours to bring you into my Lords ffavour. I wish no other for your own

[179]

Sake, so soon as this comes to yor hands, but that you will gett leave & imediately take horse & come down to Hastings & you'l certainly find us there on ffriday next. If you miss embracing this opportunity in doing yor Self service it is your own fault. It is now time to strike for the Election will be over in a ffort-night & then all will be told. My Lord Clare setts up his Uncle Pelham's son, of Lewes, who joins with Mr. Hutchinson. Yo^r writeing to yor Uncle I am afraid will availe nothing at all to yor comeing & appearing yor self : pray as I am Hon^{rble} & wish well to you, lett me begg that you'l keep this as a Secret & comunicate the contents to none more than yor Uncle, for to tell you ye truth (three words undecipherable) under Secrecy and he assures me if he can with Hon^r gett of from Sr Jos. (and nothing he does is for more than in gratitude of Sir Jos. promoting of you) he will be for my Lord Clare's Interest. I shall be at Hastings tomorrow and shall not stir from thence till Saturday (if then) where I hope to see you before me at my Quarters at ye Swan."

(ii) *Letter of John Gyles in reply to that of Anthony Trumble,* January 20, 1714-15, *Add. MSS,* 33,064, ff. 39-40.

S^r. Yours recd. and must needs confess what you write is a matter of the last Consequence and so far as it relates to me there's something of moment. But you'll easily believe my in-clinations are entirely for my Lord Clare, for I am very sensible he is a Noble person that Acts upon generous principles, and what trouble he takes and Expences he is att in these Matters of Elections is purely to serve his Country in Opposition to those who, under a pretence of the Church's Danger have visibly les-sen'd the trade and power of the Nation and have even put ye Succession in Danger, as is plainly intimated by ye proclama-tion, and I must agree with you that tis much for my Interest that I should use my endeavours with my Uncle to perswade him to be for ye Gent. recomended by his Lordship, if thereby I could obtain any place in my Lord's favour as you assure me I shall, for as his Lordship does so much for ye publick I am satisfied he does a great many particular Services, and therefore doubt not but if my ffriends wou'd serve his Lordship and mention me to him he would have some regard to me, especially if he was made sensible how by doing for me he assists severall of my family who I have help'd beyond what might be expected from my narrow Circumstances. But now what I have most to object against is that ye World will think me very ungratefull for desireing my ffriends to oppose a person that has done for me, but I desire to represent this matter to you that I may be cleared in your opinion of such an imputation. Sʳ Joseph, tis true, hath gott me a place of ffifty pounds a year, but I am certaine tis not in ye power of a Clerk to make fforty Shillings of his perquisite, and as you know how dear tis living in Town & especially by ye Exchange how we are obliged to go genteel in Cloaths and wear good Linnen and what I pay besides out of my Sallary in ye Country you'll easily conclude I have no Extraordinary place, besides for three years I may without vanity say I have well deserv'd my Money, if tis possible for a man to gett halfe a Crown by Constant application from 9 in ye morning till 7 or sometimes 10 at night, and after this I can't see I am put in hopes of any Advancement, so that I shall labour here to dye poor. Now in recompense of this Service my Uncle has all along espoused Sʳ Josʰⁱˢ Interest in 3 or 4 Elections and I believe to his cost, whereby Sʳ Jos. has had opportunity to do himself and family great services. Therefore, since tis my Inclination and so apparently my Interest, and as I think I may do it without being too ungratefull, I am resolved, and have here sent a letter to my Uncle to desire he will joyne with those that favour my Lord's Interest, and I hope if Mr. Pelham shall be chose you'll take occasion to recoṁend me to my Lord or Mr. Pelham, and I am certaine you can't serve any one who will be more sensible of ye obligation than

(P.S. I could not posibly come my selfe. Wee have all our Accts. to make up for paymt. of ye Interest, and likewise our Election for Directors is very near. I hope you wont coṁunicate this letter to my prejudice and I beg you'll give me a Line by next post.

Appendix D

A "Scheme of Regulation"

Evidently drawn up in accordance with the Duke's request of March 11, 1732, and based upon a proposed annual budget of £12,000. (*Pelham Papers*, 33,137, ff. 365-372.)

Housekeeping

Butcher ....£	50 a month		£600 a year	
Fishmonger	30		360	
Poulterer	30		360	
Baker	15		180	
Butterman	10		120	
Milkman	2	10s	30	
Pastry Cook	1	10	18	
Herbman and Fruiterer ..	12		144	
Oylman and Grocer	15		180	
Cheesemonger	4		48	
Brewer	5		60	
Malt & Hopps at Clare-mont	20		240	
Tea, Coffee and Chocolate	10		120	
Servants board wages	16 13 8d		200	4s
Soap	7		84	
Lamp oyl	4		48	
Charcoal	10		120	
Apothecary	10		120	
	£252 13 8		£3,032 4	

Wax lights	120
Tallow Candles	200
Wood and Coals	500
Wine of all sorts, etc.	800
Liverys and servts. wages	1,000
Extraordinary contingencies of all sorts and Sussex journeys	1,247 16
	£6,900

Stables

Oats and Beans	300	
Hey and Straw	278	8
Servants' Boardwages	200	4
Smith and Farrier	120	
Coachmaker's contract	90	
Stable Rent	100	
Servants' Wages	112	
Hounds	235	
Hunting stables	250	
Pointers	50	
Tradesmen, Extraordinarys and Contingencies of all sorts	272	8

£2,000 per ann.

Claremont

Servants' wages and boardwages in the House

Housekeeper and Wife	50		
Porter and his assistant	38		
Two House maids	30		
Two Watchmen	36/10		
Brewer	48/4		
Helper at the Brewhouse and Laundry	20	222	14

Keeping of the Wood and Plantations. Geo. Arnold's wages and boardwages, and also the charge of the Pheasantry and aviary included..	300	
Keeping of the fruit and kitchin Garden	160	
Keeping of the Flower Garden......	30	
Tradesmen, artificers, repairs about the house and in the wood, new works, Bills for trees, Plants, flowers, and all manner of incidents	287	6

£1,000

(The produce of the farm is to defray the charge of servants, horses, and all manner of disbursement there.)

Sussex	£300
Pin Money	800
His Grace's Private Account, Gifts, Pensions, and Charity included.	1,000
	£12,000

"A Scheme for the Family. Claremont, June 5, 1734," Add. MSS, 33,137, ff. 397-8 (*Pelham Papers*).

The House Servants and their wages

Men Servants

Burnet, (Household) Steward..	50	
Northcote, clerk of the Kitchen..	50	
Tiphaine, confectioner, etc.	60	
Bone, Tiphaine's assistant	20	
Walbank	25	
Brett	20	
French Cook	50	
Morris, the under cook	20	
London Porter and Usher of the Hall	16	
Butler in livery	8	
4 Footmen	30	
2 Chairmen	50	
2 Watchmen	36	10
Lamplighter and Drudge	10	

Women Servants

Mrs. Elliot	30	
7 House maids	42	
3 laundry maids	18	
	535	10

Stables

9 Coach Horses, at £28......... 252
3 Padds at £26 78
12 Common Horses 120
Stable rent 60
Coach maker's Contract 70

                                                 580

Stable Servants' Wages

Jemmy Cook by Agreemt for Cloths, Wages and Board Wages, etc. 50
Coachman 10
Postillion 6
2 Helpers 14
Ned Hollybone 7
2 Boys 10

                                                 97

Stable Servants' board Wages

Coachman at 8s per week 20 16
Postillion, 2 Helpers, & Ned Hollybone at 7s per week each ... 72 16
Boys at 6s per week each 15 12

                                      124 16

Liverys

Porter and Usher of the Hall ..
5 Footmen, butler included .....
Coachman ....
Postillion ....
2 Helpers ....
Ned Hollybone ....
2 Boys ....
2 Chairmen ....
   (16 Liverys in all)

                            at £18
                            per livery

                                           288

Claremont

Swaine and his wife	50		
2 Housemaids	30		
Nicholas	20		
Peter Rowles	20		
Brewer	38		
Helper and Drudge	20		
2 Watchmen	36	10	
George Arnold	30		
Kitchen Garden	150		

Keeping of the Wood, viz':
14 men 8 months at 1/4
    per diem, each
4 men 4 months, ditto.

....	221	17	4

	616	7	4

The Farm to keep itself

Housekeeping in general	2,000		
Wine and other liquors	600		
Fewel of all sorts, wax and tallow Candles included	600		
Her Grace's Pin Money	500		
His Grace's own private account	600		
Extraordinary Contingencies and Incidents of all sorts	1,458	6	8

Total	£8,000		

Bibliography

I Sources

A. Manuscript Sources

  1. British Museum

Newcastle Papers, volumes 32,679, 32,685, 32,686, 32,687, 32,738, 33,058, 33,060, 33,063, 33,064, 33,073, 33,085, 33,137, 33,146, 33,151, 33,152, 33,166, and 33,320.

Hardwicke MSS, volumes 35,406, 35,584, and 35,838.

Stowe MSS, volume CCXXII (*Hanover Papers*, vol. I).

      volume CCXLVII (*Craggs Papers*, vol II, 1719-20).

      volume CCLI (*Trans. of State Letters*, 1723-48).

Miscellaneous *MSS, Egerton MSS*, vol. CMXXI (*Accounts of the Civil List Salaries, Bounties, etc.*).

      Sloane MSS, vol. 4,076.

      Add. MSS, 5,832 (*Collections of Various Kinds*, vol. 31, bequeathed by Rev. W. Cole).

      Add. MSS, 6,834, Plut. CLXX (*Mitchell Papers*, vol. 31).

      Add. MSS, 38,507 (*Townshend Papers*, vol. 16).

  2. Public Record Office

State Papers Domestic, George I.

State Papers Domestic, Regencies, 1716-1760.

State Papers Domestic, Entry Books, 1661-1828.

Records of the Lord Chamberlain's Department.

      Miscellanea, 1516-1900.

      Registers, 1641-1875.

Records of the Privy Council Office.

      Registers, 1540-1836.

  3. Clare College, University of Cambridge.

Admission Books.

  4. Somerset House Records

Will of John, Duke of Newcastle, Probated July 6, 1715. (Prerogative Court of Canterbury, 202, Fagg, 1715).

Will of Thomas, Baron Pelham of Laughton, probated March, 1712 (P.C.C., 58, Barnes, 1712).

B. Printed Sources
(NOTE: Unless otherwise indicated, the place of publication is London.)
Belles-Lettres
Eusden, Lawrence—*A Poem on the Marriage of . . . the Duke of Newcastle to Lady Henrietta Godolphin.* 1717.
Garth, Sir Samuel—*Poetical Works.* Edinburgh, 1773.
Gay, John—*Trivia, or Art of Walking the Streets of London* (in *Poetical Works,* ed. G. C. Faber). 1926.
Pope, Alexander—*Works.* Ed. Elwin and Courthope. 10 vols., 1881-86.
Swift, Jonathan—*Prose Works.* Ed. Temple Scott. 12 vols., 1908.
Williams, Sir Charles Hanbury—*Works.* 3 vols., 1822.

Letters, Diaries, Autobiographies and Memoirs
Athenaeum, The—Letters of Sir John Vanbrugh. Aug. 30, 1890, pp. 289-91, and Sept. 6, 1890, pp. 321-322.
Bolingbroke, Henry St. John, Viscount—*Miscellaneous Works,* vol. iv, 1773.
Bradshaw, J.—*The Letters of Philip Dormer Stanhope, Earl of Chesterfield, with the Characters.* 3 vols., 1891-2.
Bramston, Sir John—*Autobiography of.* Camden Soc., 1845.
Burnet, Gilbert, Bishop of Sarum—*History of His Own Time.* 2d ed., Oxford, 1833. 6 vols.
Calamy, Edmund—*An Historical Account of My Own Life, with Some Reflections on the Times I have lived in* (1671-1731). 2 vols., 1829.
Cartwright, James J.—*The Wentworth Papers.* 1883.
Cowper, Mary, Countess—*Diary, 1714-1720.* Ed. by Hon. Spencer Cowper. 2d ed., 1865.

Coxe, Wm.—*Memoirs of the Administration of the Rt. Hon. Henry Pelham, collected from the family papers and other authentic documents.* 2 vols., 1829.

Ibid.—*Memoirs of Horatio, Lord Walpole.* 2 vols., 1808.

Ibid.—*Memoirs of the Life and Administration of Sir Robert Walpole, Earl of Orford.* 3 vols., 1798.

Graham, John Murray—*The Annals and Correspondence of Viscount and the first and second Earls of Stair.* 2 vols., 1875.

Hervey, John, Lord—*Memoirs of the Reign of George II, to the Death of Queen Caroline.* Ed. J. W. Croker. 2d ed., 3 vols., 1848.

Hutchinson, Lucy—*Memoirs of the Life of Colonel Hutchinson, Governor of Nottingham.* Ed. C. H. Firth. 2 vols., 1885.

Marchant, Thomas—*Diary* (in *Sussex Archaeol. Coll.,* XXV). 1875.

Marchmont Papers, The—A Selection from the Papers of the Earls of Marchmont, in the possession of the Rt. Hon. Sir George H. Rose. 3 vols., 1831.

Montagu, Lady Mary Wortley—*Letters, 1714-1727.* 3d Wharncliffe ed. 3 vols., 1861.

Newton, Lady Evelyn—*Lyme Letters, 1660-1760.* 2 vols., 1925.

Savile Correspondence. Camden Soc., 1858.

Sayer, Charles L. (ed.)—*The Correspondence of John Collier, 1718-1780.* 2 vols., 1907.

Sidney, Henry—*Diary of the Times of Charles II.* Ed. R. W. Blencowe. 2 vols., 1843.

Spershott's Memoirs of Chichester, with notes by H. Haines and F. H. Arnold (in *Sussex Archaeol. Coll.,* XXIX, pp. 219-223, and XXX, pp. 147-160). 1879-90.

Steele, Sir Richard—*Epistolary Correspondence.* Ed. by John Nichols. 2 vols., 1809.

Swift, Jonathan—*Correspondence.* Ed. by F. E. Ball. 6 vols., 1910-14.

Thomson, Mrs. A. T.—*Memoirs of Sarah, Duchess of Marlborough, and of the Court of Queen Anne.* 2 vols., 1839. (Contains valuable correspondence.)

Vanbrugh, Sir John—*Complete Works.* Vol. iv, the Letters, ed. by Geoffrey Webb (Nonesuch Press). 1928.

Waldegrave, James, Earl—*Memoirs from 1754-58.* 1821.

Walpole, Horace, 4th Earl of Orford—*Letters,* complete with Bibliography. Ed. by Mrs. Paget Toynbee. Oxford, 16 vols., 1903-05. Supplementary volumes, I and II, Oxford, 1918. Vol. III, 1925.

Ibid.—Memoires of the Last Ten Years of the Reign of King George II, ed. by Lord Holland. 3 vols. 1846.

Ibid.—Reminiscences, written by H. W. in 1788 for the Amusement of Miss Mary and Miss Agnes Berry. Oxford, 1924.

Whiston, William—*Memoirs of the life and Writings of Mr. W. W., containing several of his friends also, and written by himself.* 2d ed., 1753.

History, Topography, Travel, and Description

Boyer, Abel—*The History of The Reign of Queen Anne, digested into Annals.* 10th year.

Boyer, Abel—*The Political State of Great Britain, being an Impartial Account of the most Material Occurances, Ecclesiastical, Civil, and Military.* 1711 *et sqq.* Vols. 2, 6, 8-10, 12-17, 19, 21, 23, and 24.

Burnet, Dr. John—'*Odoiporountos Meleemata, sive iter Surriense et Sussexiense, peregrinantur, rusticantur.* 1752. (Translated portions in *Sussex Archaeol. Coll.,* VIII, 250-265.)

Chamberlayne, John—*Magnae Britanniae Notitia, or the Present State of Great Britain, with divers Remarks upon the Antient State thereof.* 26th ed., 1723.

Clarendon, Edward, Earl of—*History of the Rebellion and Civil Wars in England.* Oxford, 6 vols., 1888.

Deering, Charles—*Nottinghamia vetus et nova, or an Historical Account of the Ancient and present state of the town of Nottingham.* Nottingham, 1751.

Defoe, Daniel—*A Tour Through the Whole Isle of Great Britain,* 2 vols., 1927. (Based on the original ed. of 1724-26.)

Luttrell, Narcissus—*Brief Historical Relation of State Affairs, from Sept., 1668, to April, 1714.* Oxford, 6 vols., 1857.

Macky, John—*A Journey through England.* 1722.

Mayor, John E. B.—*Cambridge under Queen Anne.* Cambridge, 1911. (Consists largely of contemporary accounts.)

Miege, Guy—*The Present State of Great Britain and Ireland.* 10th ed., 1745.

Saussure, César de—*A Foreign View of England in the Reigns of George I and George II.* Trans. by van Muyden. 1902.

Pamphlets

Anonymous—*Index Rerum et Vocabulorum, for the Use of the Freeholders of Counties.* 2d ed., 1722.

Ibid.—*Reasons humbly offered why the Sheriff of the County of Sussex at an election of a knight or knights of that shire should be enabled to adjourn the poll at the desire of one or more of the candidates, from Chichester to Lewes or from Lewes to Chichester, vice versa.* n.d. B. M. Catalog gives 1720.

Ibid.—*Robin Hood and the Duke of Lancaster, a Ballad (etc.).* 1727.

Ibid.—The State of the Case between the Lord Chamberlain and Sir Richard Steele, as represented by that Knight. Restated in Vindication of King George and the . . . Duke of Newcastle. 1720.

Ibid.—The Whole Life and Noble Character of John, Duke of Newcastle. 1711.

Ibid.—A Tale of Two Tubs, or the B----s in Querpo. 1749.

Hervey, John, Lord (?)—*An Answer to one Part of a Late Infamous Libel, entitled, "Remarks on the Craftsman's Vindication of his Two Honourable Patrons," in which the Character and Conduct of Mr. P(ulteney) is fully vindicated.* 1731.

Hutchinson, Archibald—*A Collection of Advertisements, Letters and Papers, and some other facts relating to the last Elections at Westminster and Hasting, published from the 20th of February to the 24th of March, 1721.* 1722.

Periodicals

Annual Register, The. Vol. V, 1762.

Gentleman's Magazine, The. Vols. III, VII, and LIV.

London Magazine, The. Vol. for 1768.

London Daily Journal, The.

London Daily Post, The.

Collections and Records, mostly official

Bateson, Mary (ed.)—*A Narrative of Changes in the Ministry, 1765-67, told by the Duke of Newcastle in a series of letters to John White, M.P.* Camden Soc., 2d ser., 1898.

Cobbett, William (ed.)—*The Parliamentary History of England, from the Norman Conquest in 1066 to the Year 1803.* Vols. VII and VIII, 1811.

Duckett, Sir George, Bart. (ed.)—*Penal Laws and Test Act; Questions touching their Repeal, propounded in 1687-88 to the Deputy-Lieutenants and Magistrates of the Counties of Cumberland,*

Westmorland (etc.). *From the original returns in the Bodleian Library.* 1882.

Dunkin, E. H. W. (ed.)—*A Calendar of the Deeds and other Documents in the possession of the Sussex Archaeological Society.* Lewes, 1890 (in *Sussex Archaeol. Coll.*, XXXVII, pp. 39-110).

Historical Manuscripts Commission Reports (referred to in footnotes as "H.M.C.").

2d Report: *Clare College MSS; Stair MSS.*

3d Report: *Chichester MSS.*

5th Report: *Field MSS; Sutherland MSS.*

7th Report: *Denbigh MSS; Webb MSS; Egmont MSS.*

8th Report: *Blenheim MSS.*

10th Report: *Steward MSS; Bagot MSS.*

11th Report: *Townshend MSS.*

12th Report: *Cowper MSS; Coke MSS.*

13th Report: *Portland MSS*, vol. ii; *Lennard MSS.*

14th Report: *Trevor MSS; Onslow MSS; Corporation of Lincoln MSS.*

15th Report: *Portland MSS*, vols. iv, v, vii and viii; *Buccleuch-Queensbury MSS*, vols. i and ii; *Carlisle MSS; Stuart Papers*, vols. i to vii, inclusive; *Bath MSS; Franklin-Russell-Astley MSS; MSS in Various Collections*, vol. viii; *Clements MSS.*

16th Report: *Egmont MSS*, vol. i.

17th Report: *Polwarth MSS*, vol. i.

House of Commons, Journals of the. Vols. 18, 19 and 20 (1714-27).

House of Lords, Journals of the.

Legg, L. G. Wickham (ed.)—*British Diplomatic Instructions, 1689-1789.* Vol. iv, France, 1721-1727. Camden Soc., 1927.

Somers Collection of Tracts, The. 13 vols., 1809-15.

State Papers of the Reign of William and Mary, Calendar of, Domestic Series. 1689-97. 1895-1927.

State Papers of the Reign of Queen Anne, Calendar of, Domestic Series. Vol. I, 1916; vol. II, 1924.

Statutes of the Realm, The. 1101-1713. 9 vols., 1810-22.

Treasury Papers, Calendar of, 1714-19, 1883; *1735-38,* 1900.

II. Secondary Authorities

Aitken, G. A.—*Life of Richard Steele.* 2 vols., 1889.

Albery, Wm.—*The Parliamentary History of the Borough of Horsham, 1295-1805.* 1927.

Bailey, Thomas—*Annals of Nottingham.* 4 vols., 1852-55.

Barker, G. F. R. and Stenning, Alan H.—*The Record of Old Westminsters, a Biographical List of all those who are known to have been educated at Westminster School, from the earliest times to 1927.* 2 vols., 1928.

Beeching, H. C.—*Francis Atterbury.* 1909.

Berry, Wm.—*Pedigrees of the Families in the County of Sussex.* 1830.

Brosch, Moritz—*Lord Bolingbroke und die Whigs und Tories seiner Zeit.* Frankfurt-am-Main, 1883.

Brown, Cornelius—*Lives of Notts. Worthies and of celebrated and remarkable men of the County.* 1882.

Cambridge Modern History, The. Vol. VI, The Eighteenth Century, 1909.

Charteris, Evan—*William Augustus, Duke of Cumberland: His Early Life and Times, 1721-1748.* 1913.

Ibid.—William Augustus, Duke of Cumberland, and the Seven Years War. 1925.

Cheal, Henry—*The Story of Shoreham.* Hove Combridges, 1921.

Cokayne, G. E.—*Complete Baronetage.* 6 vols., Exeter, 1900-09.

Ibid.—Complete Peerage of England, Scotland, Ireland, Great Britain and the United Kingdom, extant, extinct, or dormant. New ed., rev. and enld. by the Hon. Vicary Gibbs and H. A. Doubleday. 1913.

Collins, Arthur—*Historical Collections of the Noble Families of Cavendishe, Holles, Vere, Harley and Ogle.* 1752. (Scarce. The copy used was that at Cornell Library.)

Ibid.—The Peerage of England. (Numerous editions.)

Cooper, Wm. D.—*Parliamentary History of the County of Sussex and of the several Boroughs and Cinque Ports therein.* Lewes, 1834.

Corbett, Sir Julian S.—*England in the Seven Years War, a Study in Combined Strategy.* 2 vols., 1907.

Crake, W. V.—*The Correspondence of John Collier, five times Mayor of Hastings, and his Connections with the Pelham Family* (in *Sussex Archaeol. Coll.,* XLV, pp. 62-105, and XLVI, pp. 238-239). 1902.

Dallaway, James—*History of the Western Division of the County of Sussex.* 2 vols. in 4, 1815-30.

Dictionary of National Biography, The. 1887.

Feiling, Keith—*History of the Tory Party, 1640-1714.* Oxford, 1924.

George, M. Dorothy—*London Life in the XVIIIth Century.* New York, 1925.

Giuseppi, M. S.—*A Guide to the Manuscripts preserved in the Public Record Office, London.* 2 vols., 1923-4.

Glenbervie, Sylvester Douglas, Lord—*Diaries.* Ed. Francis Bickley. 2 vols., 1928.

Gomme, George L. (ed.)—*The Gentleman's Magazine Library, being a classified collection of the chief contents of the G. M. from 1731 to 1768.* Eng. Topog., part xii (Surrey and Sussex), ed. by F. A. Milne, 1900.

Goulding, R. W.—*Henrietta, Countess of Oxford, 1694-1755.* (In *Transactions of the Thoroton Society,* vol. 27.) Nottingham, 1924.

Guthrie, Wm.—*A Complete History of the English Peerage.* 2 vols., 1763.

Horsfield, T. W.—*History and Antiquities of Lewes and its vicinity.* 2 vols., Lewes, 1824-27.

Humphreys, Arthur L.—*A Handbook to County Bibliography.* 1917.

Leadam, I. S.—*The History of England, from the Accession of Anne to the Death of George II.* 1921.

Lodge, Sir Richard—*The History of England, from the Restoration to the Death of William III.* 1923.

Lovegrove, Gilbert H.—*The Life, Work and Influence of Sir John Vanbrugh, 1663-1726.* 1902.

Lower, Mark A.—*Historical and Genealogical Notices of the Pelham Family.* Privately printed, 1873.

Ibid.—*The Worthies of Sussex: biographical Sketches of the most eminent natives or inhabitants of the County, from the earliest period to the present time.* Lewes, 1865.

Lucas, Reginald—*George II and his Ministers.* 1910.

Mahon, Philip Stanhope, Viscount—*History of England, from the Peace of Utrecht to the Peace of Versailles.* 5th ed., 7 vols., 1858.

Marks, Arthur H.—*Historical Notes on Lincoln's Inn Fields.* 1922.

Marsden, R. G.—*The Vice-Admirals of the Coast* (in *Eng. Hist. Rev.,* vols. 22 and 23, 1907-08).

Michael, Wolfgang—*Englische Geschichte im Achtzehnten Jahrhundert.* Band I, Hamburg and Leipzig, 1896. Band II, theil 1, Berlin, 1920.

Ibid.—*Walpole als Premier-minister* (in *Historische Zeitschrift,* dritte folge, 8 band, der ganze Reihe 104, pp. 504-36). Munich and Berlin, 1910.

Morgan, Wm. T.—*English Political Parties and Lead-*

ers in the Reign of Queen Anne, 1702-1710. New Haven, 1920.

Morley, John—*Walpole.* 1919.

Namier, Lewis B.—*The Structure of Politics at the Accession of George III.* 2 vols., 1929.

Noble, Mark—*Continuation of James Grainger's Biographical History of England.* 3 vols., 1806.

Official Returns. Accounts and Papers. 1878. Vol. XVII, part 2.

Oldfield, T. H. B.—*An Entire and Complete History, political and personal, of the boroughs of Gt. Britain, together with the Cinque Ports.* 2d ed., 2 vols., 1794.

Ibid.—*The Representative History of Gt. Britain and Ireland, being a History of the House of Commons and the Counties, Cities and Boroughs of the U. K. from the Earliest Period.* 6 vols., 1816.

Oldmixon, John—*History of England.* 3 vols., 1735.

Porritt, Edward and Annie G.—*The Unreformed House of Commons.* Vol. II, England and Wales. Cambridge, 1909.

Ruville, Albert von—*William Pitt, Earl of Chatham* (Eng. trans.). 3 vols., New York, 1907.

Sanders, Lloyd C.—*Patron and Place-hunter, a Study of George Bubb Dodington, Lord Melcombe.* New York, 1919.

Scott, W. R.—*The Constitution and Finance of English Joint Stock Companies to 1720.* 3 vols., Cambridge, 1911.

Sussex Archaeological Collections, The. Published by the Sussex Archaeological Society of Lewes. 1848. Vols. 7, 8, 11, 14, 19, 25, 30, 37, 55.

Sykes, Norman—*Edmund Gibson, Bishop of London, 1669-1748, a Study in Politics and Religion in the 18th Century.* Oxford, 1926.

Tindal, Nicholas—*The History of England, by Rapin de Thoyras, continued from the Revolution to the Accession of King George II.* 1747.

Torrens, W. M.—*History of Cabinets, from the Union with Scotland to the Acquisition of Canada and Bengal.* 2 vols., 1894.

Tunstall, Brian—*Admiral Byng and the Loss of Minorca.* 1928.

Turberville, A. S.—*The House of Lords in the 18th Century.* Oxford, 1927.

Turner, Rev. Edward—*High Roads in Sussex at the End of the 17th and at the Commencement of the 18th Centuries* (in *Sussex Archaeol. Coll.*, XIX, pp. 153-169). 1867.

Venn, John and J. A.—*Alumni Cantabrigienses, a Biographic list of all known students, graduates, and holders of offices at the U. of C., from the earliest times to 1900.* Part I, to 1751. Vol. III, 1924.

Victoria History of the County of Nottingham, The. 2 vols., 1910.

Victoria History of the County of Sussex, The. Vol. II, 1907.

Ward, Adolphus W.—*The Electress Sophia and the Hanoverian Succession.* 2d ed., 1909.

Ibid.—Great Britain and Hanover: Some Aspects of the Personal Union. Oxford, 1899.

Webb, Sidney and Beatrice—*English Local Government from the Revolution to the Municipal Corporations Act: The Parish and the County.* 1906.

Whitworth, Charles—*The Succession of Parliaments, being Exact Lists of the Members Chosen at a General Election, from the Restoration to the Last General Election, 1761, with other useful matters.* 1764.

Williams, Basil—*The Duke of Newcastle and the Election of 1734* (in *Eng. Hist. Rev.*, XII, 448-488). 1897.

Ibid.—The Life of William Pitt, Earl of Chatham. 2 vols., 1913.

Winstanley, D. A.—*Chatham and the Whig Opposition.* Cambridge, 1912.

Ibid.—*The University of Cambridge in the 18th Century.* Cambridge, 1922.

Yorke, Philip, 2d Earl of Hardwicke—*Walpoliana.* 1783.

Yorke, P. C.—*The Life and Correspondence of Philip Yorke, Earl of Hardwicke, Lord High Chancellor of Great Britain.* 3 vols., Cambridge, 1913.

INDEX

[201]